What People Are Saying About Carol Burton McLeod and *Guide Your Mind, Guard Your Heart, Grace Your Tongue*

Carol McLeod has developed a writing style that penetrates the core of issues that so often hinder our walk with the Lord. She presents a clear case for the examination of our mind, heart, and mouth. Carol begins with, "This book may not be for you," but within a few pages, readers will quickly identify her words as a message from heaven. Her new book is fresh manna and profitable for our soul. It is beautifully written, encouraging, convicting, and, above all, helpful. I think the apostle Paul would read this book and smile at her understanding of the importance of healing our thought life. Buy several copies of this book and share it with friends and family.

—*Dr. Steve Greene*
Publisher and Executive Vice President, Media Group, Charisma Media

Carol McLeod brings readers into a space that affects us all but is rarely given serious consideration—the ability to connect our thought life and emotions with our outward expressions. In today's society of social media and unmonitored responses, she leads the reader through a journey of aligning our mind, heart, and tongue with our call to live a God-honoring life.

—*Dr. Deana L. Porterfield*
President, Roberts Wesleyan College and Northeastern Seminary

Carol McLeod is an important voice in the church today. A great communicator? Yes! A convicting voice for truth? Yes! Carol is the real, genuine, and authentic deal. Not only has she survived some of life's biggest challenges—she's thriving! *Guide Your Mind, Guard Your Heart, Grace Your Tongue* gives us insight into how she's done it and is doing it!

—*John Hull*
Former host and CEO, *100 Huntley Street*
Lead Pastor, Eastside Baptist Church, Marietta, Georgia

I need this book, and you probably do, too. Our thoughts, our emotions, and our words have the capacity for great good—and great evil. Using both humor and hard-hitting facts, Carol McLeod shows us how to allow God's truth from the Bible to shape these parts of ourselves for the greatest good. Best of all, Carol comes alongside us as a sister in the struggle. This book is already causing me to change how I think, feel, and speak—I imagine my family and friends will be quite grateful!

—*Sarah Sundin*
Award-winning writer and author, *The Sea Before Us*

In the most distracted culture in the history of the world, Carol McLeod's new book, *Guide Your Mind, Guard Your Heart, Grace Your Tongue*, could not be more timely. The ability to manage our thoughts, what we say, and how we impact others is the great struggle of our moment in history. This book is your guide to thinking right thoughts, saying right things, and making a difference in the world. Don't miss this opportunity to discover what really makes an impact.

—*Phil Cooke, Ph.D.*
Filmmaker, media consultant, and author,
One Big Thing: Discovering What You Were Born to Do

Guide Your Mind, Guard Your Heart, Grace Your Tongue is a practical and help-filled guide for how to t ke the Word of God into every emotion we experience. (arol shares her life of wisdom and insight in a way that makes you laugh and then apply the truth she reveals. This book is terrific counsel for any stage of life.

—*Lorna Dueck*
CEO, Crossroads Christian Communications Inc. and YES TV

You will not have to read far into the introduction of *Guide Your Mind, Guard Your Heart, Grace Your Tongue* to realize that Carol's new book has you locked firmly in its crosshairs. Target acquired. What then...? Solutions! Practical, anointed, encouraging, and insightful solutions. Carol, like you and me, has not lived an ethereal life paved with petunia petals. Her perspective is not from the pinnacle but from the streets, homes, and families where we all live. Carol has a gift for helping people, so don't be surprised when this book truly helps you.

—*Chris Busch*
President and CEO, LightQuest Media

Carol McLeod's latest book, *Guide Your Mind, Guard Your Heart, Grace Your Tongue*, is a must-read for everyone. A timely message in today's broken world, this book will speak to your heart like no other. Filled with Scripture, humor, candidness, and her incredible wisdom and experience, it will impact everyone who reads it. Carol is a gifted speaker, writer, and encourager, and it is easy to see how her blog is in the Top 50 Faith Blogs for Women around the globe. Thank you, Carol, for blessing us all with your wisdom, experience, and giftedness.

—*Robbie Raugh, RN*
Integrative Health and Nutrition Practitioner
Host, *The Raw Truth Health and Fitness*
Speaker and author, *The Raw Truth Recharge:*
7 Truths to Health and Fitness

This latest release from Carol McLeod is perhaps the most important one. We are guided daily by our hearts and minds, and so often we speak too soon with our mouths. Only under the guidance of the Holy Spirit can our heart, mind, and tongue be submitted to the will of God. In this book, Carol provides daily practical disciplines to help us live godly lives, fulfilling His destiny for us.

—*Donna Russo*
Festival Director and CFO of Kingdom Bound Ministries
www.kingdombound.org

In this powerful book, Carol drives you inch by inch through the battle-field of your mind to absolute victory. While she teaches with authority, she lets us in on the secrets behind it—life lessons she has learned. This book is not just about Carol's ideas. It is about how to get the Bible into the nitty-gritty of our everyday lives. *Guide Your Mind, Guard Your Heart, Grace Your Tongue* will leave rubber marks on the road of your life.

—*Kathryn M. Graves*
Author, *Chasing Beautiful*
www.KathrynGraves.com

Struggling with negativity? In *Guide Your Mind, Guard Your Heart, Grace Your Tongue*, Carol McLeod reminds us of the power of the words we speak to ourselves and to others. Her book offers valuable strategies to help us deal with our negative self-talk, which can contaminate our hearts, minds, and souls, while jeopardizing our most important relationships. And as we begin to speak God's truth to our souls, we can experience peace in our hearts, our minds, and our relationships.

—*Karen Jordan*
Speaker and author, *Words That Change Everything*

Sometimes we need a friend who will tell us what we *need* to hear—not just what we *want* to hear. Carol McLeod is that friend, and she imparts those important truths with love that is backed by biblical principles. In *Guide Your Mind, Guard Your Heart, Grace Your Tongue*, she shares with great transparency the mistakes she has made and the lessons God has taught her. And then she equips us with the tools to become women with hearts and minds that have been transformed by Him, and tongues that have been tamed by grace. Don't miss this book!

—*Michelle Cox*
Author, *When God Calls the Heart:*
Devotions from Hope Valley and *Just 18 Summers*

In *Guide Your Mind, Guard Your Heart, Grace Your Tongue*, Carol McLeod leads us out of bondage and into freedom—real freedom. This book exposes the things that keep us from being all we were made for and releases us to transform our lives.

—*Anita Agers Brooks*
Award-winning author
Inspirational speaker and international business/life coach

Carol McLeod is a breath of fresh truth! As a Christ-follower, I am constantly battling the inner voices of gossip, pride, and emotion. *Guide Your Mind, Guard Your Heart, Grace Your Tongue* gently reminds me to replace these voices with God's truth and character. Thank you, Carol, for your transparency and wisdom. This must-read book is from one of the best!

—*Keri Cardinale*
Worship leader and speaker
Radio host, WDCX, Buffalo, NY

GUIDE YOUR MIND
GUARD YOUR HEART
GRACE YOUR TONGUE

Carol Burton McLeod

WHITAKER
HOUSE

Boldface type in Scripture quotations indicates the author's emphasis.

The forms LORD and GOD (in small capital letters) in Bible quotations represent the Hebrew name for God, *Yahweh* (Jehovah), while *Lord* and *God* normally represent the name *Adonai*, in accordance with the Bible version used.

Most Greek and Hebrew definitions are taken from Rick Renner, *Sparkling Gems from the Greek* (Tulsa, OK: Teach All Nations, a division of Rick Renner Ministries, 2003), the resources of www.blueletterbible.org, or *Strong's Exhaustive Concordance of the Bible*. The definitions of *august* and *venerable* in chapter 7, "Practice Makes Perfect," of *fear* in chapter 13, "The Fear Factor," of *disgust* in Chapter 15, "Be Disgusted—Be Very, Very Disgusted," and of *surprise* in Chapter 16, "Don't Be Surprised!" are from dictionary.com.

GUIDE YOUR MIND, GUARD YOUR HEART, GRACE YOUR TONGUE

Carol Burton McLeod
carol@justjoyministries.com
www.justjoyministries.com
Just Joy! Ministries
PO Box 1294
Orchard Park, NY 14127

ISBN: 978-1-64123-000-1 • eBook ISBN: 978-1-62911-990-8
Printed in the United States of America
© 2018 by Carol Burton McLeod

Whitaker House
1030 Hunt Valley Circle
New Kensington, PA 15068
www.whitakerhouse.com

Library of Congress Cataloging-in-Publication Data (Pending)

1 2 3 4 5 6 7 8 9 10 11 ᴜᴊ 25 24 23 22 21 20 19 18

This book is lovingly and gratefully dedicated to the brilliant, devoted, and enthusiastic staff of Just Joy! Ministries:

Angela Storm
The Steady One, The Organizer, and the CFO

Monica Orzechowski
The Creative Genius Behind It All

Linda Zielinski
Woman of Excellence and of Impeccable Detail

Sarah Grice
Prayer Warrior, Dreamer, and Designer of Beauty

Christy Christopher
Hell-Shaker, Door-Opener, and Lion-Tamer

Susie Hilchey
Travel Companion, Day-Brightener, and One-Woman PR Team

Kim Pickard-Dudley
The Wise One, The Strong One, and the Mentor to us all

Danielle Stolz
A-Work-Ethic-like-No-Other, Social-Media Genius, Daughter of the Heart

You are truly the greatest team of world-changing women that I could ever hope to work with.

Thank you for your support, your prayers, your talents, your time, and your extraordinary joy!

You are the heart and soul of Just Joy! Ministries, and I am humbled by your commitment. I am not sure what I did to deserve each one of you, but I am grateful for your friendship and for your dedication.

"Because I knew you / I have been changed for good"!

CONTENTS

PART THREE: GRACE YOUR TONGUE!

FOREWORD

One of my friends told me about an eye-catching sign she came across at the entrance to a country road in the early springtime. The sign read: "Choose your rut carefully; you'll be in it for the next thirty miles." My mind swirled when I heard this story because I've known people who've been in a rut for thirty *years*, not just thirty miles. And climbing out is hard.

More often than not, our rut has to do with the faulty way we process what's happening in our minds and hearts—and what we subsequently allow to come out of our mouths. Then we experience the age-old problem of being sincerely sorry for something we've said. Afterward, we may think we've learned our lesson, but then something unexpected happens, and we find ourselves once again speaking out of turn—creating hurt or even causing blame to be mistakenly placed on someone else.

I learned that lesson the hard way. After many years of working in ministry leadership, I was asked my opinion about whether or not a certain woman was ready to become the chairperson of a large, growing organization. I spoke up quickly—too quickly—and said, "I wonder if we should consider other people because her children have made some unwise choices, and it makes me question her ability to maintain control of her own home." I honestly believed what I said, and the committee instantly dropped her name as a candidate and went on to consider other applicants. Eventually, a far less qualified person was asked to take on the leadership position.

That incident caused me to question my motivation, my spiritual heart, my attitude, and my reasoning. Had I responded out of a critical spirit, jealousy, legalistic judgment—or out of a genuine belief that the woman was unqualified? In retrospect, her children were actually pretty normal.

Soon afterward, the bottom dropped out of my life. My husband, Gene, and I had returned home from an out-of-state speaking engagement and had retired for the night. We were sound asleep when the phone rang. Gene answered the call, then pulled the receiver away from his ear. Choking back a sob, he said, "Jason has just been arrested for the murder of his wife's first husband. He's in jail in Orlando." Nausea swept over me, and as I got out of bed, my legs would not hold my weight. Our only child, a graduate of the U.S. Naval Academy, had pulled a trigger in a public parking lot, and a man had died. After two and a half years and seven postponements of his trial, Jason was convicted in the state of Florida of first-degree murder and sentenced to life in prison without the possibility of parole.

In the middle of my grief, I experienced the variety of ways in which the people who received our deeply sorrowful news responded to us. A few individuals merely quoted lots of Bible verses and gave us advice on raising children in a biblical way. Their thoughtless words cut deeply. Some people looked at us with judgment, while others had eyes of compassion. Many wept with us, feeling our grief as their own. Certain people said very little but began helping in tangible ways. Most expected us to immediately drop out of Christian leadership, but some advised us to "stay in the fight, because it's the only way to defeat this devious attack from the enemy."

What I learned from that experience was that the people who quickly spoke up and spewed out opinions and suggestions were usually the least helpful. But the people who kept their minds, hearts, and words centered on what God was leading them to think, do, and say were the ones who ministered to us in the most powerful ways. By holding their tongues, guarding their hearts, and asking God for wisdom, they poured healing salve into our troubled souls.

You might not receive a middle-of-the-night phone call like mine, but you will no doubt face other personal challenges. You'll also have numerous opportunities to respond, offer advice, give counsel, and speak up about people, issues, and causes. In *Guide Your Mind, Guard Your Heart, Grace*

Your Tongue, Carol McLeod does a masterful job of helping us learn how to think in a renewed way—a biblical way that will forever change how we live, including how we respond to our family members, friends, coworkers, and neighbors. With vulnerable transparency, she shares the mistakes she's made and the lessons she's learned. And she explains the best biblical choices each of us can make as we live in this world alongside other people who yearn to be understood, valued, and cared for.

As you read this book, you'll not only discover a new way to think, but you'll also learn powerful biblical principles with which you can guard your heart. As you apply these principles, your life will be enriched, and your speech will be rehabilitated, becoming more grace-filled. And everyone around you will benefit from what you've learned and put into practice. It's a transformational way of thinking and living!

Always remember the best advice: *"Guard your heart above all else, for it determines the course of your life"* (Proverbs 4:23 NLT).

—*Carol Kent*
Speaker and author, *He Holds My Hand:
Experiencing God's Presence and Protection*

PREFACE: THIS BOOK MAY NOT BE FOR YOU

This book may not be for you if...

+ you never think a negative thought.
+ you never spend one second of your life worrying about the people you love.
+ you have never lost your temper.
+ you never allow bitterness to affect a relationship.
+ you are able to completely forgive someone the instant he or she offends you.
+ you are never moody and have never given a family member the silent treatment.
+ you are never cynical about the politics of the day.
+ you refuse to gossip—every minute of every hour of every day.
+ you have never yelled at your children or your dog.
+ you have never talked negatively about your spouse.
+ you have never criticized your parents behind their backs.
+ you have never spoken a word that you regret.

If all these statements are true of you, then you possess a stunningly perfect mind and constantly balanced emotions—and your words are always accurate and uplifting. (Perhaps you are the one who should be writing this book, rather than reading it! You can close it right now.) However, if you are like me, and you regularly deal with such issues, then you have come to the right place! This book was written by a woman who has been in the trenches of life and is a veteran of mind, heart, and tongue problems. *Guide Your Mind, Guard Your Heart, Grace Your Tongue* does not offer pat answers but presents powerful strategies that will reroute pandemic thinking and cure rotten emotions.

Most Christian women have regrets the size of Mount Rushmore: they regret how they have used their time, they regret how they have spent their money, they regret how much chocolate they have eaten—but most of all, they regret the words that they have spoken to the people they love the most and know the best. Every woman with a beating heart has spoken words "under the influence" of slurred thinking and warped feelings. And every woman wishes that she had the magical power to take those lethal words back.

But the tongue may not actually be the fundamental problem in our lives. The true plague is most likely the thoughts we think and the emotions that brew on the backburners of our hearts. Foundationally, we must understand that the tongue is merely the mirror of our thoughts and emotions. In order to speak words that are graced for godly purposes, we must first investigate the DNA of our minds and hearts. This book provides such a way for women to deal with their sometimes out-of-control thought lives, their deceived emotions, and their undisciplined tongues. While various books might discuss one of the three areas—the mind, the emotions, or the tongue—it is vital to consider the influence that each has on the others.

The Lord created your mind, your heart, and your mouth for specific and God-honoring purposes. When your thoughts, your emotions, and your words are working together for a sacred objective, your life can be transformed and make a glorious impact on your family, on others in your sphere of influence—and on people for generations to come!

ACKNOWLEDGMENTS

I have been blessed with an impressive parade of outrageous, genuine, and extraordinary family members and friends who have made my life a delight, my workload lighter, and my calling a reality.

Craig: My best friend, my life's partner, my loudest cheerleader, and my husband. Other than accepting Jesus as my Lord and Savior, you are the best decision that I have ever made. Thank you for choosing me, for loving me, and for serving me. Let's do forty more years together!

Matthew: You are a leader among leaders, and I love watching the great man that you have become! God needs more men just like you. Wherever you go, whatever you do, know that I am praying for you and cheering for you. I believe in you, my firstborn son.

Emily: You are a picture of the healing power of God! Thank you for loving Matt so well and for raising Olivia, Wesley, Boyce, and Elizabeth Joy to be world changers. Your strong faith inspires me. I believe in you, my daughter and my friend.

Christopher: Your talents, your heart, and your creativity are unmatched in my book. It's an honor to be your mom and to have the delight of praying for you and for cheering you on. I believe in you, my favorite worship leader.

Liz: I love being with you and watching you love all of Brooklyn in your own unique way! Thanks for loving Christopher and for raising Amelia and Jack to be thoughtful, kind, and godly. Your sweet friendship is a gift to me. I believe in you, my sensitive and caring daughter of the heart.

Jordan: Your life is the dynamic example that God really does answer prayers. Being your mom has been one of the richest treasures of my entire life. Your talents, commitment to excellence, and creativity are a rare and compelling combination. I believe in you, my miracle child.

Allie: When you walked into the McLeod family, love walked in with you! You love so well, encourage without pause, and pray with purpose. Thanks for loving Jordan so well and for raising Ian to be a man of God. Your heart is pure gold in my book. I believe in you, my Allie-girl.

Joy: When you were just a little girl, you gave me a gift from the dollar store; it was a soap dish that had these words painted on it: "A daughter is a little girl who grows up to be your best friend." How true that is of us! I love being your mom and your friend. God is using you, Joy, and I believe in you, my daughter and my kindred spirit.

Chris: You are the son-in-law for whom I prayed for many years. What a delight that God answered my prayers with *you*! Thank you for loving Joy so well and for celebrating her. Know that I believe in you, Chris, my favorite son-in-law, and in your call in life.

Joni: You are the best surprise that I have ever received! You have kept me young and have added a rich dimension to all of my days. I am watching your life with grand anticipation of all that you will accomplish for the kingdom. God has great things for you, Joni Becca…never doubt it! You are always in my heart. I believe in you, my world-changing girl.

Olivia: Someday you will be the one writing the books in this family! Your sweet spirit and obedient heart are a delight to everyone who knows you. You are so dear to me, Olivia, and I love being your Marmee.

Ian: God is going to use you, Ian, so keep close to Him all the days of your life. Your tenderness is a great strength, and your giggle is infectious! Keep reading, keep drawing, and keep dreaming. I love being your Marmee.

Wesley: What a spark of joy and enthusiasm you are to the McLeod family! Your insight and quest for knowledge are game-changers, for sure. Can't wait to watch you in the Final Four someday! I love being your Marmee.

Amelia Grace: Keep singing your songs...keep being kind...keep dreaming...keep drinking in the life that God has given to you. You are an amazing, girl, Amelia, and I just love being your Marmee.

Boyce: I love your perspective on faith, on prayer, and on life! You might be small, but you are mighty on the inside! Keep being the warrior that God created you to be. You are uniquely created to do great things for the kingdom of God! I love being your Marmee.

Elizabeth Joy: I love your spunky ways, your little-girl opinions, and your joyful chatter. You were made for greatness, dear one; don't ever forget it! I love being your Marmee.

Jack: Always remember that when you are on God's team, nothing is impossible for you, my Jack! Obey your mom and dad and enjoy being a boy! Thanks for loving Christmas with me. I love being your Marmee.

Mom and Leo: Thanks for loving me and for believing in me. My heart just aches to be with you, but know that I can always feel your prayers.

Nanny: Your example of godly living has inspired our entire family! Keep praying for all of us!

Norman Burton: My wonderful dad who now lives in eternity with Jesus. I wouldn't be the woman I am without having had you as my earthly father. All the credit goes to you, and all the glory goes to God.

Wesley McLeod: Craig's dad in heaven. You were the steadying force of the family McLeod. Your strength and wisdom are with us still today. See you soon!

John Mason: My friend and literary agent who has opened door after door after door for me! You and the Holy Spirit are a great team!

The staff at Whitaker House: Thanks for taking a chance on this persuasive, enthusiastic, and persistent author! Your friendship and your professionalism mean the world to me. I am honored and blessed to be a Whitaker House author.

Suzanne Kuhn: You are a breath of fresh air in a world of stale ideas. You have placed feet on my dreams and have given brand-new life to my seasoned hopes.

LightQuest Media: Thank you for supporting me in the teaching of the Word of God through every avenue available in the twenty-first century.

Chris Busch: The words *thank you* will never be enough.

And then, to a ravishingly beautiful bouquet of friends who fill my life with fragrance and delight: *Shannon Maitre, Carolyn Hogan, Janie Sperrey, Lisa Keller, Jill Janus, Dawn Frink, Marilyn Frebersyser, Lynn Fields, Patricia Apy,* and *Camella Binkley*—you are all priceless gifts from a loving and extravagant Father.

And to *Jesus, my Lord and Savior!* Thank You for calling me, equipping me, anointing me, and choosing me for Your grand purposes. I live to make hell smaller and heaven bigger! I live to honor You with every breath, with every word, and with every minute of my life!

INTRODUCTION: WHAT ARE YOUR ISSUES?

The way our minds, emotions, and tongues function is perhaps the greatest indicator of our spiritual health and psychological strength. If our minds are clean and clear, they will undoubtedly influence both our emotions and our tongues in a positive way. When our thoughts are motivated by positive purposes, our thought life will be fruitful, and when our emotions are well-ordered, our words will be a blessing to others. As a matter of fact, the tongue does not influence either our thought life or our emotions; rather, it is controlled by the ideas and perspectives we allow to exist in our brains and by the emotions we embrace. Thus, if our minds are cluttered with unproductive or damaging thoughts, and if our emotions are unsettled, we can find ourselves facing any one of the following issues.

ISSUE #1: MIND GAMES

Tell the truth... Has your mind ever taken you in the wrong direction? Perhaps you have been bombarded by worry or other destructive thought patterns, so that you often find yourself thinking self-defeating, critical, or angry thoughts. Maybe you are the type of person who is always vehemently convinced that something horrible is waiting for you around the next corner; Yet, when you turn that particular dreaded corner of life, you are surprised to find that no hideous event is waiting for you. Ashamedly, you realize that you invested countless days of emotional energy anticipating the worst-case scenario, when, in fact, all you ended up experiencing was a fairly good day.

Tell the truth... Have you ever convinced yourself that someone hated you? Perhaps *hate* is too strong a word, but, at the very least, you persuaded your extremely gullible self to believe that someone was offended by your despicable personhood, and therefore you began to double-check the effectiveness of your deodorant every time you approached his or her frigid presence! And then, when your self-esteem was at an all-time low, and you were sure that there was absolutely nothing likable about yourself, this apparently aloof acquaintance was, inexplicably, as welcoming and kind to you as a long-lost friend! You wondered if you had totally misinterpreted that individual's view of you.

Tell the truth... Are you held in bondage by fearful and appalling thoughts, in which, for example, your husband loses his job, your children are kidnapped, or you receive a doctor's report with the big "C" stamped on it?

Tell the truth... Have you ever found yourself tormented by horrific, dark thoughts and wondered if you were distantly related to Edgar Allen Poe or Stephen King? Perhaps your mental processes go something like this:

I am going to fall down these stairs.

Someone I love is going to disappear.

My purse will be stolen, and my credit card and all of my bank accounts will be compromised.

Life is going too well, so I am sure that something bad is going to happen to me!

It could be that your mind never travels down those dark, worrisome routes, but your imagination is absorbed by something else: you fantasize! Are you the type of person who has spent your entire life spinning mental golden threads of fiction about your first love, or that guy in the gym with whom you made eye contact yesterday, or some unattainable hottie on television? Perhaps you imagine yourself as mistreated and forlorn, when, suddenly, on the big screen of your mind, that rugged and ravishing new movie star (at least his on-screen version) comes to your rescue and whisks you away! Have these imaginary scenarios—or something similar—become a recurring thought pattern for you? *Tell the truth!*

ISSUE #2: EMOTIONAL ROLLER-COASTER RIDES

Let's move next to some issues of the heart, or emotions. Perhaps you think that your mind is filled with positive thoughts and your tongue is well-regulated, but you admit that your emotions are out of control, and they have been directing the course of your life. Your constantly fluctuating emotions often lead you on a roller-coaster ride—climbing, dipping, spinning, and curving—from the thrill of the mountaintop to the valley of despair.

For example, if your teenager is ten minutes overdue from an activity, you begin to break out in a cold sweat and have even been known to call the local police station to see if an accident has been reported. Or, perhaps, every year on the anniversary of your beloved father's death, rather than being grateful for his long and productive life, you find yourself crying, eating all the carbs in sight, and mournfully moping around the house. Or maybe your emotional story is more like these scenarios: When you come home from a long day at work, if the house is picked up and the laundry is folded, you are cheerful and easy to live with. But if the house looks like a tornado roared through it, you become the Wicked Witch of the West!

ISSUE #3: SPEECH ERUPTIONS

You might feel that your thought life is in order and your emotions are in check, but you sorrowfully admit that your tongue is unruly. As you frequently lash out at your children, vilify your spouse, or scream at your poor dog, the words roar and echo through the caverns of your soul, and you wonder, *Who is that person, and why does she hate her family so much?*

Perhaps you even verbally accost strangers from time to time. For example, when you have waited too long in the grocery store line, your tongue becomes a hot poker of blame aimed at the poor girl who is making minimum wage and, quite frankly, could not find another job if she tried. Instead of exhibiting the fruit of the Spirit, you feel compelled to vent, telling her why you will never come back to this "sorry place," in what specific ways she has absolutely ruined your day, and why she had better hope she never meets you in a dark alley!

Similarly, when the single mother who works at the fast-food drive-through mistakenly gives you the wrong change, you sweetly ask, "May

I please speak to your manager?" Although your voice is controlled, your words are not, and by the end of your five-minute diatribe, the cashier who flunked consumer math is in tears and has lost her job. But you spoke your mind...and isn't that the important thing?

MARIONETTE ON A STRING

Which of the above is your primary issue? Is it the negative state of your thought life? Is it your out-of-control emotions? Or is it your unrestrained tongue? Perhaps you have some experience grappling with all three. Maybe you felt you had finally taken control of your tongue, but you became painfully aware that the town dump was still alive and well between your two ears. Then, when you eradicated all the "stinking thinking" from your brain, your raw emotions reared their ugly heads again, and you hung on, white-knuckled, for the ride of your life! Personally, too often, I have been forced to watch myself with great incredulity as my tongue became the marionette of my swamp-like brain and of my unbalanced emotional soul. My slippery tongue often comes to life by the pull of an emotional switch or by the manipulation of an errant thought.

CRANIAL-CARDIO-ORAL SURGERY

If you sadly nod your head in agreement because you are dealing with any of the mind, heart, or tongue maladies I have mentioned, I believe you are an excellent candidate for a miraculous procedure known as *internal biblical laser surgery*, which is performed only by the Great Physician. Here's the good news: no matter what our issue(s), God is just itching to roll up His sleeves and perform a radical, cleansing, healing work in us! When God cleanses His dear children, He eliminates the foul odors and germs that have lingered around the hallways of our lives for much too long.

Guide Your Mind, Guard Your Heart, Grace Your Tongue is filled to overflowing with pertinent and powerful Scripture passages because, truthfully, the Bible is the only remedy that can heal our universal human maladies. Contrary to popular perception, the Bible does not merely address issues like evil serpents, miracles, floods, giants, fiery furnaces, visions, and heaven. I can guarantee you, God's Word has a voluminous amount of practical encouragement—applicable for believers of any time and culture—that will enable us to live abundantly and victoriously this side of heaven.

You will be able to guide your mind, guard your heart, and grace your tongue when you allow the Bible to laser its way through all of the ugly "stuff" in your life. Stored within the Scriptures is a vast treasure that will enable you to think the right thoughts, to control your emotional extravagance, and to never again regret another word that you speak.

> *The heart of the righteous ponders how to answer, but the mouth of the wicked pours out evil things.*   (Proverbs 15:28 esv)

The Bible does, indeed, give instructions concerning our thought life; the Bible does, indeed, coach us in how to maintain a healthy emotional makeup; the Bible does, indeed, have much to say about the power that the tongue holds. Reading, studying, and memorizing the Bible is the miracle cure for which we have been longing in order to heal our disorderly thought life, our emotional instability, and our "mouth disease."

A truly wise person is someone who no longer believes the lies of Satan but actually thinks like God thinks, based on His thoughts and will, expressed in His Word. Wisdom will become an intrinsic part of your mental makeup when you have taken every thought captive to the obedience of Christ (see 2 Corinthians 10:5), and when you have been transformed by the renewing of your mind (see Romans 12:2). You will receive an extraordinary ability to guard your out-of-control emotions, and you will be empowered to speak words of grace, wisdom, and patience.

Yes, there is only one possible cure for any mental infection that exists in the recesses of that gray matter between our two ears, or for any clog in the arteries of our spiritual hearts, or for any bitter words that want to escape from the opening that lies right underneath our nose—and that miraculous remedy is the Word of God. In this book, I endeavor to teach you how to access that potent remedy.

IN RHYTHM WITH GOD'S HEART

With this promise of healing through God's Word, we are confronted with a difficult but significant choice: will we allow God's Holy Spirit to teach us to guide our thoughts, to guard our heartfelt emotions, and to grace our tongues? If so, we will need to allow Him to address all three areas in our lives, since it is virtually impossible to control one member of that powerful triumvirate without dealing with the other two in the process. All three are intimately and inseparably connected. If you long to live the abundant life that Christ died to give you, then you must agree to receive peace and order for an unchecked mind, to allow the renewal of a heart that has been diseased, and to learn to govern a tongue that has careened out of control.

That is why Guide Your Mind, Guard Your Heart, Grace Your Tongue is divided into three specific sections. The first section, entitled "Guide Your Mind!" deals with issues related to your thinking habits and patterns. It will help you examine exactly what you have allowed to take up space in your vital gray matter and how you can replace negative thoughts with positive, uplifting ones. The second section, called "Guard Your Heart!" will assist you in controlling your emotional responses to life, while offering a healthy emotional prescription that will enable you to live the way God intended you to. The last section, "Grace Your Tongue!" will explain how to clean up your "verbal vomit," such as that which you have spewed on unsuspecting people in your world. Each chapter contains vivid references to the spiritual cure found on the sacred pages of the Bible; additionally, each chapter closes with a Scripture verse that places an exclamation point on that chapter's theme.

When you have a developed a wise mind-set due to being saturated with the Word of God, it will be impossible for you to continually embrace a foolish heart. Why? Your heart takes its cues from your thought life, which is the nerve center of your existence. As the internal biblical laser surgery takes place, and as wisdom rules and reigns in your brain, then your mind and heart will work together in complete harmony. Your heart will look into the mirror of your mind, and your emotions will reflect the thoughts your mind is thinking. The process may take a while...but it *will* happen! You will find that, when your heart and mind are in sync, your tongue will become a shadow-dancer for this dynamic duo. Your lips will speak the wisdom that flows from your renewed and reconstructed mind and heart.

This laser surgery is not an outpatient procedure—it will require a lifetime commitment to receiving the miraculous healing power of God's presence and Word. As you read this book, my prayer is that your mind will be guided by Christ's thoughts, your heart will be guarded and transformed by His heart, and your tongue will be graced for His high purposes.

You have the capacity to actually think the thoughts of God, to experience the joy of your heart beating in rhythm with His heart, and to speak His words of encouragement to others. Let's get to it!

The heart of the wise instructs his mouth and adds persuasiveness to his lips. (Proverbs 16:23)

PART ONE
GUIDE YOUR MIND!

1

A BRAND-NEW BRAIN!

I am not the neatest person in the world, are you? The sad truth is that I did not receive the "cleaning gene" that most women do. More often than not, there are dishes in my sink, clothes on my bedroom floor, and yesterday's towels strewn across my bathroom. (I am blushing right now.) Some days, my bed is haphazardly made, but most often, it is left askew from my postmenopausal sleeping patterns. Additionally, my kitchen floor perpetually needs sweeping, and my laundry is a never-decreasing mountain on the laundry room floor.

It's not that I am opposed to cleaning, I just always have more important things to do, like answer e-mails or read a book or talk to one of my children on the phone! I know…I know…I know…. If I would just spend a little bit of time every day on my home, I might be able to keep it in order. I get that; I do! I have a friend who has tried to train me from the earliest days of my marriage that if I would just spend one hour a day first thing in the morning on cleaning and straightening, my house would never get disgustingly out of control. I did try that strategy for a day or two, but within about fifteen minutes of my first attempt, I was distracted by a magazine article or by a piano piece that was calling my name.

As much as I find absolutely no enjoyment in cleaning my home, I do, indeed, enjoy the results when I discipline myself to roll up my sleeves and get to work. I love it when my blue bathroom towels are all folded and put away neatly and in order. I love looking into my bedroom and seeing a bed that is made with precision—with no wrinkles to be found! And oh, the rapture that fills my soul when my kitchen floor is swept and there are no dishes lingering in my sink! And did I mention that I love the smell of a sparkling-clean bathroom, of freshly washed laundry, and of dusting polish?

Why do I love the results but absolutely hate the process? Why, indeed? It is, quite simply, because of the daily effort and focus required.

Our minds are much like the homes in which we live: we must daily keep up with the process of organizing our mental clutter and cleaning up the cerebral dirt and grime that accumulates in our thought patterns, not to mention scrubbing the dark and dusty corners of our brains; otherwise, spiritual havoc will quickly ensue. If we take even one day off from the intensive process of keeping a pure mind, we will be in danger of losing the battle altogether. But while the process of sanitizing our brain may be exacting and frustrating, the results will be absolutely fabulous!

ALL THINGS NEW

Not only does Jesus desire to remove junk from your brain, but He also longs to add goodness and peace to the fabric of your mind. He wants His very presence to be the motivating force within your thought processes. If you will allow Jesus to fill your mind with His power and presence, you will be a living, breathing demonstration of His knowledge and wisdom while you live on planet earth.

The foundational Scripture that we will apply to the renewing of our minds is this: *"As* [a person] *thinks within himself, so is he"* (Proverbs 23:7). If you are thinking the thoughts of Christ Himself, then you will demonstrate His character and purposes every day of your life this side of heaven. You will be Jesus's show-and-tell, and He will reveal Himself through your life. Jesus will tell His story through you—what a divine promise and possibility!

If you have asked Jesus Christ to come into your heart and to forgive you of your sins, then you have become a Christian, or a Christ-follower. You are in agreement with God and with His Word that Jesus Christ is the only Son of God, the Savior, and that He died on the cross of Calvary to reconcile you to the Father. You also realize that when Jesus died on the cross, it was to ensure that you would be able to live with Him forever. As a believer in Jesus Christ, you know that you are certainly not perfect, but that He is indeed perfect.

When you surrendered your life to Jesus Christ, you also surrendered your mind to Him. On that day of new birth, spiritually speaking, your mind was born again, restored, and renewed. From that momentous time forward, even your thought processes should have changed. Yet, although we are given the undeniable gift of eternal life the instant we are saved, we unfortunately don't automatically begin to think *all* of the right thoughts or embrace *all* of the right heart attitudes at the onset of this new life. This is because our minds are still susceptible to fleshly desires and motivations.

Thus, as Christians, we have an understanding of salvation and of the price Jesus paid to ensure forgiveness of sin for all who would come to Him. We also have an understanding of our future life in eternity with God—a future secured for us in our salvation. But what about right now? What about today? How do we appropriate salvation in the present tense of life? In what way does our salvation relate to a renewed mind?

Let me share with you an amazing piece of theology that might help all of this make sense: eternal life does not begin at death; it begins the instant you accept Jesus into your heart. And, if you can be victorious in the battle over your brain, you will experience life abundantly before you even arrive at heaven's shore!

A FUTILE WALK

So this I say, and affirm together with the Lord, that you walk no longer just as the Gentiles also walk, in the futility of their mind....
(Ephesians 4:17)

In the above verse, Paul uses bold and significant language, declaring that he has heard from God Himself about this topic. The particular matter that Paul addresses concerns the believer's "walk" in life. The Greek word translated *"walk"* means to conduct oneself or to pass one's life; it can also mean to be occupied.

Paul is talking to you when he says that you were never intended to spend your life according to the futility of your mind, like the "Gentiles" do. If you choose to conduct yourself in this worthless manner, your mind will be devoid of truth and of appropriate thinking. The verse strongly implies that your mind will be a place of perverse thoughts and depravity. A futile mind is one that is in a weakened condition, thinking frail thoughts and lacking vigor.

Thus, if your mind is occupied with lies and other inappropriate thoughts, this is a futile and destitute way of living. If you have given your mind over to perversity, you will quickly become a frail Christian who lacks both vigor and purpose. I have an inkling that when we get to heaven, we will sadly realize that we settled for so much less than God's best in this area of our minds. Therefore, if your mind is guilty of any of the descriptions that the word *futility* encompasses, you need to enter fully into the mind of Jesus Christ. You need to change your thought patterns and enthusiastically embrace His thoughts.

> *...being darkened in their understanding, excluded from the life of God because of the ignorance that is in them, because of the hardness of their heart; and they, having become callous, have given themselves over to sensuality for the practice of every kind of impurity with greediness. But you did not learn Christ in this way....* (Ephesians 4:18–20)

Your life starts in your mind! If you want to live a vibrant, joyful life that smacks of the nature of God, it will always begin in your brain. I would do absolutely anything at all *not* to be excluded from the life of God! I long to live out God's dreams for my life, and therefore I must order my thinking according to His plan and boundaries. I must walk away from depraved and perverse thinking; I must think only true thoughts that honor God, so that I am able to live an energized and zealous life in tandem with the Father.

If we keep listening to God and continue to feed on His Word, we will be renewed in our minds day by day. If we commit ourselves to worship and prayer, our minds will perpetually become stronger and more vibrant. If we proactively choose to attend a life-changing Bible study and are committed to a body of believers, our minds will begin to change for the better.

> *...if indeed you have heard Him and have been taught in Him, just as truth is in Jesus, that, in reference to your former manner of life, you lay aside the old self, which is being corrupted in accordance with the lusts of deceit, and that you be renewed in the spirit of your mind.*
> (Ephesians 4:21–23)

Again, what a divine possibility! We have the human potential of being renewed in the spirit of our minds when we listen to the Lord with undivided attention and then allow ourselves to be taught by Him. We must predetermine to listen to Him when He speaks, to educate ourselves according to His teachings, and to remind ourselves daily that truth is found only in Christ Jesus. Sincere renewal inevitably begins in Jesus Christ and is unequivocally sealed in Him. There is no other way to discover the secret of living a transformed and powerful life than to discover it in Jesus.

I must concur with the principle found in John 3:30: *"He must increase, but I must decrease."* Every day of my journey upon earth's shore, I must declare, "More of His wisdom and less of my foolishness! More of His truth and less of my fantasies! More of His power and less of my weaknesses!"

A MIRACLE IN THE MAKING

The regeneration of our mind will build an entirely new and improved way of thinking for us. We will begin to bless others when they wrong us and forgive those who affront us. We will commence to love those who are cruel to us, and we will choose to bless offenders rather than criticize them. The renewal that is taking place in our minds is much more impactful than mere positive thinking because our regenerated thinking patterns have roots in Christ and not in self. It is not just an act of commitment but a lifestyle of surrender.

> *For those who are according to the flesh set their minds on the things of the flesh, but those who are according to the Spirit, the things of the Spirit. For the mind set on the flesh is death, but the mind set on the Spirit is life and peace.* (Romans 8:5–6)

As your mind is being gloriously renewed, it is time for you to take yet another step of maturity in Christ—to make a decision to stop thinking about self and to start thinking Spirit thoughts. This step will require an act of your will that might cause you to sweat and groan as you labor to change what you think about, but it will deliver glorious joy and peace to your everyday life.

Realize that there is a price to pay if you long to partner with God in completing the transforming work of Christ in your life. That price is called "desire." You must "want" your mind to be set on the Spirit more than to be set on the flesh. You must have a moment of complete surrender when you painfully but powerfully assert, "I want You, God! I am sick and tired of my faulty mind and thoughts! Give me Your brain, Father! Help me to set my mind on the Holy Spirit of power!"

YOUR MIND-SET

But the mind set on the Spirit is life and peace. (Romans 8:6)

When a person holds to a certain set of beliefs, it is known as a *mind-set*. A mind-set determines how a person acts, and it also shapes their value system; a mind-set motivates an individual and influences who or what they choose as their sources of knowledge and authority. A mind-set can affect a person's view of all their experiences, and it often dominates both their private and public life.

My father had a Depression-era mind-set, and it influenced everything he did. He ferociously saved money, refused to spend a penny on even some of the necessities of life, and would reuse things over and over and over again. Because of my dad's particular way of thinking, we were required to use our teabags no less than three times before they were thrown away. How did we accomplish this? My dad would place a clean towel on top of the refrigerator every Sunday night, and it was there that we were required to place the once-used or twice-used teabags to dry out and then be used again. Clearly, my father lived by that Depression-era mind-set!

Perhaps you might possess what is considered a traditional Southern mind-set, and be known for extending hospitality and for a darling sweetness in your personality that is as syrupy as the sweetest of teas. Most likely, you liberally sprinkle your conversations with expressions such as "Bless your heart," "I'm fixin' to do somethin'," and "y'all."

Similarly, if our mind is set on the Holy Spirit, our actions and our speech will reflect that distinct outlook. The more we enter into the mind of Christ, the more we will expand our capacity to demonstrate His life to our world. Do you long to live life as it was truly meant to be lived, as purposed by the One who created you? If you desire to experience overwhelming peace in your heart, in your home, and in your relationships, you must set your mind on the Spirit! There is no other way to encounter peace than to emphatically choose to set your mind on Him.

You must be more impacted by the Word of God than you are by anything else, if you long for your mind-set to reflect only Christ and His lovingkindness. Your past should not have the same degree of influence, the culture should not sway you, and your current living conditions should not hold the ability to influence your mind, as does the Word of God.

ALL WE HAVE TO OFFER

Therefore, I urge you, brethren, by the mercies of God, to present your bodies a living and holy sacrifice, acceptable to God, which is your spiritual service of worship. And do not be conformed to this world, but be transformed by the renewing of your mind, so that you may prove what the will of God is, that which is good and acceptable and perfect.

(Romans 12:1–2)

The body to which Paul is referring in Romans 12 represents the total person. The stark reality is that our bodies, including all of our bodily systems and abilities, are all that we actually have to offer to the Lord. We must willingly and cheerfully give to Him our minds, our emotions, our tongues, our plans, our hearts, our potential, and all of our discipline. The four most important words that we will ever speak to the Savior are: "I am Yours, Lord!"

The greatest challenge when dealing with a living sacrifice is that it can walk off the altar! Since you are that living sacrifice, you must be prepared to say those four important words more than once in a lifetime. Every time your flesh tries to take back control of your mind, declare, "I am *Yours*, Lord!"

We must daily lay aside our own desires, in complete and utter submission to God, and then we must give to Him all of our energy and the entirety of our resources. This is the only reasonable way to respond to God, and it is an act of high and holy worship. If you believe that worship is merely choosing to sing a song on a Sunday morning with the other members of your church, you have it all wrong. If you equate worship with the copycat act of raising your hands just to impress the person next to you, you have it all wrong. Worship, at its beautiful and sacred core, is giving all of you to all of God. Worship is consecrating even the thoughts that you think to Him, and to Him alone.

In the ancient Hebrew sacrificial system, the animal sacrifices generally entailed the death of the animal, such as a sheep or an ox. When we become a "living and holy sacrifice" to God, that sacrifice involves dying to anything that does not reflect the mind of the Spirit, including our faulty thought life. Pleasing Christ is more than prohibiting ourselves from participating in behavior that is inappropriate for a believer; honoring Christ is deeper than determining that we won't, for example, do drugs, cheat on our taxes, or participate in adulterous living. The desire to glorify Christ includes the desire to renew our minds by choosing the mind-set of the Holy Spirit. It is not mere actions that have the power to transform us into the likeness of Christ, but rather it is the renewal that takes place in our minds when the Holy Spirit is allowed to take control of them.

THE POWER OF RENEWAL

Karen was an active young mother who had been raised in the church and who had memorized many Bible verses as a child. As she grew to adulthood, Bible memorization became less important to her, although her fervent walk with the Lord continued. Karen was a loving wife to her husband and a devoted mother to her three active children. She worked a part-time job at an insurance agency, was PTA president, taught Sunday school, and played the organ at church. Eventually, all of these responsibilities combined to place extreme pressures on her life; the busyness of her daily activities began to consume her—to choke the very life out of her. When she was no longer mentally and physically capable of juggling all her activities, she suffered a complete nervous breakdown and spent three weeks in the hospital trying to regain her vitality and mental stability.

The doctors treated Karen's mental condition by administering strong doses of calming drugs, but due to the side effects of these drugs, she was nearly comatose for the entire three weeks. Her husband eventually asked the doctors to wean her off of the drugs so that she could once again engage in life. As Karen started to regain consciousness, she began to repeat the Bible verses that she had memorized as a child. The words of faith that had laid a solid spiritual foundation in her life now began to heal her mind. Over and over and over again, Karen would repeat these life-giving words of Scripture:

> God has not given us a spirit of fear, but of power and of love and of a
> sound mind. (2 Timothy 1:7 NKJV)

I can do all things through Christ who strengthens me.
(Philippians 4:13 NKJV)

But You, O Lord, are a shield about me, my glory, and the One who lifts my head.
(Psalm 3:3)

For the word of God is living and active and sharper than any two-edged sword, and piercing as far as the division of soul and spirit, of both joints and marrow, and able to judge the thoughts and intentions of the heart.
(Hebrews 4:12)

Karen discovered that a renewed mind had the power to heal her, strengthen her, and enable her to continue living with strength and joy. When she was released from the hospital, she possessed a new vibrancy. She altered her schedule and chose to eliminate several optional activities to keep from becoming overcommitted again. The new joy in Karen's life was clearly apparent. Even her children were aware that they had a brand new mom!

MORE THAN A VITAMIN

You can experience the power of a renewed mind, as well. The most important and potent spiritual vitamin that you can ingest in order to maintain a healthy brain is the Word of God. The Bible has miraculous and supernatural power to keep your mind on the right thought pathways and to provide stability where there has been confusion. God's Word is the truth that your brain has been desperately seeking! As you meditate on and memorize the Word of God, your way of thinking will actually change. As we will discuss in more detail later, you don't primarily read the Bible for *information* but for *transformation*. You will certainly be informed as you read the Bible, and you will access historical facts as well as great theological truths in it, but the foremost way that your life will be impacted is by the transformation that will take place in your mind, soul, and spirit.

And do not be conformed to this world, but be transformed by the renewing of your mind, so that you may prove what the will of God is, that which is good and acceptable and perfect. (Romans 12:2)

This verse encourages us that, when our mind is transformed, we will begin to become experts at knowing what the will of God is. The Greek word translated *"transformed"* means "the change of moral character for the better." As this mental transformation takes place, you will have an assurance of what the plans and purposes of God are for your particular life, enabling you to follow them. As others observe this rebirth of your brain, they will begin to come to you for spiritual insights and encouragement. When the Holy Spirit has remodeled your brain, you will then be able to impact the lives of others as they listen to the wisdom that has been given to you by the mind of Christ Himself.

Thus, while the goal is a transformed mind, the benefit package includes knowing God's will. Your mind comes into agreement with the will of God, which the Bible says is *"good and acceptable and perfect."* God has plans for you that are always good, that are acceptable to Him, and that are a perfect fit for you! And it all starts in your brand spanking new mind!

A MIND AND A MOUTHPIECE

For who among men knows the thoughts of a man except the spirit of the man which is in him? Even so the thoughts of God no one knows except the Spirit of God. (1 Corinthians 2:11)

In this fundamental verse, Paul once again addresses the purpose and intent of the mind. He reminds even those of us who are living in the twenty-first century that the only One who knows the thoughts of God is the Spirit of God. When you know the Holy Spirit and have allowed Him to take over your life, this incredible Teacher will give you first-hand knowledge of what is in the mind of God! The Holy Spirit is longing to share with you the thoughts of the Father, but He is able to do so only when you are in daily communion with Him. Perhaps it is time for you to stop talking incessantly throughout your prayer times and to simply listen to the voice of the Holy Spirit.

Now we have received, not the spirit of the world, but the Spirit who is from God, so that we may know the things freely given to us by God.... (1 Corinthians 2:12)

God's thoughts are not hidden, nor are they a riddle; our loving Father is the greatest Communicator in all of eternity. He enthusiastically and generously yearns for His children to know exactly what He is thinking. God doesn't play hide-and-seek with us, nor does He play hard to get. He is easier to understand and more accessible to know that you have ever imagined! He simply desires that you desire Him. He wants to hang out with you every day of your earthly existence. He wants you to be in close friendship with the Holy Spirit, who is an expert at knowing the mind of God.

We understand that relationships with friends and family members flourish when we definitively commit to spending time together. When I make a lunch date with a friend, it communicates to her that she is important and valuable to me. When I look at my husband's face and listen as he talks, it tells him that I love him and can't wait to hear what he is going to say next. When I put away my cell phone and simply have a cup of tea with my mom as we laugh and share memories, she feels loved and appreciated by me, her daughter.

A relationship with the Father takes much the same commitment of undivided attention, and it also requires the priority of spending quality time together. Again, God wants to hear you say, "Father, I choose *You!*" When you choose God before you choose social media, extracurricular interests, hobbies, or even necessary commitments in life, He will freely give you His thoughts, opinions, and wisdom.

> *...which things we also speak, not in words taught by human wisdom, but in those taught by the Spirit, combining spiritual thoughts with spiritual words.* (1 Corinthians 2:13)

This verse distinctly points to what should be our primary goal when dealing with our minds and our mouths. Our ambition should be to think spiritual thoughts that are birthed in the mind of God and are delivered to us by the divine communication skills of the Holy Spirit. Then, it is our human responsibility to make sure that those sacred and wise thoughts freely come out of our mouths in various situations in life. We no longer speak our own minds or our own hearts, but we become a mouthpiece of the Holy Spirit.

When we have cleaned our brains completely and made room for the thoughts of God, then our words become tools of wisdom and comfort.

They no longer criticize or condemn or even present a human perspective but are miraculously able to teach people God's truth, to comfort those in pain, and to heal those who are emotionally wounded, because that is exactly what the Holy Spirit does. And you, my friend, have been hanging out with Him! The Holy Spirit has rubbed off on you, and you have become like Him. The Holy Spirit is a contagious Spirit, and He wants you to catch everything that He has! That's a wonderful possibility, indeed!

> *But a natural man does not accept the things of the Spirit of God, for they are foolishness to him; and he cannot understand them, because they are spiritually appraised.* (1 Corinthians 2:14)

It has been all good news so far in our study of 1 Corinthians 2! We have learned that the Spirit of God knows the mind of God and that He can't wait to share all of it with us. We have discovered that when our mind comes into communion with the Holy Spirit, not only is our mind renewed but our words are transformed, as well. We actually begin to speak concepts that were birthed in the mind of God. However, now we are in for some sobering news.

If you are not connected to the mind of God through the channel of the Holy Spirit, you will never understand the spiritual words of God. If you ignore the function of the Holy Spirit, you will be unable to achieve a good connection with heaven and the mind of God. You will be left frustrated because there will be too much static on your direct line to the Father. Charles Finney wrote, "The unspiritual are deaf men judging music."

The good news is that the bad news doesn't last for long. Paul next presents a one-two punch when it comes to our ability to think the very thoughts of God Himself:

> *But he who is spiritual appraises all things, yet he himself is appraised by no one. For who has known the mind of the Lord, that He will instruct Him? But we have the mind of Christ.* (1 Corinthians 2:15–16)

The powerful, heavenly implications of this verse are nothing less than astonishing. We have the potential to think like God the Father thinks! When we partner with the Holy Spirit in our mental processing, we are able to understand situations, people, and events just as Jesus does. We have the miraculous ability to receive the wisdom of the ages. As mere mortals, we have been bequeathed the glorious discernment of the Holy Spirit. We can have God-sized dreams and divine creativity in our pea-sized brains!

When the channels are open between you and heaven, you are invited to tap into the infinite mental powers of the God who created such glorious demonstrations as diamonds, giraffes, and stars. You have been given the wisdom of the Father who invented the water cycle and electricity. Your creative Partner is a Genius who paints sunsets and renews the seasons every year. You have the mind of Jesus Christ.

This benefit is only one prayer away: "Oh, Lord, give me Your mind! I deeply desire Your thoughts and Your wisdom. Holy Spirit, guide me into all truth."

A BOY AND HIS MOM

It is impossible to compartmentalize the effect of having the mind of Christ to one area of our lives because it seeps over into every area, including academics. When my husband, Craig, was the youth pastor of a church in the Deep South at the beginning of our ministry together, we became close friends with one of the families who attended that church. The father, Harold, was an engineer and served as a church elder. The mother, Sarah, was a stay-at-home mom. Harold and Sarah's family was built around Mary, their teenage daughter; Michael, their middle-school-age son; and Ricky, their ten-year-old son. Sarah also found great delight in being a foster mom to many, many babies who just needed extra love.

When their son Ricky was in the fourth grade, Harold and Sarah were called in for a conference with his teacher. The teacher made them feel comfortable but wasted little time with small talk. She quickly let them know that Ricky was not doing well in school. Furthermore, she informed the shocked parents that Ricky was showing symptoms of some serious learning disabilities and that he likely would never graduate from high school. The compassionate yet truthful teacher had great concerns about Ricky's future ability to succeed in middle school and suggested that they look into a special school for their delightful, lively child.

As Harold and Sarah processed this diagnosis, they decided that, to succeed in his studies, what Ricky needed was the mind of Christ. So Ricky and his determined mother began to memorize Scripture together. Sarah placed Scripture verses on every kitchen cabinet and on the bathroom mirror in their home. Thus, while Ricky was eating breakfast, he was looking around at the Word of God. While Ricky was facing the bathroom mirror, brushing his teeth, he saw only Bible verses.

Sarah was so focused on helping her son to be able to process information in a normal way that she even climbed up a ladder and attached Bible verses to the ceiling over Ricky's bed so that, every night before he fell asleep, he would see the Word of God, and every morning, when this little man woke up, his first sight would be the truth of God's Word.

When Ricky entered fifth grade, his parents began to see a miracle in the making. His grades slowly began to improve, and he was able to pay attention in class, in spite of the usual distractions. Ricky began to repeat at the kitchen table what he had learned in class, and he developed a voracious appetite for learning. His improvement continued, and he eventually graduated in the top ten of his high school graduating class of nearly five hundred students! He later graduated magna cum laude from a private university and earned his MBA from one of the most prestigious universities in the nation. Today, Ricky is the CEO of a major pharmaceutical company, all because he had parents who believed in the importance of tapping into the mind of Christ.

> *I have more insight than all my teachers, for Your testimonies are my meditation.* (Psalm 119:99)

THE BEST FOR LAST

Although we have already studied the principles found in verses 11–16 of 2 Corinthians 2, let's go back in that chapter and read verses 9–10. I wanted to save the very best for last!

> *But just as it is written, "Things which eye has not seen and ear has not heard, and which have not entered the heart of man, all that God has prepared for those who love Him." For to us God revealed them*

through the Spirit; for the Spirit searches all things, even the depths of
God. (1 Corinthians 2:9–10)

God reveals to us—His beloved children—all that He has for us through the Holy Spirit. The Spirit is intimately acquainted with the deepest parts of God, and so He is more than able to teach what is in the heart of the Father. But what this type of relationship requires is constant communion. We must choose to stay in continual contact with the Holy Spirit, who is in continual contact with the Father.

If you have a genuine desire to know a person well and intimately, then you will be eager to spend time with them and will do so whenever possible. When I first met Craig McLeod during my college years, he was all that I could think about and talk about! I couldn't get enough of him, and I communicated with him in any way possible. I loved being in his presence, I took every phone call from him that came into my dorm room, and I adored the letters he sent me. It was through deep communication that I got to know the man that Craig McLeod was. I became acquainted with his plans, his desires, his heart, and his wisdom.

In contrast, I know a lot about Abraham Lincoln as a role model and as a president; however, I have never had the pleasure of spending time in the company of the Great Emancipator. I know Abraham Lincoln only through the writings of historians and from the way he is depicted in movies. Due to the fact that I will never meet this incredible man in person, I will never hear his voice or know him personally. However, you and I have a daily opportunity to get to know our loving heavenly Father, the Creator of the universe. So, if you want to get to know God, spend time with His Holy Spirit. The connection will be glorious!

OUR GOAL

In the same way the Spirit also helps our weakness; for we do not know how to pray as we should, but the Spirit Himself intercedes for us with groanings too deep for words; and He who searches the hearts knows what the mind of the Spirit is, because He intercedes for the saints according to the will of God. (Romans 8:26–27)

In this passage, we see that we have the added gift of knowing that the Holy Spirit is praying for each one of us! When the Holy Spirit prays, He prays according to the will, the heart, and the mind of God Himself. Our goal is to do warfare and win the battle over our minds, so let us determine to destroy the lies and attacks of the enemy. Our focused objective is not to settle for mere positive thinking but to be in moment-by-moment communion with the Holy Spirit, with His wisdom and power. The cry of our hearts should be, "Holy Spirit, fill my mind with the thoughts of God Himself!"

Those who seek the LORD understand all things.   (Proverbs 28:5)

GUIDE YOUR MIND: PERSONAL APPLICATION

1. Imagine that you are a professional organizer, and that your mind is your client. Do a walk-through and evaluate how cluttered your mind is with thoughts that are unaligned with God's thoughts. What are some of the erroneous ideas that have been allowed to gather dust there? After considering these questions, begin to devise a decluttering plan. Decide which false thought you will help your "client" to remove *today*.

2. What Bible verse can you use to help you declutter your mind and keep it in sync with the mind of the Father?

3. Willingly offer to the Lord your mind, your emotions, your plans, your heart, your desires, your tongue, your potential, and all of your discipline. Say with a sincere heart, "Lord, I am fully Yours!"

4. We have learned that the Holy Spirit longs to share with us the thoughts of our heavenly Father, but He can do so only when we are in continual communion with Him. Choose to spend more quality time with God. Additionally, during your prayer times, begin to incorporate periods of listening for the voice of the Holy Spirit.

5. When was the last time you clearly heard the voice of the Holy Spirit? What did the Holy Spirit say to you?

2

YOU ARE NOT YOUR PROBLEM

THE BLUEPRINT CREATED BY YOUR THOUGHTS

Your thought life has massive implications—both internally and externally—and that is why, when God desires to do a work in you, He always begins with the head. Your head, or your brain, is not only the Grand Central Station of your nervous system, but it is also the decision-making part of you.

For as [a person] *thinks within himself, so is he.*   (Proverbs 23:7)

The above incredible truth, found in Proverbs, the book of wisdom, indicates that your thought life has the authority to create the kind of life you will live! Accurate, yet sobering, this statement points to the fact that you will eventually become the exact representation of the blueprint that your thoughts have created.

This idea is not some New Age philosophy; it is a reality, and a God-given determinate of the course of your life. If you think negative, critical thoughts, you will become a negative, critical person. If you are living in a fantasy world, you will find yourself mired in the quicksand of never-never land rather than walking in God's destiny for your life. Your life *will* reflect the thoughts that you think about yourself and others—for better or worse.

One of the challenges of dealing with an errant thought life is that no one *sees* your thought life but you! We're not always motivated to change negatives about ourselves that aren't obvious to others. Other sin issues are more visible and apparent than the state of our thoughts, which are hidden in the recesses of our brains. For example, if you have a problem with overeating, it shows itself in the mirror, on the scale, and in the abandoned clothes in your closet. If you have a problem with lust, it reveals itself in the way you dress, the books you read, and the movies you watch. If you have a problem with anger, someone you love very much will probably bear the brunt of your rage sooner or later. If you have a problem with overspending, every bill collector in America has your phone number and takes gleeful pleasure in calling you each evening during the dinner hour. However, if you are embracing the deceitful and destructive thoughts that Satan offers you, it is easy to camouflage those thoughts and to pretend there is absolutely nothing wrong inside you. Yet, while a decaying thought life may be hidden in your brain, as mentioned earlier, it certainly has the potential to control the scope of your entire life.

WINNER TAKES ALL

For our struggle is not against flesh and blood, but against the rulers, against the powers, against the world forces of this darkness, against the spiritual forces of wickedness in the heavenly places. (Ephesians 6:12)

Your loving heavenly Father's ultimate plan for your mind is to fill your thoughts with His Word and with the power and authority that belongs to a believer in Jesus Christ. But just as God has a plan for your mind, so also does Satan, the Father of Lies. A battle over your mind is going on between God and Satan, good and evil, truth and fiction, righteousness and fantasy. Therefore, it's important to recognize that, according to Ephesians 6:12, you are really not your problem! Your problem is a spiritual battle, which has been orchestrated and masterminded by the devil and then carried out by his little band of wicked wimps. The devil understands the reality we discussed above—if he can influence your mind, his prospects are good for controlling your entire life. Remember, *"as* [a person] *thinks within himself, so is he"* (Proverbs 23:7).

Let me reassure you that your struggles with your thought life do not affect God's love for you; they will not remove the Holy Spirit's presence from within you or negate your eternal salvation in Christ. However, you *must* realize there is a full-blown assault taking place to capture the DNA of your brain—and, for the victor of that battle, "winner takes all"! That is, the winner will occupy all of your time and determine the overall state of your mind; this means the winner will hold all of your potential to change the world and will either provide you with joy—or steal it from you. Thus, the winner of the battle for your mind will hold all of your promise in life. We don't want Satan to have the victory in that struggle! We need to regain control of our thought patterns from the enemy.

How you deal with the battle that is raging within the confines of your mind will determine the environment of key circumstances and relationships in your life, including, for example, the health of your marriage. If you can halt your daily mental disappointment and verbal criticism directed toward a husband who burps, leaves the toilet seat up, and never seems to pay the bills on time; if you can cease to mentally disparage your spouse for his clutter around the house and the weight he has gained since the honeymoon, you can change the state of your marriage—and you will have the opportunity to allow your marriage to reflect the atmosphere of heaven! If you long for a peaceful home, you must acknowledge the biblical principle that peace begins within you. Your cerebral reasoning, to a large extent, will predetermine whether or not your home is filled with stress or with strength. The same is true in all other areas of your life.

THE WEAPON OF FALSEHOOD

I have had the character-building privilege of knowing a woman who believes that years ago, I did something to intentionally hurt her. She thinks that I did not handle a situation well, and she has never allowed me to forget that specific time when, apparently, I was wrong and she was right. As I look back at the experience that has caused her such pain, I honestly believe that I was loving and kind toward her and was doing my best to handle a difficult situation. She remembers it differently. I have apologized many, many times for any hurt that I might have caused her. I have taken her to lunch and apologized and have given her a gift that reflected my love for her. I have written her several notes asking for forgiveness and reminding her that she is important to me. I have responded to her caustic e-mails with love and gentle care. Still, every time I hear from her or spend time with her, she brings up that situation in a "woe is me" kind of way. After all these years, and after many heartfelt apologies, I now dread hearing from her. When her name pops up in the in-box of my e-mail, I groan and hold my head in my weary hands. I don't want to spend time with her—would you? And I am ashamed to admit that I have withdrawn from any type of relationship with her.

Why did all of this happen to a formerly sweet relationship? I believe it is due to her thinking processes. She falsely perceived something that never actually happened and has allowed this deception to corner her into believing that she is a victim. Her struggle is not really with me but rather with the Father of Lies; it is an ongoing battle being waged within her mind. Accordingly, I must remind myself that my struggle is not actually with her but with our unseen enemy, who loves to sow seeds of discord in relationships and to separate friends. The enemy does not fight fair because his chief weapon of mental warfare is falsehood. In fact, Satan is so desperate to gain control of your thoughts that he will throw every lie at you that he thinks he can con you into believing.

SATAN CAN'T READ YOUR MIND—BUT HE DOES OBSERVE YOUR LIFE

Protestant evangelical theology maintains that Satan is not able to read a person's mind because Satan is not all-knowing. Only God is omniscient, and He alone is acquainted with all the knowledge and thoughts that are stored in an individual's brain. However, one of Satan's favorite pastimes is to perceive Christians' thought patterns and weaknesses by observing their words and actions, so he can learn how to better attack us. For example, he will detect that you are crazy about your kids and that you protect them with great diligence. And, because the devil has been watching mothers for millennia, he knows how to trick a mother into believing lies about her children. Accordingly, he throws deceptive, cunning thoughts into your brain, hoping you will accept them as true, thoughts like the following:

"Your little boy is going to get sick."

"Someone is going to steal your son."

"Your daughter is going to rebel when she is a teenager."

"Your little girl is not as smart as her cousin!"

Such negative, fictional thoughts are hurled straight at your mind with full satanic force. It is up to you to decide whether or not you will allow those thoughts to simmer on the back burner of your brain. If you allow those wretched suggestions to weave themselves into the fabric of your mind, they may change from a passing, wicked lie into a very real and haunting possibility, as you project these ideas onto your children.

Because Satan is cunning and crafty, he not only has the ability to take the information that he has observed and then hit us with sometimes ridiculous but always irrational ideas, but he also takes great pleasure in tormenting us with lies that may seem feasible to us, such as the following:

"It's because you have gained so much weight that your husband does not talk to you anymore when he comes home from work."

"Your husband forgot your mother's birthday, and he doesn't even take out the trash anymore; he neglects you and your family!"

"Your husband does not really care about you; he is just going through the motions when he tells you he loves you."

CHANGE YOUR THOUGHT PATTERNS

It's time for a change in our thought patterns! It's time to reject Satan's suggestions and to receive God's truths. The transformation begins with a divine examination, performed by the greatest and most trustworthy Physician of all time. When Satan spews his awful lies into your vulnerable mind, he uses just enough of the truth to build his deceitful case. With the help of the Great Physician, you can object loudly and defiantly with the truth found only in the Word of God! We are not finished with this subject yet, because in the chapters that follow, we will learn more about how our spiritual enemy works and how to stand against him with God's Word.

The mind of the prudent acquires knowledge, and the ear of the wise seeks knowledge. (Proverbs 18:15)

GUIDE YOUR MIND: PERSONAL APPLICATION

1. Think about your everyday attitudes, words, and actions. What do they indicate about the state of your thought life?

2. What hidden, negative thoughts have you been allowing to direct your life?

3. Which fear-based thought has the greatest ability to throw your emotions and your life off-track?

4. What life event or relationship has most drastically impacted your thought life? Was it a positive impact or a negative impact? If it was a negative impact, how can you free yourself of this type of thinking?

5. Reread Ephesians 6:12, and then memorize this verse and other Scriptures that directly address your negative thoughts and fears.

> For our struggle is not against flesh and blood, but against the rulers, against the powers, against the world forces of this darkness, against the spiritual forces of wickedness in the heavenly places.

3

MR. DECEIT

SUBTLE DECEPTIONS

Since the birth of time, Satan has targeted God's people—beginning with the mother of humanity—with his preposterous lies. (Did you actually think he would be willing to treat you any differently?) The one with whom you struggle in the battle for your mind is known as, among other things, "the accuser of the brethren (see Revelation 12:10), "Wormwood," "Old Slew Foot," and "the deceiver." For the purposes of this chapter, we'll refer to him Mr. Deceit. Let's eavesdrop on a conversation between Mr. Deceit and Mother Eve, the first woman ever created:

> *Now the serpent was more crafty than any beast of the field which the* Lord *God had made. And he said to the woman, "Indeed, has God said, 'You shall not eat from any tree of the garden'?"* (Genesis 3:1)

As he did with Eve, when Satan attacks the thought processes of your mind, his strategy is to cause you to question the Word of God. Satan is sinister and manipulative, and therefore he begins by placing minute suspicions into your mind:

"You know, God does have favorites—and you are not one of them."

"God is good to you only when you are good."

"The Great Physician heals only a select few, and you didn't win the healing lottery."

"It's okay…go ahead—pay your bills and skip giving an offering at church this week. Tithing isn't all that important."

You must *never* entertain a thought that places doubts in your mind concerning the infallibility and the validity of the Word of God. God's Word is true all the time! Don't doubt the solid fact that the Scriptures are absolutely trustworthy for every situation in life. Every word, every verse, every chapter, and every book in the Bible holds eternal truth. There is no "maybe" about it! You must unwaveringly decide this issue for yourself once and for all: "If God said it, then I believe it, and that settles it!"

Of course, if you are not *reading* your Bible, then how will you even know what it says? The most powerful way to combat the lies of the enemy is by wholeheartedly embracing the strategy of reading your Bible on a daily basis. If you have a never-ending struggle with your thought life, you won't conquer it without knowing the Word of God. I find that the more I read my Bible, the more this dastardly struggle diminishes. If I am in the heat of a particular skirmish for my thought life, I often choose to read my Bible more than once a day! I place three-by-five-inch cards with Bible verses on them in strategic places in my home so that I can just pick one up as I walk by and review it. I have been known to tape Bible verses to my kitchen cabinets, to the dashboard of my car, and to the bathroom mirror. I am in this battle to win it, and the only weapon that will destroy Satan is the Word of God! By believing God's Word, you can build a solid foundation for your capacity for healthy thinking.

SETTING OURSELVES UP FOR DEFEAT

Let's continue to listen in on the conversation between Mr. Deceit and Mother Eve:

The woman said to the serpent, "From the fruit of the trees of the garden we may eat; but from the fruit of the tree which is in the middle of the garden, God has said, 'You shall not eat from it or touch it, or you will die.'" The serpent said to the woman, "You surely will not die! For God knows that in the day you eat from it your eyes will be opened, and you will be like God, knowing good and evil." When the woman saw that the tree was good for food, and that it was a delight to the eyes, and that the tree was desirable to make one wise, she took from its fruit and ate; and she gave also to her husband with her, and he ate.

(Genesis 3:2–6)

Satan's wily plan is to convince you that it is not absolutely necessary for you to obey *every* word that God speaks. He tries to chip away at your trust in God, and if he can place a shadow of a doubt in your mind, then he is on his way to accomplishing utter ruin in your thought life. When you enter into a discussion with Satan, and then allow his perverse words to simmer in your brain, as Eve did, it will result in defeat in the following three areas of your life.

1. SATAN'S LIES CAN AFFECT YOUR EYES

First of all, Satan's lies can influence how you see your circumstances.

*When the woman **saw** that the tree was good for food, and that it was a delight to the **eyes**....* (Genesis 3:6)

Satan's lies affect your eyes. The enemy's lies make things look attractive to you that ordinarily would not be appealing. You may begin to have thoughts like the following:

There is a handsome new guy at work! I know that I am married, but having coffee together is no sin; after all, everybody does it.

That trainer at the gym is just so darn cute! Does it really matter that he doesn't go to church?

I absolutely love watching the shopping network! I can't wait until I can purchase at least fifty more of those dolls they are featuring!

I am going to buy that two-hundred-and-fifty-dollar dress in a size small; after all, someday it will fit me, and then I will be glad that I have it!

Satan kneads and coddles our minds in order to change our perception of right and wrong. He is twisted and perverse, and, alarmingly, he tries to convince believers that his twisted, perverse lies smack of reasonable truth. Satan endeavors to tempt your mind with the pleasures of the moment, and to blind you to the long-term consequences of his deceit. If you are not reading your Bible on a daily basis, Satan definitely has the potential to convince you that he has a better idea than you have previously considered. However, when you have immersed yourself in the Word of God, you will know that every word Satan speaks is a venomous lie, and you will have the wisdom to reject his profane suggestions.

2. SATAN'S LIES CAN CHANGE YOUR DESIRES

Second, Satan's lies can change your desires from those that are healthy and eternal to those that are sick and temporal.

*...and that the tree was **desirable** to make one wise....* (Genesis 3:6)

Eve morphed from being a healthy woman who enjoyed the eternal pleasure of God and delighted in the company of her husband into a vulnerable woman who yearned for something that was outside the boundaries of God's plan for her. All of us who have spent more than thirty seconds conversing with Satan, the Father of Lies, have probably been guilty of a similar change of desire. We might begin to think things like the following:

I will agree to have sex with my boyfriend. If I don't, he will find somebody else.

Reading steamy romance novels can't be all bad. It's just a bit of vicarious, romantic pleasure.

Looking at pornography from time to time doesn't harm anyone.

It's okay if I charge a cruise with my girlfriends on my new credit card. I'll pay it off someday.

3. SATAN'S LIES CAN LEAD TO SELF-JUSTIFICATION

The third downfall of listening to Satan is that you will attempt to influence others based upon your own deception and self-justification.

*...she **gave also to her husband** with her, and he ate.*   (Genesis 3:6)

When we try to compel others to agree with our insane reasoning, it is an indication that we are trying to justify our acceptance of Satan's ideas. We might suggest to others things like these:

"Girlfriend, you look so sexy in that outfit! If you've got it, show it, is what I always say!"

"It's okay if you gamble on the basketball game. Everyone does it! You aren't hurting anyone, and neither am I. I've heard that even our pastor does it!"

"It's fine to use your credit card to pay for that great outfit! I always do it! I know that you are behind on your bills, but you can make it up."

It is a fatal flaw of human nature to think that if we can convince someone else to join in our sin, it somehow justifies that sin. When Eve handed the apple to her handsome husband and convinced him to eat the forbidden fruit, in her mind, it delegated her guilt to him and relieved her of her shame.

SHAME ON YOU

Then the eyes of both of them were opened, and they knew that they were naked; and they sewed fig leaves together and made themselves loin coverings. (Genesis 3:7)

When you listen to the lies of Satan and allow his deceitful implants to remain in your brain, not only will you see God's plan differently, not only will you desire things that you should not desire, not only will you try to influence others to buy into the lies, but the saddest truth of all is that you will have a genuine reason to feel shame. After being influenced by Satan, you will be ashamed of who you have become, and you will feel a need to try to cover yourself, camouflaging that shame. You will cloak yourself by imitating the behavior of the evil one who influenced you—you will cover your shame with a lie. It might go something like this:

"Well, honey, I don't know what that charge on the credit card statement was for. It must be a mistake."

"I had to work late."

"But, Mom! I really was over at Lisa's house…. You never believe me! Don't you even trust me?"

HIDE AND SEEK

[Adam and Eve] *heard the sound of the LORD God walking in the garden in the cool of the day, and the man and his wife hid themselves from the presence of the LORD God among the trees of the garden.* (Genesis 3:8)

When you enter into a conversation with Satan, allowing him to place doubts in your mind concerning God's Word, it will affect your communion

ord. God will still be there, waiting for your companionship and
bend time with you, but you will be deceived into believing that you
need to hide from Him, and you may begin to entertain thoughts like these:

Reading the Bible really doesn't help me.

*It seems like when I pray, He doesn't hear me. My prayers just hit the
ceiling.*

I think that I will take a break from church this week.

A STRATEGY OF ATTACK

*For though we walk in the flesh, we do not war according to the flesh,
for the weapons of our warfare are not of the flesh, but divinely powerful for the destruction of fortresses. We are destroying speculations and
every lofty thing raised up against the knowledge of God, and we are
taking every thought captive to the obedience of Christ.*

(2 Corinthians 10:3–5)

These three verses, written by Paul through the inspiration of the Holy
Spirit about two thousand years ago, hold the compass that unmistakably
points us in the right direction whenever we deal with an assault by Satan
on our thought life. If you are tired of struggling with the enemy's barrages
against your mind, these verses will give you the strength you need to press
on as an overcomer in Christ.

For though we walk in the flesh, we do not war according to the flesh.

With our minds, we both conceive of and receive thoughts; then, we
either reject those thoughts or accept them. The place where we have given the
largest amount of ground to Satan, by accepting many of his false ideas, is our
mind—that most dangerous place of all. The mind is dangerous because it is
part of our fleshly system, or fallen human nature. Yet this is actually great
news if you are in the middle of spiritual warfare, because although your mind
has been clogged by countless conversations with Satan, you will not have to
fight him in the weakness of the flesh—you can defeat him in the power of
the Spirit! It is fighting Satan in the flesh that wearies you and drains you of
all of your purpose and all of your productivity. When you attack Satan in the
Spirit, rather than in the flesh, you will find yourself strengthened, and you
will miraculously begin walking in the authority of Christ.

For the weapons of our warfare are not of the flesh, but divinely power-
ful for the destruction of fortresses.

This particular Scripture firmly states that we are to attack the lies of
the enemy with something that is *"divinely powerful"*! This one-two punch
of "divinely" and "powerful" is best translated from the Greek as "absolutely
God"! Again, there should not be one bit of your flesh in the fight; you can
stand with the sword of the Spirit, the Word of God, in your hands and
let that sword rip Satan into shreds on your behalf. (See Ephesians 6:17.)

When you fight your battle with *"divinely powerful"* weapons, you will
demolish "strongholds" in your thought life. A stronghold is an area in your
mind that Satan controls because he stated his argument in a deceptive
conversation with you, and you believed his misleading hypothesis. Many
Christians embrace the lies of Satan and rehearse them over and over and
over again until those lies have become strongholds in their mental real
estate. Again, if Satan can gain a foothold in our minds, he will likely control our lives, because *as we think within ourselves…so are we.* Thus, you
literally give to Satan a parcel of real estate in your brain when you allow
yourself to think thoughts of fantasy, worry, criticism, or anything else
false and negative. All that Satan is capable of giving you is deception; all
that God is capable of giving you is truth.

We are destroying speculations and every lofty thing raised up against
the knowledge of God, and we are taking every thought captive to the
obedience of Christ.

When we have given Satan a piece of real estate in our gray matter, our
thoughts will inevitably begin to contradict the truth of the Word of God.
Our heavenly Father took a great risk when He gave us the freedom to
think for ourselves. This privilege of being able to choose our own thoughts
confirmed the gift of our being made in the image of God Himself. We are
set apart from animals with this extraordinary gift of having the ability to
choose our own thoughts.

We do not fight our Satan-induced doubts with drugs, with neuro-
logical reconnections, or with a lobotomy! Instead, we bring down every
thought that is contrary to the knowledge of God and destroy speculations

at their very root. Once and for all, we need to do what the Word of God says to do with the lies of Satan: Destroy them! Take them captive! We must take captive our outrageous and unhealthy thoughts and make them obedient to Jesus Christ.

As you strategically choose your thoughts, your goal is to fill your mind to a greater degree with the principles and truth found only in the Bible. If you have a "default" setting in your brain, it should always be set to the Word of God!

> *Examine me, O* Lord, *and try me; test my mind and my heart. For Your lovingkindness is before my eyes, and I have walked in Your truth.* (Psalm 26:2–3)

GUIDE YOUR MIND: PERSONAL APPLICATION

1. Consider and identify the following: (1) your general concept of God; (2) how you feel about your current life circumstances; (3) your strongest desires; and (4) any negative behaviors you may have been justifying to yourself. In what ways have any of these areas been influenced by erroneous thinking, planted in your mind by the enemy? Match a Scripture to each of your answers—either one that affirms it or corrects it.

2. In what ways have you tried to cover a wrong action with a lie, in an attempt to deny or hide it?

3. If you are currently "hiding" from God because you have sinned, run back to Him, right now! Receive His loving embrace and forgiveness and be restored to Him.

4. Implement a counterstrategy to the enemy's lies by making a point to read the Bible daily and to actively believe God's Word, in order to build a foundation for healthy thinking.

5. In addition to reading the Bible daily, I dare you to share a Bible verse that is meaningful to you with a friend or family member this week!

4

"GET YOUR TRASH OUT OF MY YARD!"

Have you ever met someone whose personality and very presence just lit up a room? Have you ever had the delight of knowing someone who never failed to amuse you and frustrate you at the very same time? Such is my dear friend, Kathy Rae, who happens to be one of my favorite people in the entire world. She is my husband's first cousin, although they really grew up more like brother and sister. Kathy is an only child, was raised in a pastor's home, and is truly one of the funniest individuals you could ever hope to meet. She is so filled with both sputter and sparkle that I have often accused her of "making coffee nervous." No one does that but Kathy!

Kathy and I had children at the same time, and we delighted in raising our precious little people and homeschooling them together. Many an afternoon, you would find us at one or the other's house, combining our knowledge and skills to do a science experiment or create a craft, or just having a much-needed mental break while our children played together.

One lovely autumn day, shortly after school had started, my children and I spent the afternoon with Kathy and her three children at their home. Kathy has a beautiful piano room that overlooks the street through glistening windows that span the front of her house. As we stood by the door, saying good-bye for the tenth time, the local school bus pulled up and deposited about a dozen middle-school children from the neighborhood in front of Kathy's house. As these future leaders of America paraded off the bus and passed in front of her pristine yard, they left a trail of homework papers, candy wrappers, and pop cans. I looked at Kathy's face and saw it quickly turn an audacious array of colors, from pink to red to purple. I immediately began praying for those kids.

She yanked open her front door and firmly ordered, "Hey! You need to pick up your trash!"

The group of outstanding young people looked her way but kept right on walking, ignoring her determined, easy-to-understand instructions.

Next, Kathy raised her voice and shouted, "I said, 'You need to pick up your trash!' Turn around and pick it up!" This time, when the stellar students heard the angry inflection, they started to walk faster, attempting to get out of range of her voice.

Finally, Kathy stomped onto her front porch with her cell phone in hand and blared, her voice rising to a grand crescendo, "I know all of your names. I know your mothers. I know where you live. Now…get your trash out of my yard!"

Those formerly cocky kids backtracked, picked up their trash, and then smiled and waved politely, albeit nervously, as they ran down the street.

This humorous but true story teaches a powerful lesson as we tackle the sludge that has been allowed to remain in our brains. Whenever Satan tries to clutter up your brain with thoughts of doubt, worry, or fantasy, you need to think of Kathy's approach in order to get rid of the enemy's "trash." Take the Word of God in your hands, stomp, and shout, "I know who you are! You are the deceiver of the brethren and the father of all lies! Get your trash out of my life!"

How absurd it would have been to say to those middle-school hooligans, "It's okay, you sweet little darlin's. You can leave your trash in my yard. I'll take it all—old banana peels, rotten food, even trash from the bathroom. Just leave it right here to decorate my yard!" Yet, when we allow Satan to trash-talk his way into our lives and then leave the rotten residue of his cunning in our minds, our lives will exhibit the stench of his existence. Do not embrace the lies of Satan! Stand toe-to-toe and nose-to-nose with that dirty rotten scoundrel, and spit in his face as you proclaim, "Get your trash out of my life!"

BLITZKRIEG

Again, picture your mind as a battleground on which good thoughts are clashing against bad thoughts and where truth is contending with fantasy and fiction. In this volatile setting, the devil shoots a lie your way, while you try your absolute best to refute it with a sound fact.

"Your kid isn't going to graduate from high school," says the Father of Lies.

"Oh yes, he will! And he will go to Yale and become president," is your emphatic reply.

Hmm, that reply sounded a bit more like fantasy than fact.... Let's try that comeback again.

"Yes, he will graduate from high school, and he will be on the honor roll and even become valedictorian! So there!"

Once again, that verbal reaction sounds more like wishful thinking than it does truth. Most wishful thinking is certainly positive and may lead you in a healthy direction, but it is still not strong enough to stand up against the lies of Satan. When dealing with the enemy, fighting back with well-intentioned fantasy is like throwing water balloons at a vicious and dangerous terrorist. Your mind is a battleground, and you will never be able to take captive the enemy's lies with any of your own human, even though extremely positive, thoughts. You will need a different strategy than positive thinking provides.

Here is example of another type of response that is ineffective against the enemy. What if Satan, sneering and rubbing his hot little hands together, whispers this falsehood into your command central: *"That recurring headache that you have...it's really brain cancer"*?

How will you respond?

"Oh, shut up, you old liar, you," might be the best you can come up with at that moment. Yet calling Satan names is a powerless approach to his dastardly words. In fact, he rather delights in the name-calling and would probably even respond with a chuckle or two. You need something more powerful than your self-righteous thinking in order to conquer the manipulation and deception of Satan.

What is necessary to clean up the sinkhole that your brain has become is, again, nothing other than the dynamic, always-powerful, mighty, unable-to-be-defeated Word of God! Once more, let's picture the battle zone that has tortured your brain. Good is fighting valiantly against evil.

Right is in a wicked dogfight with wrong. Truth and lies are in an all-out struggle of epic proportions.

What if the Father of Lies smirks at you and repeats, *"Your kid isn't going to graduate from high school"*? You can answer, according to the undeniable truth of God's Word, "God is able to do abundantly in my son's life, beyond all that I can ask or think, according to the power that works within him." (See Ephesians 3:20.)

Or suppose the devil looks at you as an object of ridicule and continues his tormenting routine, saying, *"That recurring headache that you have…it's really brain cancer. You know that are going to get cancer! Everyone in your family has died of cancer, and you will be the youngest ever to die!"* You have the spiritual authority to tackle him soundly, taking him out at the knees, by saying, "Jesus Christ is the Great Physician, and the Bible says that by His stripes I am healed! He heals all of my diseases!" (See Isaiah 53:5; Psalm 103:3.)

Here are some other examples that will give you the strategy you need to embrace:

Satan begins to gloat as he looks down his massive red nose at you and mocks, *"You are going to have a rotten Christmas this year because you have no money!"* You can respond to his no-good piece of nothingness by hitting him between the eyes with this: "But my God will supply all my need according to His riches in glory!" (See Philippians 4:19.)

Or, the Father of Lies has the audacity to whisper in your ear on Valentine's Day, *"You are worthless. Nobody will ever marry you or love you!"* You can hit him below his infamous little red belt by saying, "The Word of God says that I am royalty and that He has chosen me for His own possession!" (See, for example, 1 Peter 2:9; Deuteronomy 7:6.)

With his knees shaking and his voice quaking, Satan makes one last-ditch attempt on your thought life, and croaks, *"You will never amount to anything! Your third grade teacher knew you were a big, fat failure, and it is true. You are a loser with a big "L" on your forehead!"* As a believer whose mind is ruled by the truth found only in the Bible, you can come in with this knockout punch: "I know the plans that God has for me! He has plans for welfare and not for calamity, to give me a future and a hope!" (See Jeremiah 29:11.)

THE ONLY WAY

I hope you are beginning to see that the only way you will ever have victory in your mind is by taking captive the lies of Satan with the Word of God. If you are one of the vast multitude of Christians who daily struggle with worry, fear, fantasy, negativity, or a critical spirit, there is only one strategy for conquest: to discipline yourself to read your Bible and to fight Satan's lies with the truth found in God's Word.

Again, if you try to fight this mental disorder with wishful thinking, with name-calling, or with mere delusion, your mind will resemble the Battle of Gettysburg—you will find yourself knee-deep in the bloody aftermath of the struggle, and, without a decisive victory, you will have to face the same type of opposition on another battlefield of life. Moreover, you will slog hopelessly through dead dreams and other mental destruction, with no clear direction for future conquests; and you will be armed only with depression. Conversely, when you come against Satan's thought patterns and processes with the all-powerful Word of God, the only blood you will encounter will be the victorious blood of Jesus Christ, conquering on your behalf!

But thanks be to God, who always leads us in triumph in Christ, and manifests through us the sweet aroma of the knowledge of Him in every place. (2 Corinthians 2:14)

GUIDE YOUR MIND: PERSONAL APPLICATION

1. List some of the "trash" that Satan has left in the "front yard" of your mind, such as thoughts of doubt, worry, fantasy, and resentment.

2. Why is it dangerous to leave the enemy's trash in the "front yard" of your mind? Will the trash of the enemy have any long-term effects on your life? What might those long-term effects be?

3. In what ways have you tried to clear away the enemy's rubbish from your life? Has the method been successful? Or has it been more like wishful thinking or a mere emotional response?

4. Dispose of each piece of " trash" that Satan has deposited in your mind by replacing it with a specific Scripture verse or passage that

speaks the truth of God about it. Commit these Scriptures to memory so you can speak them whenever similar thoughts surface. Develop a pattern of quoting Scripture to the enemy whenever he attempts to toss more garbage into your mind.

5

WORTH THE FIGHT

There will be a fierce fight involved if your goal is to achieve a spanking-clean brain. This fight is not a minor skirmish, nor a mere tussle; it is all-out warfare between you and the one who knows that if he can control your mind, he will be able to control your very life. Although the conflict in which you are engaged will be intense and, at times, more vicious than you can imagine, let me tell you two amazing and vital facts about it.

First of all, the enemy has already lost! This liar of gargantuan proportions has already been defeated; his power has been stripped from him by the Champion of eternity, Jesus Christ. Your role in this lopsided battle is simply to come into agreement with the One who is victorious.

The second fact is that the only strategy the enemy engages in is deceit; anything he says to you is an utter and ridiculous lie.

You are guaranteed the victory in this battle before you even begin the fight simply because you have Jesus on your side. If you long to clean up your mind and think the thoughts of God Himself, then you must partner with Jesus and the Holy Spirit in this triumphant battle. The battle is fought in three theaters of conflict: first, the theater of truth versus error; second, the theater of prayer; and third, the theater of worship.

1. THE THEATER OF TRUTH VERSUS ERROR

WHAT A WONDERFUL WORD!

Let me remind you that when a worry or a negative thought comes into that space between your two ears, it is futile to fight it with mere positive thinking. Human strength and insight are not enough to win this vital conflict over your mind; it must be fought and won through the victorious, true thoughts of God found in His invincible Word.

May I let you in on a wonderful secret? I can assure you that the disciplines of reading and memorizing the Word are more essential than any of your other daily disciplines, such as your morning exercise routine, your diet, or your work ethic. You will absolutely never win a spiritual battle in any arena in life without partnering with the truth on the sacred pages of the Bible. Before you go into battle, you must give the Holy Spirit something to work with! The Spirit will help you in every situation, in every skirmish, in every challenge, and in every conflict, but you must read the Word of God and memorize verses from among its treasure chest; otherwise, even the Holy Spirit may wonder what to do with you!

> *For the word of God is living and active and sharper than any two-edged sword, and piercing as far as the division of soul and spirit, of both joints and marrow, and able to judge the thoughts and intentions of the heart.*   (Hebrews 4:12)

A VITAL AND DYNAMIC SOURCE

The Word of God is not a dead, flat book; it is a vital and dynamic source for living a victorious human life. The Bible will enable you to actually "test" your thought life and determine which thoughts should be allowed to remain in your brain and which should be escorted right out of your gray matter. The Bible is able to expertly expose any thoughts that are improper or unhealthy.

We discussed previously that, as believers in Jesus Christ, we don't primarily read the Bible for *information* but for *transformation*. Embracing a daily commitment to reading the Bible will change your thought life in a way that nothing else is able to do. The Word of God is a powerful healing medication and an effective cleansing agent that will enable your brain to perform the divine functions for which it was created. But apart from the Word of God, your brain will be diseased and ineffective.

2. THE REALM OF PRAYER

A POWERFUL SPIRITUAL WEAPON

Prayer is the second theater in which you will need to launch a massive attack against the enemy. It is a powerful weapon against the assaults of Mr. Deceit, because it is through prayer that mountains move, massive seas divide, and death is conquered. When an ordinary believer spends time on his or her knees simply communing with the Father, demons tremble and resources multiply; bodies are healed and prodigals come home. Prayer should be in your arsenal of spiritual weapons every time you encounter the unfair fighting tactics of the enemy against your mind.

First of all, as you brandish the weapon of prayer, identify which satanic "ground forces" have been sent to occupy your brain. Make a list of the very things against which you are fighting. Some of the items that might be found on your list are worry, judging, rejection, a critical spirit, self-righteousness, negativity, and fantasy. Then, in prayer, ask the Great Physician to heal you of all of the germ-infested thoughts that have attacked your mind. Ask your loving Father to release you from processing every event in your life through your particular brand of mental captivity. You might pray something like this:

> Father, I come to you in the mighty name of Jesus, and I ask You to release me from my mental infirmity of _____.
> I ask You to clean up my brain and help me to think healthy and life-giving thoughts. Forgive me, Jesus, for always defaulting to a negative stream of thinking. Holy Spirit, give me the power to think God's thoughts from this day forward. In Jesus's name, I pray. Amen.

FERVENT AND EFFECTIVE

If the mental affliction with which you have been battling is excessively deep and has become a stronghold in your brain, it might take disciplined and daily prayer over a period of time for you to ultimately be cleansed and set free from your mental syndrome. But effective, fervent prayer victoriously holds the key to your ability to live a vibrant life that finds its source in a healthy mind.

> *The effective ["effectual fervent" KJV] prayer of a righteous man can accomplish much.*   (James 5:16)

3. THE REALM OF WORSHIP

SPIRITUAL CLEANSING

I have white kitchen cabinets that fill nearly the entire wall of the room in which I cook, entertain, and enjoy rich conversations with others. My kitchen also boasts a pure white countertop that runs the circumference of the room. In addition to the white cabinets and countertop, the emphatic exclamation mark of my kitchen is a sparkling-white sink. White…white… white. When you walk into my kitchen, you might imagine that you have been transported to the wonder of the inside of a snow globe!

Before I tell you my dilemma, perhaps you have already discerned the nature of my challenge regarding this room: How in the world is it possible to keep a snow-white kitchen sparkling clean, with no food spatters, coffee discoloration, or spots of dirt marring its look? How is it achievable to keep all of that white surface space free of stains, residue, and the yellowing that comes with age?

In my fierce battle against household grime and dirt, I have become familiar with every modern cleaning product. Simple soap and water refuses to effectively scour my kitchen, most generic cleaning agents do not remove the stains from the white surfaces, and even high-powered cleaning options have been futile to aid my attempts to maintain a kitchen with a blizzard-like appearance. Over the course of the decade that I have been operating in my perpetually white kitchen, I have discovered only one thing that will do the trick, one product alone that will clean to perfection my alabaster culinary heaven: the miracle agent known as "bleach." Bleach is the only cleanser powerful enough to keep my cabinets, countertop, and sinks clean and sparkling white all the time. Every time.

SING LOUDLY!

You, my friend, face a dilemma in your mind that is very similar to the one I confronted with my kitchen: How is it possible to keep one's mind free of the dirt and grime of daily living and experiences? Let me joyfully reassure you that it is indeed possible for those who are brave enough and defiant enough to use the spiritual equivalent of bleach to clean away the mental mildew and residue that has collected in their brains. That equivalent is to sing praises to God!

When you begin to think critical and self-destructive thoughts, you can change the atmosphere in your gray matter by singing spiritual songs—loudly. When the enemy begins to lie to you and tries to get you to agree with his ridiculous thinking, cut him off at the pass with the power of praise. Mental bacteria and worship are mutually exclusive; it is impossible for these two opposing factions to live in the same brain at the same time. Would you rather have a thought life filled with the germ-infested scum of Satan, or with the pure and majestic melody of heaven itself?

There is a profound and rich passage related to this topic that may be found in the recesses of the biblical book that was written by the prophet Isaiah. In my years of studying the Bible, I have learned to deeply appreciate the creativity of Isaiah as he learned to partner with the Holy Spirit in conveying a certain message. Much of Isaiah's book is difficult to understand, and at times we might wonder how Isaiah's insights apply to life in the twenty-first century. However, if you will absorb this anointed book in small gulps and read it contextually, as I have, you will discover that it has great meaning for today. Here is the first part of that profound Scripture passage:

> You will have songs as in the night when you keep the festival, and gladness of heart as when one marches to the sound of the flute, to go to the mountain of the LORD, to the Rock of Israel. And the LORD will cause His voice of authority to be heard…. (Isaiah 30:29–30)

Isaiah and the Holy Spirit are calling the people of God to perpetual worship. This message was not only given for the people living in biblical times, but it is as vital today as it was then. Isaiah is reminding us in the contemporary world, as well all those who will live in years to come, that when we choose to make the sound of worship with our ordinary lives, it will enable us to meet with the Lord on the mountain of His presence. When we choose to worship above the roar of circumstances, it is in that place that the authority of the Lord's voice echoes across our humanity.

Isaiah continues to teach on the power of worship:

...and the descending of His arm to be seen in fierce anger, and in the flame of a consuming fire in cloudburst, downpour and hailstones.

(Isaiah 30:30)

Isaiah firmly declares what happens when an individual chooses to worship; God goes to battle for that person who has determined to sing loud praises, no matter what the enemy continues to chatter on about. But this isn't all that Isaiah has to say about worship.

For at the voice of the LORD Assyria will be terrified, when He strikes with the rod. And every blow of the rod of punishment, which the LORD will lay on him, will be with the music of tambourines and lyres; and in battles, brandishing weapons, He will fight them. (Isaiah 30:31–32)

The above verses are powerfully proclaiming that the Lord will literally beat down the enemy to the rhythm of your praise! When your mind is dragging you through sludge, and your thoughts are filled with fantasy, worry, and bitterness, instigate a one-person worship service! When you sing, God enters into the battle against the enemy and shows that dastardly gene-pool-of-nothingness exactly who is the Boss of you!

The enemy wants to steal your song, because he is fully aware of how powerful that song can be in the battle for your mind. Don't let the enemy have your song or your mind! In the very moment when the enemy speaks, you, my friend, should determine to drown out his lies with vibrant worship for our loving and wise Father.

A DAILY BATTLE

Daily vitamins are called "daily" for a reason—they do the job they were created to do only when they are taken every day. We all know that a person with diabetes needs to take insulin daily, and a person with high blood pressure or high cholesterol has to take the corresponding medication daily. The battle against infection and disease is day to day, and patients with chronic conditions must submit to their doctors' orders every day of their lives. It is the same way in our endeavor to fight the good fight that ultimately results in our gaining back control of our minds—it is a continuous, daily battle.

Thus, as I have been emphasizing, you must ingest the Word of God every day in order to have a mind that thinks the thoughts of God. You must be committed to daily times of prayer and intercession in order to receive power thoughts from the throne room. And, you must choose to worship loudly and joyfully every day in order to clean up your brain from the mess the enemy has left there.

Incline your ear and hear the words of the wise, and apply your mind to My knowledge; for it will be pleasant if you keep them within you, that they may be ready on your lips. (Proverbs 22:17–18)

GUIDE YOUR MIND: PERSONAL APPLICATION

1. Recognize that the battle for your mind will always take place in three theaters of conflict: (1) the theater of truth versus error; (2) the theater of prayer; and (3) the theater of worship.

2. (a) In the theater of truth versus error, as you daily read God's Word, allow it to examine your thought life and determine which thoughts you will allow to remain in your brain and which you will refuse to allow to enter or stay there.

   (b) Choose a verse from this chapter that seems to speak personally to you. Memorize this verse and then write it out on five different three-by-five-inch cards. Place these cards in places where you will see them often and be reminded of God's truth.

3. (a) In the theater of prayer, ask the Lord, the Great Physician, to heal you of the destructive thoughts that have attacked your mind. Pray along the lines of the following prayer, which we read in this chapter. Remember that it may take daily prayer over a period of time for you to be fully cleansed and set free.

   > Father, I come to you in the mighty name of Jesus, and I ask You to release me from my mental infirmity of [worry, judging, rejection, a critical spirit, self-righteousness, negativity, fantasy, or anything else]. I ask You to clean up my brain and help me to think healthy and life-giving thoughts. Forgive me, Jesus, for always defaulting to a negative stream of thinking. Holy Spirit, give me the power

to think God's thoughts from this day forward. In Jesus's name, I pray. Amen.

(b) Find a prayer partner and ask this friend to pray with you over your mind and the thoughts that you think. Be accountable and truthful with this trusted friend as you cleanse your mind with the power of prayer.

4. (a) In the theater of worship, choose to praise and worship God above the roar of negative thoughts and circumstances in your life. Sing to God—often and loudly! Drown out Satan's lies with truthful, vibrant worship for your all-powerful Father. When you sing, God will enter into the battle against the enemy and defeat him.

    (b) What is your favorite worship song? Write out the lyrics to that song and allow the Holy Spirit to use those words to cleanse your mind from all that has lingered there.

6

HAVE YOU MADE UP YOUR MIND?

One of the most important aspects in this battle to regain control of your thought processes is to *think about what you are thinking about*. As a believer in Jesus Christ, you are responsible for your own thought life; no one else will be held accountable for the thoughts that you allow to simmer on the back burners of your highly productive brain. It is true that some of your actions may be prompted by peer pressure, and it is just as true that some of the words you speak might be a justifiable reaction to another person's influence; however, only you have the authority to determine what goes on between your two ears.

Often, we give ourselves healthy boundaries for the actions we choose to demonstrate and the words we choose to speak to others. However, the boundaries that we set for ourselves must not be limited to those two areas; creating mental boundaries is also a part of our quest to live a healthy life. Although your mind might be a secret, cavernous place, it still needs specific boundaries within which to operate.

The thoughts that you choose to think on a given day will determine your attitudes and moods for that day. A thought always precedes an emotion; remind yourself daily that a solid thought becomes an authoritative emotion before it is ever expressed through your mouth. Thus, every word that you speak has its conception in your brain; the birthing room of every emotion and every conversation is found in the Petri dish of your mental choices. Again, your emotions originate as thoughts, and your words tend to follow your emotions or feelings, so the processing sequence goes like this:

Thought —> Feeling or Attitude —> Action or Spoken Words

MIND CONTROL

The prophet Daniel and his three friends, Hananiah, Mishael, and Azariah, were four of the Hebrew youths who were carried off to the Babylonian empire at the captivity of Judah. These three young men were extraordinary in every way; they were leaders intellectually, morally, and spiritually.

> *Then the king [Nebuchadnezzar] ordered Ashpenaz, the chief of his officials, to bring in some of the sons of Israel, including some of the royal family and of the nobles, youths in whom was no defect, who were good-looking, showing intelligence in every branch of wisdom, endowed with understanding and discerning knowledge, and who had ability for serving in the king's court; and he ordered him to teach them the literature and language of the Chaldeans.* (Daniel 1:3–4)

Babylon was a godless and evil culture ruled by the cruel and despotic King Nebuchadnezzar. This royal villain had an intentional plan for the Hebrew youths whom his empire had kidnapped; his plan was to brainwash them and convince them to think the very thoughts of the Babylonian empire. Nebuchadnezzar was determined to change the way these young men thought, to rearrange their belief system, and eventually to destroy their very identity. The king knew a truth that you and I often ignore: whatever we believe, we will become; the creed that we ascribe to will certainly determine our character.

Identity begins in the brain and in the scope of one's thinking processes. Thus, the evil king, Nebuchadnezzar, and the spiritual enemy that you daily face, are in agreement about this one unchangeable aspect of life, which is true regardless of what century you live in: if you are able to alter people's thinking, you can change the particular way they perceive themselves. Consequently, if your enemy can "brainwash" you and convince you to think like him, he will also own your identity.

However, Daniel was an extraordinary and unforgettable young man with an excellent spirit. When he was confronted with the destructive plot of the king of Babylon, this is what he decided to do:

> But **Daniel made up his mind that he would not defile himself** with the king's choice food or with the wine which he drank; so he sought permission from the commander of the officials that he might not defile himself. (Daniel 1:8)

This young, impressionable adolescent made up his mind not to defile himself! He determined that he would not be polluted with the food of the culture, the wine of his captors, or the thinking of the compromised empire. Daniel knew that he had been chosen for greatness in the unseen kingdom and refused to fellowship even mentally with those who planned to steal his identity.

Have you made up your mind not to defile yourself? Have you predetermined that you will keep yourself separate, both mentally and physically, from the plans of the enemy to draw you into his culture? *Make up your mind* that your mind has been set aside for greatness in the kingdom of God; refuse to allow even a morsel of the enemy's deceit or a drop of the devil's trickery to enter your sanctified brain.

> As for these four youths, God gave them knowledge and intelligence in every branch of literature and wisdom; Daniel even understood all kinds of visions and dreams. Then at the end of the days which the king had specified for presenting them, the commander of the officials presented them before Nebuchadnezzar. The king talked with them, and out of them all not one was found like Daniel, Hananiah, Mischael and Azariah; so they entered the king's personal service. (Daniel 1:17–19)

The four young men who had been violently taken from their homes were used to change the course of Jewish history. There were others who had been kidnapped, as well, and who also came from excellent families. There were other young men who had been well-educated and who were also filled with potential; however, these other unnamed and forgotten young men apparently caved in to the thinking of the Babylonian empire and were never heard from again. They had been brainwashed by the enemy.

> *Then the king promoted Daniel and gave him many great gifts, and he made him ruler over the whole province of Babylon and chief prefect over all the wise men of Babylon.* (Daniel 2:48)

This is an amazing piece of historical information! Daniel, the youth who had made up his mind to remain undefiled at the risk of his very life, was now the beneficiary of the king's favor and blessing. The Babylonian kingdom, which had held Daniel hostage, now recognized him as a man of authority and influence. Daniel's voice of leadership was heard above all the other voices of his culture, and this amazing miracle was set into motion when he made up his mind to honor God. Daniel actually defied the culture in which he lived by remaining true to the Lord in his mind. It was, indeed, a valiant and defining choice that the young Daniel made!

When you make up your mind not to be defiled by the false outlook of the culture in which you live, you are offering yourself as a living sacrifice to be used by the King of Kings. When you resolve to think pure thoughts and to commit your brain to being a reservoir of righteousness and honor, you are positioning yourself for promotion, favor, and destiny in God. You will be promoted from being a powerless captive of Satan's attacks to becoming a ruling comrade of the King! You will evolve from being an ordinary person into an extraordinary servant. You will no longer be identified as "kidnapped" or "vulnerable," but you will take on the leadership qualities of the King Himself. But first, *you must make up your mind*. You must determine ahead of time, by the power of the Holy Spirit, which thoughts you will allow to remain in your mental cavity and which thoughts must be banished from your brain. Such a personal decision has the power to determine what type of life you will live.

Too many people mistakenly suppose, *It's not a big deal what I think. After all, it doesn't impact anyone other than me.* If you are thinking such self-defeating thoughts, I can verify that the enemy is talking to you and through you. He wants you to falsely believe that it is not a "big deal" what you think; however, always remember that the thoughts you think today will become the reality of your tomorrow. The world may be waiting for a man or a woman like you to make up your mind so that you, too, can have kingdom impact! God may be waiting for you to make up your mind so that He can use your life to change the course of history.

THE WISEST SUPERLATIVE

King Solomon is recognized both by secular scholars and church historians as one of the wisest people who ever lived or ruled. Solomon wrote most of the book of Proverbs, in addition to the books of Ecclesiastes and Song of Solomon. Kings and leaders from other nations traveled to Jerusalem to visit this wise man so that they could learn from him. They wanted Solomon's wisdom to rub off on them! Solomon's father was King David, whom the Scriptures call "a man after God's own heart." (See 1 Samuel 13:14; Acts 13:22.)

One night, early in Solomon's reign, God interrupted the king's sleep to ask him a piercing question.

In that night God appeared to Solomon and said to him, "Ask what I shall give you." (2 Chronicles 1:7)

Think about that for a minute! If God awakened you from snoring and drooling and said to you, "You can have whatever you want—just tell Me what you want," how would you reply to such an expansive request from God Almighty?

Perhaps you would ask for better health or for an Ivy League education. Maybe you would ask to be famous. Some people would certainly request the opportunity to add more stamps to their passport or to be able to experience extravagant living. I don't know of anyone who wouldn't ask for more money! Maybe on your short list of things to ask God would be for your children to live honorable lives, or for a godly spouse for yourself. Or would you ask to go on a trip to Disney World or Hawaii?

Solomon said to God, "You have dealt with my father David with great lovingkindness, and have made me king in his place. Now, O Lord God, Your promise to my father David is fulfilled, for You have made me king over a people as numerous as the dust of the earth. Give me now wisdom and knowledge, that I may go out and come in before this people, for who can rule this great people of Yours?" (2 Chronicles 1:8–10)

Solomon, with great foresight and epic humility, didn't request houses or lands but godly wisdom and knowledge. Look at God's response:

Because you had this in mind, and did not ask for riches, wealth or honor, or the life of those who hate you, nor have you even asked for long life, but you have asked for yourself wisdom and knowledge that you may rule My people over whom I have made you king, wisdom and knowledge have been granted to you. And I will give you riches and wealth and honor, such as none of the kings who were before you has possessed nor those who will come after you.

(2 Chronicles 1:11–12)

God took note of what Solomon had in his mind! Now, the truth is that God knew what was in Solomon's mind before he even expressed it, but the Lord was interested in hearing audibly the thoughts of Solomon's mind. God is likewise interested in hearing the thoughts of your mind. What you think in the deepest part of you is important to God!

When, in that innermost part of your being, you long for wisdom and knowledge in order to make godly decisions, you are setting yourself up for so much more than even wisdom affords! God takes note of men and women who desire wisdom, and He abundantly blesses them beyond what they asked for, thought, or imagined!

You will receive from God more than you had imagined when you have the right thoughts and when you have wise requests in mind. You are no different from Daniel or from Solomon; you have been given the remarkable opportunity to make up your own mind while you are living on planet earth. The thoughts that you think will determine the outcome of your life in a way that potentially nothing else has the power to do.

Today is the day to think about what you are thinking about, and to make up your mind! Today is the day to ask God for His wisdom so that you will be able to live a life with the kingdom impact of Daniel and King Solomon. Just like they were, you are part of God's incredible and forceful plan—so think like it!

I, the LORD, search the heart, I test the mind, even to give to each man according to his ways, according to the results of his deeds.

(Jeremiah 17:10)

GUIDE YOUR MIND: PERSONAL APPLICATION

1. "Whatever we believe, we will become." Think of two or three ways in which this truth has manifested in your own life.

2. We have learned that the process by which we become what we believe is as follows:

   Thought —> Feeling or Attitude —> Action or Spoken Words

   We can guard what we become by creating mental boundaries for ourselves based on the truths of Scripture. Have you established mental boundaries for the thoughts and ideas you accept into your mind? If not, start to construct them now. List some scriptural truths that will form the foundation of your mental boundaries.

3. The only way you can be successful in maintaining your mental boundaries is to do what Daniel did—*make up your mind* that you—and your mind—have been set aside for greatness in God's kingdom. You must predetermine to keep yourself separate, mentally and physically, from the plans of the enemy to draw you into his culture of lies and deceit. Today is the day to make this defining choice.

4. Write down one false thought that you will never accept again as long as you live. Now, rip up that piece of paper and throw it in the trash.

5. Write down one truthful thought that you will be committed to think every day for the rest of your life.

7

PRACTICE MAKES PERFECT

Piano lessons were as much a part of my childhood as were my regular habits of eating dinner with my family, brushing my teeth, and going to Sunday school! Every Thursday afternoon, beginning when I was just a little girl, I would dutifully and carefully cross the street in front of my house, walk past the village post office, and then go down three more houses until I reached the home of Darwin and Marianne Townsend for my 4:00 p.m. piano lesson. The Townsends weren't just any small-town pianos teachers, however—they were my close relatives, Uncle Doug and Aunt Marianne. My beloved and talented "Auntie," as I called her, not only taught me to play the piano, but she also taught me to love the books of Laura Ingalls Wilder, to write with perfect penmanship, and to fully engage in the study of Latin.

I took piano lessons from the enthusiastic and cheerful Auntie until I was ready for *John Thompson's Book Four*; then it was time for me to advance in the world of music. At that point, at about ten or eleven years old, I began to study under the true virtuoso, my beloved Uncle Doug. Uncle Doug taught me to love Gershwin, Chopin, and Rachmaninoff. When he was feeling especially beneficent, he allowed me to play the show tunes of the day, such as "Climb Every Mountain," "Getting to Know You," and "Put on a Happy Face."

But most important of all, during my years of studying music at Uncle Doug's Steinway grand piano, I learned the importance of scales, arpeggios, and etudes. Over and over and over again, my fingers were required to play scales in four octaves without making a mistake. The arpeggios were even more exacting and took much more practice than did the simple scales. I will never forget the hours that I spent practicing fundamental piano skills from the *Czerny Book of Exercises and Etudes*. These strict exercises are unrivaled for helping aspiring pianists attain a high level of function and mobility in their playing, enabling them to excel at technique.

But what I really learned every Thursday afternoon for over a decade was the importance of practice. When piano students make a daily commitment to lengthy practice sessions, it changes everything about their capacity to tackle the great masterpieces of creative genius! Were it not for the hours of disciplined—and often boring—practice that I engaged in while other children were playing Monopoly and kickball or watching reruns of *I Love Lucy* on TV, I would never have become an accomplished pianist.

Similarly, to develop noble thought processes, your mind needs to spend some time in disciplined and mundane practice under the tutelage of the Great Virtuoso!

MIND SCALES

PURPOSEFUL THINKING

When can you find time for these "thinking" practice sessions? Consider these questions: when your mind is at rest and idle, what should you be thinking about? When there is nothing on the front burner of your brain, what should occupy the space in your remaining cerebral matter? If you are a student or a scholar, when you are not solving quantum physics equations or memorizing Shakespeare or conjugating Greek verbs, what should your mind be occupied with? When you are in the shower, unloading the dishwasher, or putting on makeup, what should you be dwelling on? What mental habits should you engage in while folding laundry, filling up your car with gas, or trying—futilely, at times—to fall asleep at night? In other words, what should be the "default" of a mind at rest?

Rejoice in the Lord always; again I will say, rejoice! (Philippians 4:4)

Paul and the Holy Spirit have provided a profound challenge for your mind whenever you are idle, restless, or bored: rejoice in God! In your own "down times," have you ever considered defaulting to worship? A believer's mind at rest should be a mind filled to overflowing with praise and with the unction to rejoice. When your mind finds itself idle, it should immediately turn to thoughts of God's greatness, goodness, love, and mercy.

Defaulting to worship is especially important when our idle minds start to wander in a negative direction. Therefore, the first thing is to ask yourself, "At what point, in a twenty-four-hour period, does my mind generally lead me in the wrong way?" For many people, that perilous period is when they are attempting to gently fall asleep at night. It is in those moments, when the lights are darkened, the television is off, and the computer has been put away, that one's mind has the tendency to stray into danger zones. It is when you falsely believe that there is nothing else to think about that your mind finds something to worry about, someone to fantasize over, or some human pain to rehearse. As you lay your head upon your pillow each night sometime before the stroke of midnight, are you filled with fear over what may or may not happen? Do you erroneously make a list of all the things that your spouse has done to offend you that day? Do you painfully complain to God about the many benefits in life that have not come your way?

Identify your personal mental danger zone and then make an important note to worship God in that place, instead! Chose to praise rather than to worry or fantasize, and determine to rejoice rather than to take mental revenge on someone. Your mind needs to become a house of worship rather than a place where an accident is waiting to happen!

A PROACTIVE CHOICE

But an hour is coming, and now is, when the true worshipers will worship the Father in spirit and truth; for such people the Father seeks to be His worshipers. God is spirit, and those who worship Him must worship in spirit and truth. (John 4:23–24)

The *choice* to worship occurs in our mind, but our spirit always desires to worship. In John 4:23–24, there are two words that are vital to the human worship experience: one is *"spirit,"* and the other is *"truth."*

The word *"spirit"* in this passage refers to that part of a human being that is the life principal bestowed upon man by God. The spirit is the house where faith and the Word of God are at home. When your spirit worships, it is reflexive—nearly a divine instinct. Your spirit worships intuitively in response to God, just as your heart perpetually and regularly beats and just as your lungs continually take in air to enable your body to keep living.

The word *"truth"* in this passage means "according to the fact and in the mind." It refers to a person's choice to worship in the soul part of their being, which is a starkly different place from that of their spirit. My mind does not always desire to worship, but it must rise above its own objections and—in spite of circumstances, feelings, or disappointments—make a decision to praise.

While your spirit is a perpetual worship festival just waiting to happen, your mind has to *proactively* choose to participate in the celebration; you need to have made a predetermined decision to worship if you want to be consistent and effective. In the above verses, Jesus indicates that true worship is when your mind joins your spirit in a vibrant celebration of praise and rejoicing! Thus, He essentially defines "true" worship as worship that you enter into whether you feel like it or not.

SWEET REASONABLENESS

Let your gentle spirit be known to all men. The Lord is near.

(Philippians 4:5)

At first glance, you might wonder what this Scripture has to do with one's mind and the practice of purposeful thinking, but as we study its deeper meaning, it will actually become quite clear. The word *"gentle"* in this verse means "patient in mind." The Holy Spirit and Paul are in eternal agreement that our minds must be places of gentleness and patience.

This particular theme and exhortation challenges me deeply because of the type of woman I am. I must sadly admit that I often *appear* gentle in dealing with someone, when in actuality my mind is racing, condemning, judging, critiquing, admonishing, and condemning. I could win an Academy Award for "appearing" to be gentle and patient! The Holy Spirit, who is the greatest Teacher in all of eternal history, firmly coaches believers to embrace a genuinely gentle and patient mind. When I allow gentleness to be nurtured in my mind, it actually controls and stifles my capacity to be an angry and aggressive person. I begin to think gentle and forgiving thoughts toward other people, and my words come from a place of patience rather than a place of frustration. If I am able to supernaturally cultivate a patient mind, it will also activate my propensity to love others in the manner that Jesus loves them.

I remember coming across one source that defined the Greek word for *"gentle spirit"* in Philippians 4:5 as a "sweet reasonableness." I like that definition because it resonates deeply within a woman with my particular weaknesses. God is calling each one of us to be "sweetly reasonable" and to allow that sweet reasonableness to be cultivated in our minds. We are called to embrace reasonable expectations toward those in our world, and the Holy Spirit expects that we should sweetly express those expectations. For example, when someone offends you, you are required by the Holy Spirit to respond with a gentle and caring word of encouragement or a gesture of kindness.

NOTHING! ANYTHING! EVERYTHING!

Be anxious for nothing, but in everything by prayer and supplication with thanksgiving let your requests be made known to God.

(Philippians 4:6)

From the time it was first penned by the apostle Paul, this well-known verse has encouraged Christians throughout the centuries. It holds dynamic power to assist you as you endeavor to guide your mind, using it as a receptacle for godly thoughts and for pure, clear thinking processes. It is what I like to refer to as the "Nothing! Anything! Everything!" verse:

+ Be anxious about absolutely *nothing*!
+ Don't you dare worry about absolutely *anything*!
+ Pray about absolutely *everything*!

Do you understand the forceful and effective command that Paul is presenting? He is literally saying, "Cut it out, will you?! Just cut it out! Quit worrying and start being thankful! Cease being a person of fear, and start being a person of prayer!"

The question is this: "Will you agree with Paul and the Holy Spirit, and will you become a person who refuses to worry, who throws away anxiety like yesterday's trash, and who enthusiastically prays with thanksgiving? Will you?"

This injunction comes from the heart of a man who is spending unwanted time in prison due to serving the Lord. There is double reason, in the natural, for worry and fear in this situation. Not only is Paul unfairly chained in prison, but he is writing to a group of people who are about to undergo severe and cruel persecution themselves! Paul's advice to this group is that there is nothing in life that deserves an expenditure of worry. The words of Paul ricochet through the centuries as he reminds all of us today who are committed to serving Jesus Christ that our minds were never made for worry—they were made for worship! Thus, when our mind chooses to worry, it is not operating within its God-ordained function. Worry is simply attempting to carry the burden of the future by oneself in a receptacle that was not made to hold worry.

Would you ever endeavor to serve gravy with a slotted spoon? Would you ever try to serve hot coffee on a paper plate? Or would you ever think it feasible to substitute sand for gasoline in the gas tank of your car? You must know for what purpose your mind has been made and use it for that purpose alone. Your mind was made to worship—not to worry!

Worry can be defined as "anxious and harassing care." Is it possible, as a mother or father, as a husband or wife, as a single person, as the citizen of a nation, never to worry again? It must be possible, or Paul wouldn't have said not to worry! His advice holds life-changing influence for those who will believe in the power of prayer and in the mental cleansing power of worship.

Therefore, if your child becomes sick, you don't have to worry—you have the privilege of praying with thanksgiving! If your spouse loses his or her job, you don't have to worry, because you are called to a lifestyle of praise and prayer! If you unexpectedly receive a large bill in the mail, or if your teenager is found with pornography or alcohol, instead of falling into anxiety or anger, your immediate response can be one of worship and intercession. Don't worry about *anything*, but pray about *everything*! What a grand and abundant lifestyle we are called to live! There is nothing like it, so please don't settle for anything less than this energetic and electric life of "Nothing! Anything! Everything!"

This brings us to a question that we must all answer, one that is hidden in the coaching of Paul: "Does prayer work or not?" If you can answer this simple question of faith in the affirmative, then you must agree that worrying is a waste of valuable time that could be spent in fruitful prayer, with vibrant thanksgiving. Prayer is Paul's anecdote to worry, and in the above passage, he is trying to convince you that God cares for you and that prayer to the Father is indeed effective. He is assertively arguing that the God who cares about you is infinitely bigger than any problem you will ever face in life.

The only way not to be anxious about anything is to wholeheartedly pray about everything. The amazing thing about worry is that it doesn't work! Worry is a noneffective and futile way to spend one's life and mental energy. To worry is to think the thoughts of the enemy, and it is to stupidly agree with the deceiver's perspective of the battle in which you are engaged. But faith is thinking the thoughts of God Himself! Faith is bringing your mind into agreement with the purposes and plans of your loving Father.

God knows that anxiety and worry will turn you into a miserable, unhappy, and fearful human being. Worry minimizes the release of God's power and magnifies the lies of the enemy. The truth is that worry and thanksgiving are mutually exclusive. If you have allowed the enemy of your soul to infect you with the dread disease of worry, I can guarantee that thanksgiving is your miracle cure. I dare you to be such a thankful individual that worry will never find a place to call home in your mind. A non-negotiable goal that I have embraced in life is to be the most thankful person alive at my moment in history!

I know people who emphatically, but falsely, believe that if you sincerely love someone, you will be anxious for them when they are in trouble or need help. These people erroneously believe that the more you love someone, the more you should worry about them. Do you know anyone like that? In the following verse, the Bible takes a strong stand against such deceptive thinking.

Love…bears all things, believes all things, hopes all things, endures all things. (1 Corinthians 13:4, 7)

Love always believes for the best and has never been known to worry a day in its eternal life! A person is capable of living in that way only when he or she has taken every thought captive to the obedience of the Word of God, has developed a thinking process that embraces both patience and gratitude, is constantly rejoicing in spirit and in truth, and prays with thanksgiving. Praying with thanksgiving will powerfully force anxiety out of your mind and bequeath it with the gift of sweet, sweet peace.

I emphatically and completely believe that the Holy Spirit has recorded every Scripture in the Bible in order to present the blueprint that will enable Christians to live an abundant, joyful, peaceful, and hopeful life. God, the very One who created you, has brilliantly made your mind to be a place of thanksgiving and prayer, not a home of worry and anxiety. God knows what will cause you to live a productive life, operating at maximum capacity! If I were you, I would take God's advice on the matter.

SURPASSING PEACE

And the peace of God, which surpasses all comprehension, will guard your hearts and your minds in Christ Jesus. (Philippians 4:7)

Many of us are familiar with the term *"peace with God,"* which describes how a person is justified by faith in Jesus Christ. (See Romans 5:1–2.) However, *"the peace of God"* is a unique and thoughtful gift of God's own character.

Have you ever thought to yourself, *If I could just have peace about this situation, I would be fine?* Or perhaps you have supposed, *If I could just come to a place of peace with this event, I would be able to move ahead in life?* Worry is akin to an atomic bomb for disrupting a state of peace. Worry destroys peace before it is allowed to take root or grow or flourish in your life.

Yet, as a believer in Jesus Christ, you are invited to share in the peace of God Himself! He who is the Prince of Peace is generous and gives to you the same atmosphere that rules and reigns in heavenly places. It is a powerful reminder that His peace is perpetually available to those who rejoice always, have a gentle mind, are anxious for nothing, and pray about everything with thanksgiving. Peace is God's promise to those who actively practice the principles found in the above portions of Scripture.

Thus, the following is the heavenly equation that will deliver a supernatural and empowering peace to your life, no matter what is happening in your circumstances or what is developing in your relationships:

Rejoicing + patient mind − worry + thankful praying = the peace of God.

The type of peace that God delivers to His children will never be understood with the human mind: you will never be able to figure out exactly where the power of God's peace has come from. But you will have the solid and immovable knowledge that God's peace is well able to guard your heart and your mind in Christ Jesus. God's peace will take authority in your mind and will refuse to let any unwelcome interruptions destroy what you and God have worked together to achieve. His peace marches back and forth, continually guarding what is allowed into your mind.

This peace is vibrantly different from the peace that the world offers; the world's peace depends upon a lack of conflict or an absence of confusion in order to be a reality. God's peace, however, supersedes all natural and human events and provides a joy that allows us to carry on, even in the midst of great turmoil. God's peace delivers hope and confidence in the face of insurmountable odds. His peace strengthens His children when their burdens are heavy and when the pathways of their lives are ferociously rugged.

So, the next time your circumstances are distasteful and your emotions are roaring out of control, I dare you to default to worship, to refuse anxiety, and to practice praying on your knees with thanksgiving until you have worn holes in the carpet. I dare you! When you choose to respond to difficult situations in this godly and sacred manner, God's peace will be standing at attention at the entryway to your mind. God's peace will be going to battle for you against fear and worry. The turmoil that so aggressively intends to force its way into the cavity between your ears can be turned away time after time after time by God's ruling peace. However, when you worry rather than pray, and chose to whine rather than worship, God's peace will calmly sit down and wait until you are ready to do it His way.

Remind yourself of this formula again and again and again:

Rejoicing + patient mind − worry + thankful praying = the peace of God.

Ah...there it is! You have rediscovered the peace of God! God's peace is standing to its feet and taking its rightful position in your mind, where it will always protect you from fear and worry and anxiety.

The steadfast of mind You will keep in perfect peace, because he trusts in You. (Isaiah 26:3)

THE TRUTH, AND ONLY THE TRUTH!

Paul and the Holy Spirit are now ready for you to tackle the grandest and most exquisite concerto of all! It is time for you to be purposeful about what you dwell on. It is time for you to make godly and holy choices that signify your brain is being sanctified, redeemed, and saved. It is the moment for which heaven has been waiting, and heaven will stand and applaud as your mind begins to create this glorious melody, for which it was created:

Finally, brethren, whatever is true, whatever is honorable, whatever is right, whatever is pure, whatever is lovely, whatever is of good repute, if there is any excellence and if anything worthy of praise, dwell on these things. (Philippians 4:8)

The first thing to note in this challenging Scripture is that you only get to think about true things! There should be no fantasy, no fiction, and no fairy tales—about your life, others' lives, or any circumstance—in the brain that Jesus gave to you. (I am not referring to reading or watching works of fiction, including fantasy and fairy tales, that uplift, enlighten, or edify, as long as they ultimately cause you to be led to God and His truth.) It must be absolute truth alone for you to spend any time at all thinking about it. If you don't know that something is fundamentally true, then throw it in the trash! If you can't verify and justify a certain piece of mental information, then do not spend another millisecond letting it rest in the recesses of your brain. If a thought is not true, then it does not pass the litmus test of belonging in your mind.

HONORABLE, RIGHT, AND PURE

The second admonishment by Paul and the Holy Spirit is that your mind should focus on what is honorable. The Greek word translated *"honorable"* is *semnos*, which refers to thinking dignified and grand thoughts. *Semnos* is best translated by the English words *august* and *venerable*. (Truthfully, I had to look up the meanings of *august* and *venerable* when I discovered that these two very academic and archaic words explain what *semnos* means.) *August* means "inspiring reverence or admiration," "of supreme dignity," or "majestic"; one definition of *venerable* is "worthy of reverence because of noble character."

God has a high and noble purpose for your gray matter, and it includes majestic thoughts and godliness. Your mind is meant to be a grand place of noble and reverent thinking. It was never meant to be a trash receptacle for waste material from trite, superficial, or improper thoughts. Your brain was created for dignity, not for mental dirty laundry.

In a practical sense, this knowledge causes me to carefully examine which books I choose to read, which movies I decide to watch, and which music I listen to. I must remind myself daily that societal norms are not the standard of my walk with Jesus Christ. I must be very careful what I accept of the lifestyle, the thinking patterns, and the opinions espoused by my cultural environment.

The Greek word translated *"right"* in Philippians 4:8 is *dikaios*, which means "upright, virtuous, keeping the commands of God." My mind must be a breeding ground of righteousness. I need to ensure that every thought that I download onto the hard drive of my brain is one of virtue and in keeping with biblical principles. With every thought that comes into my mind, I must ask myself, *Would God think this thought?* If I am not able to answer in the affirmative, then the thought must immediately leave my mind. Sinful, dirty, and slanderous thoughts do not belong in the mental processes of a believer.

Your mind was meant to be a pure place, free of rotten, manipulative, resentful, and misguided thoughts. God fashioned you to be both mentally and morally immaculate; you were created to have a holy mind that is precious to God and an asset to the world in which you live! Your mind will need to take a fresh bath in the cleansing water of the Word of God every day in order to achieve this pure status. Do not settle for anything less than a radically clean mind!

LOVELY AND GOOD

God also made your mind to be one of the loveliest parts of your entire personhood. Your mind should be exquisitely pleasing and perpetually kind. It was created only for thinking beautiful thoughts, so there should be nothing in it that reeks of mental manure or decay. For example, the stench of gossip perpetuates when you allow an unkind thought concerning someone to remain within the boundaries of your brain. According to Paul and the Holy Spirit in Philippians 4:8, your mind should accept only factual pieces of information that are of good repute. Therefore, if you hear a piece of gossip, immediately discard it from your thoughts. If someone reports an unkind opinion about someone, banish it from your brain! Your mind will function at a powerful and dynamic level when you refuse negative speculations and accept only good reports. And, as we will learn later, if you don't think a thought, you will never be tempted to repeat that thought.

Loveliness requires tender cultivation and exacting attention. In order for your brain to achieve a state of loveliness, it will require your undivided focus. Keep in mind that lovely objects are usually not created overnight, and lovely gardens are never achieved by the work of forgetful gardeners. Perhaps it is time for you to partner with God to create an exquisite and rare display of His beauty in your mind.

EXCELLENT AND PRAISEWORTHY

Would you rather view the merchandise at the finest jewelry store in town or go rifling through a dumpster? Would you rather inspect the paintings at a renowned art museum or peruse the broken and stained objects in a secondhand store? God made your brain to be a place of unmatched excellence and virtue! He created this particular cellular structure of your human makeup to be a showcase of His nature, His thoughts, and His wisdom. Don't clutter up your brain with low-class thinking or with compromising attitudes. Raise your standard of thinking to that of your Creator.

Years ago, when my two older sons were attending a private academy in North Carolina, I taught Latin at that school for three class periods a day, every weekday; when I had completed my morning teaching assignments at the school, I would return home and tutor homeschool students in the ancient Roman language for an additional three to five hours every weekday. After I had fixed dinner for my family in the evening, my friendship with the Latin language continued as I graded papers, perused translations by my Latin scholars, and planned for the next day's courses. It wasn't long before I began to dream in Latin! All of my dreams were sprinkled with the beautiful language of the Roman Empire, so deeply was I immersed in the teaching of it.

Similarly, your mind should continually think in the beautiful heavenly language of applause and gratitude. Your thoughts should be so drenched with worship and grace that you even dream in your native tongue of godly optimism and rejoicing! Your brain should be trained to give standing ovations of appreciation, words of encouragement, and expressions of thanksgiving.

NOW YOU KNOW

Now you know what you are allowed to think about! Now you understand where the boundaries of a healthy brain are drawn. Now you know, my friend, what neighborhood your mind should dwell in. The dwelling address of your brain is Philippians 4:8—don't ever move away from that esteemed location!

When you begin to follow the encouragement of Paul, thinking true and honorable thoughts, it will turn your life into the best life possible— you will experience the abundant life. Your mind will move into the land of righteousness and purity, and you will become a vibrant and joyful person. If you will concentrate on allowing only excellent and lovely ideas to take up residence in your thought life, you will live the life of your dreams!

The mind of man plans his way, but the LORD *directs his steps.*

(Proverbs 16:9)

GUIDE YOUR MIND: PERSONAL APPLICATION

1. Have you answered the following question, which was posed in this chapter? "At what point, in a twenty-four-hour period, does

my mind generally lead me in the wrong way?" (For example, just before you fall asleep at night.) Write down your answer. Then prepare ahead of time specific verses and scriptural songs of praise and worship with which you can fill your mind at those times, allowing the Holy Spirit to guide you in this.

2. Begin to live a life of "Nothing! Anything! Everything!" based on Philippians 4:6:

    •   Be anxious about absolutely *nothing*!

    •   Don't worry about absolutely *anything*!

    •   Pray about absolutely *everything*!

3. What is one area in life that you will absolutely never be anxious about again?

4. What is one thing that you will never worry about again?

5. List three to five prayer requests that God has answered for you in miraculous ways.

6. Remember this heavenly equation for receiving supernatural and empowering peace in your life, no matter what your circumstances:

    Rejoicing + patient mind − worry + thankful praying = the peace of God.

PART TWO
GUARD YOUR HEART!

8

A HEART TRANSPLANT

Now that you know what it means to have a renewed mind that thinks the very thoughts of Christ, it is time for a heart transplant of the very best kind! It is time for you to make room for the heart of God in the deepest part of you. God wants to remove your hard, calloused, and worn-out heart and replace it with His perfect heart.

> *Moreover, I will give you a new heart and put a new spirit within you; and I will remove the heart of stone from your flesh and give you a heart of flesh. I will put My Spirit within you and cause you to walk in My statutes, and you will be careful to observe My ordinances.*
>
> (Ezekiel 36:26–27)

The *"heart"* that this passage describes is not the physical organ that pumps blood throughout our body and maintains our physical functions. When the Bible talks about the heart in this passage, it is referring to the core of our emotions, preferences, and desires. God has a distinct purpose for your heart, and it is vital that you discover that purpose so that you are able to live fully, richly, and abundantly in Him.

FASTER THAN A SPEEDING BULLET

Scientists tell us that our emotions travel eighty thousand times faster than our thoughts travel.[1] What extraordinary information! This explains why, when there is an emergency or when something tragic happens, we

---

1. See, for example, Robert K. Cooper, PhD and Ayman Sawaf, *Executive EQ* (NY: Grosset/ Putnam, 1997), 88–89.

are filled with raw, searing emotion but are unable to remember what to do or who to call. It also explains why a person will often operate out of emotion rather than out of principle. It's quite obvious that it would be helpful if we had something, or perhaps Someone, that could give us the power to harness our out-of-control emotional responses to life. If we don't give our emotions a speeding ticket, we will end up saying something that is totally inappropriate or reacting in a manner that causes great damage. If we don't control our emotions, our life will have the effect of a fast-moving tornado—it will wreak havoc on everything in its path.

ANCHOR YOUR HEART

As with our foundational verse for the mind, our anchor verse for the study of our heart comes from Proverbs, the greatest book of wisdom that has ever been written:

> *Watch over your heart with all diligence, for from it flow the springs of life.* (Proverbs 4:23)

The Hebrew word translated "*heart*" in this verse is *leb*, which is defined as "the soul, the seat of life, the seat of senses, emotions, and affections; the seat of will and purpose." Building upon this definition, we can conclude that the heart is the part of the human makeup that determines how a person will act in any situation in life; the heart is also an emotional thermometer and regulates to what degree we express our feelings concerning people, events, and circumstances. Additionally, the heart has been given the responsibility of regulating the affections and aversions. Thus, our heart dictates what we enjoy doing and what we vehemently refuse to take part in.

For example, why do some people absolutely love Christmas, while others dread the entire holiday season? That determination is regulated by their hearts.

What explains why you might just click with a certain person, while another acquaintance seems to be more like fingernails on the chalkboard of life? Your heart makes that call.

Your heart ordains when you overreact or under-respond; your heart decides whether you love sports or music. Your heart chooses whether your preference is breathing in deeply the brisk air of the great outdoors or enjoying a cozy afternoon inside by the fire with a good book. It is your heart that selects whether you are laid-back and messy or like to maintain a spotless, sterile home.

PRESERVE YOUR HEART FROM DANGER

The Hebrew word translated *"watch"* in Proverbs 4:23 is *natsar*, which is also often rendered "guard." This word, expressed in the imperative, contains several levels of rich meaning—and it presents a powerful challenge to anyone who knows the regret of overreacting, overspeaking, and overemoting.

First of all, *natsar* means "to watch over, keep, preserve, guard from dangers." If a dear friend or family member asked you to watch over their precious and well-loved two-year-old, would you allow that little cherub out of your sight? Would you allow that tiny bundle of energy to cross the street alone? Would you permit that darling little person to play with the poisonous cleaning supplies underneath your kitchen sink? All of those suggestions are absolutely preposterous! Guarding a cherished toddler would require your full care and unrelenting observation.

Similarly, the Holy Spirit is asking you to guard your heart—which is a treasured and precious commodity to God the Father—with your most exacting care and with perpetual oversight. When you realize the serious implications of being instructed by the Holy Spirit to *guard your heart*, it should cause you to exercise focused oversight of that essential part of your being. You must diligently watch over your heart, and at the least bit of inappropriate emotion, you must bring it back into the boundaries you have set for it according to the Word of God. Your heart, or soul, is the two-year-old of your physical makeup, and you must treat it like a willful toddler. Guard it intensely. Control its behavior. Discipline it quickly.

The problem with your heart is that it doesn't want to be guarded! Your heart is adamant about expressing itself enthusiastically and often with high drama. Your heart wants to vent and exaggerate and dramatize every situation in life. But the Bible doesn't say to "express" your heart; it says to *"guard"* your heart.

My mother has given me a very beautiful diamond ring that she bought with the money that my father left to her when he went to heaven. This ring is a family heirloom, and every day when I look at it, I am thankful for godly parents and for a generous mother. Now, if I were to loan this gorgeous and expensive ring to you, would you throw it in the trash? Would you pass it on to a friend without my permission? Would you work in your garden wearing it? Would you dig your hands into raw hamburger meat with this valuable piece of jewelry on your finger? Of course, you wouldn't! You would treat it as it deserved to be treated—with great love, care, and responsibility.

This is how you must likewise guard your heart, because it is both God's treasure and your treasure; it is of great value to you, and how you treat it matters very much not only to you, but also to those in the inner circle of your relationships. Your heart is indeed a family heirloom, and its legacy can have a great impact—not only now, but on the generations to come.

BLOCKADE YOUR HEART

The second biblical meaning of the word *natsar* is "to be blockaded." This word was often used to describe the assignment of guard ships that traveled back and forth in front of a port during times of war. The guard ships, or "sea sentries," were expected to warden a much larger expanse than just the area in front of the port. These appointed and official vessels patrolled miles and miles of water surrounding the confines of the port. They were on the lookout for any enemy activity and were prepared to go to battle in order to protect their assignment.

You, too, must blockade a large dimension of territory around your heart, constantly being on the lookout for the attempts of the enemy to enter into the issues of your life. This is especially important when you are going through a difficult time or are in a fierce battle—spiritually, emotionally, or physically.

It is in times of intense battle that the enemy is most apt to try to sneak into the area that guards your heart. During such difficult days of your life, that old deceiver will try his hardest to skulk into your emotions and win a victory. You must be especially diligent in those dangerous times when you feel most out of control of your emotions. Utilize the Word of God to set up a blockade around your heart so that no enemy forces are allowed to sneak in unnoticed. Guard your heart when your world is imploding. Guard your heart when your life is in ruins. Guard your heart when you are deeply disappointed. Guard your heart.

BE A FAITHFUL WATCHMAN OVER YOUR HEART

The Hebrew word *natsar*, which describes how a person needs to treat his or her heart, can also be translated as "to be a watchman over; to guard with fidelity." You are the only watchman that your heart will ever have, and it is vital that you never deviate from your planned course of earnestly keeping watch over all of the issues of your heart. Watch over your heart when life is easy and when it is hard; watch over your heart when you are happy and when you are sad. Refuse to allow any enemy emotions or attitudes to invade the peaceful ground that determines the issues of your life.

The Holy Spirit tells us the "how" of watching over our hearts: "guard with fidelity." This solo task of watching over your heart must be done with great faithfulness. The honorable business of defending your heart requires determination, fortitude, and dedication. The enemy troops that are storming their way toward you will endeavor to distract you from this essential assignment, which has been given to you by the Holy Spirit—but stay focused on the job. Always faithful. Always guarding. Always watchful. Always.

LIFE-GIVING OR SWAMPY?

The decision to guard your heart with honor and faithfulness will affect every other aspect of your life. The stuff that you allow to enter the recesses of your heart will determine how you act, and will undoubtedly determine your reputation. You must not only monitor what is allowed to enter your heart, but you must also guard what is allowed to exit your heart. Thus, your ability to guard the boundaries of your heart will perpetually determine the boundaries of your very life.

The truth is, if you have kept your heart from outrageous emotional reactions and have forbidden angry and hurtful attitudes to smolder in the coals of your inner being, those unseemly emotions will not come out of your heart, because they were never allowed to enter it. I have a friend who often says to me, "If ugly doesn't live in your heart, then ugly won't be able to come out of your heart." (See Matthew 15:18–20; Luke 6:45.) Yet if you have not guarded your heart well, then you certainly have embraced a skewed value system and will not be able to make decisions based upon principle and virtue; your decisions will spring from unstable emotions and selfish preferences.

When you truly keep your heart away from the enemy's influence, your life will be a fresh, life-giving fountain filled with sweetness and strength. Doesn't that sound desirable? If, however, you have allowed the enemy to infiltrate your heart with his opinions, his preferences, and his emotions, your life will then contain putrid, stagnant, and infested water that has no destination but is a cesspool filled with certain death. Yuck! Who wants a life like that! Who wants a friend like that, a spouse like that, or a parent like that!

Faithfully guard your heart, and you will become a stable and powerful woman of God who is able to navigate the challenges and difficulties in life without subjecting others to unguarded, unsteady emotions. You will be a sweet gift of strength and peace to the world in which you live! The legacy that you bequeath will continue for generations beyond the "dash" on your tombstone, and you will be forever known as a woman of virtue and honor. Guard your heart above all else, and you will have the pleasure of living an abundant and joyful life!

A tranquil heart is life to the body, but passion [envy, jealousy[2]] *is rottenness to the bones.*   (Proverbs 14:30)

GUARD YOUR HEART: PERSONAL APPLICATION

1. Before reading this chapter, did you ever consider your own heart's value to God? Based on what you have read, how would you describe the worth of your heart in God's eyes?

2. After having read this chapter, *why* do you believe that your heart is so valuable to God?

3. Proverbs 4:23 can be taken as a direct instruction from the Holy Spirit to us. Commit this verse to memory as you consider your commitment to guarding your heart:

---

2. *Strong's*, #H7068.

> *Watch over* [guard] *your heart with all diligence, for from it*
> *flow the springs of life.* (Proverbs 4:23)

4. In this chapter, various images were used to describe the ways in which the heart needs to be protected, including the guarding or watching over of treasure (a human life or valuable jewelry); a naval blockade that prevents an enemy incursion; and a watchman who keeps alert for enemy advancements. Write down some practical ways you can protect your heart using these images as a guideline.

5. After having studied this chapter, what do you believe are *"the springs of life"* (Proverbs 4:23)? Be specific in your answer.

9

ARE THERE TWO OF ME?

You are going to love this chapter! This is the chapter that you have been waiting for your entire life. This chapter will help you understand why you act the way you do, and it will give you a powerful strategy that will enable you to change your behavior when you don't understand or even like yourself.

Do you ever feel like you might have a dual personality? You can be sweeter than cotton candy to your pastor, your neighbor, and the women in your prayer group; however, when confronted with your husband's messy ways, your children's lack of discipline, or your mother's controlling interference, you become a screaming shrew with absolutely no evidence of the fruits of that delicious Holy Spirit!

In moments like those, do you ever wonder, *Who am I? Could I possibly be two different people in one body?!*

Let me assure you that you do not have a dual personality; you are simply a woman with both a soul *and* a spirit. Your soul, under the influence of the fallen human nature, will try to chain you to your emotions and lead you away from the character of Christ; your spirit always tries to imitate the truth of the Bible but will never force you to choose Christ over your disruptive emotions. It's up to you, my friend. Which do you want to be in control of your life—your soul or your spirit?

SOUL VERSUS SPIRIT

In order to understand these two vital components of our inner person, let's compare the soul and the spirit while observing their differences and specific assignments. Then, we will dig deeply into the Word of God and discover what the Bible has to say about these two parts of our human nature.

THE SPIRIT, OUR LIFE PRINCIPLE

The spirit is the life principle bestowed upon man by God; it is the part of a person that is able to perceive and grasp eternal concepts and sacred principles. Your spirit, quite simply, is the aspect of your being upon which the Spirit of God exerts its primary and life-changing influence. It is also the part of you that is assigned to guard your heart, or soul. Your spirit is higher than your soul and should be in charge of the soul in every life situation, directing your soul in what to do and how to act. We all require an enormously strong, well-fed, and fortified spirit in order to complete the task of guarding our heart.

The great theologian and thinker Martin Luther explained the nature of the spirit with these clarifying words: "The spirit is the highest and noblest part of man which qualifies him to lay hold of incomprehensible, eternal, invisible things." Your spirit "gets" God. Your spirit yearns for more time with your heavenly Father and for the sweet fellowship that He provides. Your spirit hungers for communion with the Father—and seeks it zealously, much like a starving person desperately searches for food. Your spirit is never able to drink in enough of the Word, of worship, or of times of intimacy with the Lord. Your spirit always wants more of Jesus.

The Bible describes the spirit of a man (or woman) in this way: "*The spirit of man* [the factor in human personality that proceeds immediately from God] *is the lamp of the* LORD, *searching all His innermost parts*" (Proverbs 20:27 ESV).

THE SOUL, THE SEAT OF OUR PERSONALITY

The soul is strikingly different from the spirit; whereas the spirit is a higher and more honorable part of one's unseen makeup, the soul is lower and often feeds on the empty calories of temporary issues and circumstances. The Bible often refers to the soul as the mind or heart; in fact, in Scripture, the words translated *heart* and *soul* are often interchangeable in both the Greek and the Hebrew. The soul comprises the mind, the will, and the emotions. It is the seat of your personality and the birthplace of your feelings, desires, affections, and aversions. All of your emotions are incubated in your soul. When the Bible talks about the soul, it is referring to that which influences a person's emotional responses to life.

Your soul walks by sight, feelings, and opinions, whereas your spirit walks by faith and the Word of God. Isn't that good to know? Your spirit is always trying to drag your soul into the victory of walking by faith! Again, you need a strong and well-conditioned spirit in order to control your expressive soul. A powerful and well-fed spirit is able to take charge of an immature soul and demand that it doesn't go outside of the boundaries that have been set by the Holy Spirit.

As Western Christians, we often make the horrific mistake of focusing on and feeding our souls to such an extent that we are guilty of forgetting or even ignoring the condition of our spirits. We give our spirits only the scraps that are left over from an extremely busy and challenging life.

For example, we choose to attend church if we haven't been up too late the preceding night going to a concert or to the movies. We read our Bibles if we can sandwich it in between e-mails, phone calls, and coffee dates. We pray for others on the run—if at all. And memorizing Scripture has become a lost art because we are just too busy!

Look at your life from an honest perspective and decide if you are feeding your spirit the nutrients that it needs in order to help you live an abundant and powerful life. What are your priorities? Do you need to rearrange some things in your life so that you are able to feed your spirit?

TELL YOUR SOUL TO WORSHIP

In the Psalms, David often commanded his soul to "bless the Lord." I believe the reason David did this was that his soul did not always "feel" like worshipping the Lord. Your soul is not much different than David's; and, like David, you may need to command your soul to bless the Lord! Remember, your spirit will automatically and instinctively respond to the Spirit of God in worship, while your soul generally needs that infamous kick in the pants to begin to worship!

Bless the Lord, O my soul, and all that is within me, bless His holy name. (Psalm 103:1)

In this well-known passage of Scripture, David is telling his soul that worship is valuable and that it is not an option! He compels his soul to worship the Lord, regardless of how it feels. And then, David reminds his soul to remember all that God has done on his behalf:

Bless the LORD, O my soul, and forget none of His benefits; who pardons all your iniquities, and heals all your diseases; who redeems your life from the pit, who crowns you with lovingkindness and compassion; who satisfies your years with good things, so that your youth is renewed like the eagle. (Psalm 103:2–5)

In this beautiful passage, David's strong spirit is reminding his whining soul of all of the blessings that God has given to him. Your spirit needs to do the same with your soul. For example, when you go to church on a Sunday morning after having gone through a very difficult week, you may not feel like worshipping. Perhaps life has been particularly hard; you might feel beaten up emotionally and be extremely weary in your soul. When you feel that way, it will be easy to sit in the service with a tissue in your hand and rationalize all of the reasons you falsely believe God understands why you are not singing, clapping, or raising your hands this week. If you give in to that emotional response, you are allowing your soul to have precedence over your spirit. Your spirit wants your soul to worship! Your spirit wants your soul to quit complaining and to start rejoicing! Your spirit knows that you will never win a battle in life by giving in to your emotional preferences. You will win when your soul submits to your spirit.

SOUL TALK

When your soul tries to take the upper hand, all it talks about is feeling, preference, and opinion. When your spirit joins in the conversation, it always echoes the principles and even the very verbiage found in the Word of God.

"Nobody ever thinks about me. I might as well be invisible," reports your poor, pitiful soul.

"I can do all things through Christ who strengthens me," declares your powerful and well-fed spirit.

"Well, I'll teach Sunday school, but it won't be easy, and I'm not going to like it. I am the only one who ever does any work at this church," are the languishing and woeful words of your morose soul.

"I won't grow weary in doing good, and I will serve the children under my care with a cheerful heart," asserts your energetic spirit.

"I better not give anything in the offering today because finances are tight," expresses your meager soul.

"I can't wait to give to the offering today! I might be going through a hard time financially, but I refuse to stop giving to the kingdom of God," is the affirmation of your spirit, which is in submission to the Spirit of God.

> The strong spirit of a man sustains him in bodily pain or trouble, but a weak and broken spirit who can raise up or bear?
>
> (Proverbs 18:14 AMPC)

Again, it takes a strong and healthy spirit to control anyone's soul, so your spirit must be ready at all junctures in life to exert its influence over your highly dramatic soul. Your spirit must perpetually instruct your soul how to talk appropriately and how to behave victoriously. Your spirit should constantly be in the process of reminding your soul what the Bible says.

A DIET OF CHAMPIONS

When neglected, your spirit will exist in a weakened and ineffective position. It is vital that, every day, you choose to feed your spirit those holy nutrients and sacred vitamins that will actually enhance its growth and bolster its resolve. What are those nourishing elements? Your spirit will flourish and mature when you are actively and energetically involved in worship every day. Worship is calcium to your spirit's skeletal structure. You must also give your spirit large portions and even second helpings of the Word of God. The Word will create a spirit that is unable to be defeated in any situation in life.

Don't forget that your spirit absolutely loves to feast on the delight of prayer! Prayer happens when your spirit is having an intimate dinner with the Father, and what joy abounds in that place! Additionally, tithing and fasting are two disciplines in life that will create a well-fed and powerful spirit. Moreover, your spirit craves the sustenance of faithful attendance at church—as you gain strength from fellowship with other believers—and a commitment to studying, not only reading, the Word of God.

Your soul, too, must be fed healthy nutrients in order to function at its optimum performance level. As we have discussed in previous chapters, the books that you choose to read and the movies that you choose to view are two of the ways that you feed your soul. This is why it is critical to choose well in the areas of education and entertainment. The things that you elect to ingest emotionally will determine how healthy your soul is when life becomes challenging. Your soul is also fed by human relationships, so choose people as your closest friends who are kind, who are filled with integrity, and who refuse to gossip. Friends who resort to childish behavior and who exhibit foolish attitudes will impact the health of your soul in a negative manner and cause it to languish. The germs of a weakened, diseased soul are contagious, and when you are around others whose souls are "sneezing" all over you, your soul is likely to catch the virus.

Your soul needs to submit to your strong spirit, and your spirit needs to take charge of your vacillating soul. If you have not fed your spirit the correct godly nutrients, your soul will threaten, "Mutiny!"

A PRAYER OF SPIRIT-POWER

One of the areas that vividly exhibits the difference between a well-fed spirit and an out-of-control soul is one's prayer life. You can pray with your spirit or with your soul, and God will hear both of those types of prayers. It is not a sin to pray with your soul, but when you pray with your spirit, you are praying with effectiveness and power beyond human understanding.

A soul prays with deep human emotion and often sounds like this: "Oh, God, You know that I have done my very best to be a good mother. Nobody on the face of the earth loves her children more than I do. But I just don't know what to do anymore! My kids are rebellious and ungrateful, and they are driving me absolutely crazy! Nobody in my entire family appreciates me! I just want to go on strike! I can't take this anymore, Lord! You have *got* to help me!"

Your soul, as you know, walks merely by sight, and so it processes human experiences and disappointments exclusively by what it sees and feels. Your spirit, however, lives in constant communion with the Father, so it will pray over the same situation with power and faith. When your spirit prays, it sounds like this: "God, I know that You love my kids more than I do. I know that You have plans of welfare for each one of them and that You have designed a bright and godly future for them. Lord, do what You do best! Go after my kids and bring them back to You, in Jesus's name!"

God created you for communion, for commitment, and for Christlike behavior. He has designed your internal makeup to run with confidence and faithfulness as you strengthen your spirit and allow your spirit to be in charge of your soul.

I warned you that you were going to love this chapter! Now that you know the difference between your spirit and your soul, you will be able to easily identify which is currently in charge of your life. Remember that your spirit sounds exactly like the Word of God when it talks, and that your soul often expresses itself with a victim mentality, and always demands its own way. The next time that you are in a challenging situation in life, allow your spirit to arise and tell your soul to sit down!

> *You have tried my heart; You have visited me by night; You have tested me and You find nothing; I have purposed that my mouth will not transgress.* (Psalm 17:3)

GUARD YOUR HEART: PERSONAL APPLICATION

1. Which do you think is *primarily* in charge of your personal life— your spirit or your soul?

2. Review the section "Soul Talk." Next, write down two statements your soul regularly says based solely on feeling, preference, and opinion. In response, write down corresponding statements from your spirit, based on God's Word.

3. Are you feeding your spirit all the nutrients it needs to help you live a more abundant and powerful life? If not, do you need to rearrange your priorities in order to feed your spirit? Which of the following spirit-strengthening activities could you integrate more into your life? In what ways will you do so?

    +   Bible reading and Bible study

- Worship
- Prayer
- Tithing
- Fasting
- Fellowship with other believers

4. Can you think of some other ways that you can feed your spirit?

10

A ROCK OR A STUMBLING BLOCK?

The people whose names fill the pages of the Bible were not perfect men and women; they were ordinary and flawed people whom God chose to use for His greater purposes. One such man was Peter.

Peter was an outspoken fisherman who heard the voice of Jesus call to him and say, "Follow Me!" (See, for example, Matthew 4:18–19.) Peter, who was always up for adventure, took Jesus up on His offer and spent the next three years watching Jesus in action. He was there when Jesus preached the Sermon on the Mount, when He multiplied the loaves and the fishes, and when He raised Lazarus from the dead. Peter laughed with Jesus, listened to His wisdom, and observed His power.

Peter was a man with fish guts under his fingernails and enthusiastic passion in every corner of his heart. He was the only disciple who chose to get out of the boat with Jesus in the middle of a ferocious and life-threatening storm. He also cut off a man's ear, denied Jesus three times, and was known for spouting opinions and emotions that no one had requested. He was quite the handful of personality and of "soulish" responses to life. In all the theological and historical descriptions I have read of this man Peter, the one common word I have found is *impulsive*.

Peter was on the same journey that you and I are, this side of heaven; we are endeavoring to lasso our heart issues and to guard our emotional responses to challenging circumstances.

A ROCK

Jesus and His band of brothers had gone on a walk one afternoon and were discussing the issues of the day. At one point, Jesus posed an interesting question to His dearest friends.

Now when Jesus came into the district of Caesarea Philippi, He was asking His disciples, "Who do people say that the Son of Man is?"
(Matthew 16:13)

I can imagine that some of them were anxious to answer, while others were more thoughtful in their response.

And they said, "Some say John the Baptist; and others, Elijah; but still others, Jeremiah, or one of the prophets."   (Matthew 16:14)

I wonder if Jesus paused at this point, looked down at the earth that His Father had created, and then looked into the distance. After perhaps a poignant moment of silence, He looked into their expectant eyes and made the question more personal and invasive.

He said to them, "But who do you say that I am?" (Matthew 16:15)

It is not what the crowds say about Jesus or how the culture chooses to define Him, but it is the personal response, that always matters. As Jesus tenderly interrogated His disciples, His question was posed not only to them on that dusty road to Caesarea Philippi two thousand years ago, but also to you. Who do *you* say that Jesus is?

Peter, who was never known for his lack of verbosity, felt the passion rise in his spirit, and he responded to the Spirit of Christ.

Simon Peter answered, "You are the Christ, the Son of the living God."   (Matthew 16:16)

I love Peter, don't you? He has always been my favorite disciple because of his full-throttle approach to life, his vibrant faith, and his leadership skills. In this conversation with Jesus, Peter's spirit is vividly and powerfully acknowledging the lordship of Jesus Christ.

Remember, when your spirit talks, it sounds like the Word of God and confirms the truth that Jesus brings. Peter's spirit was in robust form that day, and he couldn't wait to declare to anyone who would listen exactly who Jesus was.

I wonder if Jesus put an arm around Peter's shoulders as they continued their walk and their intimate, heart-to-heart communication.

> *And Jesus said to him, "Blessed are you, Simon Barjona, because flesh and blood did not reveal this to you, but My Father who is in heaven."*
> (Matthew 16:17)

Immediately, Jesus acknowledged that Peter had responded with his spirit, because this was information that only God could have given to him. Peter's spirit had heard from God on the matter, and he couldn't hold back from declaring what God had delivered to him. According to Peter's spirit, Jesus Christ was indeed *"the Son of the living God"*!

Perhaps Jesus began to smile, and then a heavenly twinkle appeared in His human eyes as He encouraged the man Peter. I can imagine that Jesus placed both of His hands on Peter's shoulders and looked him in the eye, Man-to-man.

> *I also say to you that you are Peter, and upon this rock I will build My church; and the gates of Hades will not overpower it.*
> (Matthew 16:18)

Like Peter, when you talk with your spirit and not with your soul, you will be walking toward your God-approved and God-appointed destiny. God is able to reveal His purposes and plans for your life when your spirit is allowed and even encouraged to take full leadership in the matters of your emotions and mouth. The Spirit of God responded to the spirit of Peter with the thrilling words that God was about to use Peter in the grand arrangement of the kingdom! Peter's life was important in the plan of God, and Jesus had a strategic position for Peter in His purposes.

When you lead with your spirit rather than with your soul, God will position you for critical importance in His kingdom. When Jesus hears an ordinary man or woman declare what God has spoken, all of heaven rises to its feet in attention, knowing that destiny is about to be established and purpose revealed.

Jesus continued speaking with Peter, saying,

> *I will give you the keys of the kingdom of heaven; and whatever you bind on earth shall have been bound in heaven, and whatever you loose on earth shall have been loosed in heaven.* (Matthew 16:19)

Not only was Peter given a position in the kingdom of God because of his strong spirit, but he was also given the authority and power of heaven! When you are walking in the truth of your spirit and not in the excesses of your soul, you will be given heaven's authority while you are still living on earth. Walking by one's spirit is a walk of divine and earth-shaking authority.

A STUMBLING BLOCK

As they continued on their walk, Jesus opened His heart to His disciples in order to gently yet firmly prepare them for what lay ahead—His sacrifice on the cross.

> *From that time Jesus began to show His disciples that He must go to Jerusalem, and suffer many things from the elders and chief priests and scribes, and be killed, and be raised up on the third day.* (Matthew 16:21)

This was horrific news to the entire group of disciples who had come to love Jesus dearly! They had given up everything to serve Him and had been eternally changed by His love, His wisdom, and the miracles He had performed. In this teaching moment, as they continued their journey in the unusually beautiful, lush region of Caesarea Philippi, Jesus told them the truth of what was to come. He would not be establishing an earthly kingdom but would suffer and be killed. Jesus knew why He had come, and He also realized that He had to prepare His closest friends for all that they were about to experience.

> *Peter took Him aside and began to rebuke Him, saying, "God forbid it, Lord! This shall never happen to You."* (Matthew 16:22)

I understand Peter, don't you? I understand the emotions that course through a person's body when appalling news is being announced. I understand Peter's stark and protective reaction to the awful words that Jesus had just spoken.

However, what is puzzling is that Peter rebuked the Lord in this sacred moment. Take it from me as one who has first-hand experience in this, it is never a wise move to rebuke the Lord. Of all the possible options that lie before you in a moment of pain or incredulity, never choose the box marked "Rebuke the Lord." Only an out-of-control soul would have the audacity to check that box!

The mistake that Peter made is a common one, and perhaps, like me, you see yourself in Peter's outrageous and foolish reaction. He was processing difficult circumstances through his soul and not through his spirit. His soul reared its ugly head, and he began to react emotionally to circumstances to which he was vehemently adverse. I wonder if Peter eventually wished he could press the rewind button and take back those words spoken out of raw emotion and gargantuan fear. So often, I have found myself in a "Peter place" in life, speaking from my soul rather than from my spirit. In such moments of coarse and unrefined rage, we are apt to speak from the instability of our souls rather than from the wisdom of our spirits.

> But [Jesus] *turned and said to Peter, "Get behind Me, Satan! You are a stumbling block to Me; for you are not setting your mind on God's interests, but man's."* (Matthew 16:23)

I have often read that verse and wondered what Jesus was implying. Truthfully, I have questioned how Jesus could have said those accusatory words to one of His favorite people! What was He thinking?! However, as I have lingered in this disturbing passage, it has become clear that Peter deserved to hear those words and that Jesus had the divine authority to speak them.

Those words, spoken from the deepest and most discerning place within the Son of God, are among the strongest that Jesus ever spoke to one of His own. Our Lord understood, from the perspective of eternity and righteousness, that Satan can disturb our emotions, but he can never influence our spirits. Allow me to reiterate that truth one more time: *Satan can disturb our emotions, but he can never influence our spirits.* The enemy will try to cause a revolution in our souls and then have that uprising spew out of our mouths. Just like Peter, when your spirit has been taught by the wisdom of Jesus, when you have been changed by the Word of God, and when you have spent time in God's joyful presence, Jesus wants to wrench you away from the influence and confusion of the enemy. Jesus is able to discern what is of the soul and what is of the spirit; and, in this startling verse, it is clear that a soul without boundaries is a soul that has been influenced by the enemy.

Jesus went to the heart of Peter's issues when He pointed out that Peter was not setting his mind on God's interests but on his own selfish perspective. Our souls focus on what we desire in the flesh; left on their own, our souls will not embrace what God desires.

Peter did not have a split personality. He was simply a man whose soul was often out of control. The deep need that he had at that moment was to experience a revolution in his soul, so that it would come under the authority of his spirit. The renewal that Peter desperately needed would indeed occur later in his life, but on this day, in this situation, his soul had won.

When Peter's spirit had declared earlier in the above passage that Jesus was the Christ and the Son of the living God, Jesus was able to bless him. The Messiah declared that Peter was a rock and that he would be given the authority of heaven. However, when Peter's soul spoke out of human pain and disappointment, Jesus called him a *"stumbling block"* and reminded him of the power of the deceiver.

We must each read this passage of Scripture in a personal way, applying the example of Peter and the response of Jesus to our individual lives. When you feed your spirit and respond to the Spirit of God with faith, you will be a rock in the kingdom of God! When your spirit is in charge, the Father will use your life to make a difference in the lives of others. However, when your soul leads the way, and you choose to spew volcanic discharge out of your mouth, you will become a stumbling block.

YOUR WAY OR HIS WAY

Jesus used this moment of awkward confrontation as one of the most vital teaching moments that He ever had with His disciples. He then spoke the riveting and familiar words that would ricochet down through the centuries into our lives today.

> *Then Jesus said to His disciples, "If anyone wishes to come after Me,*
> *he must deny himself, and take up His cross and follow Me."*
> (Matthew 16:24)

Each one of us must determine what our heart's desire is in the deepest part of our emotional makeup. If you wish to follow Christ, you must pursue Him alone. If you long for your life to count for something beyond human preference, then you will press into Christ and follow Him with a passion that most people disregard. You will be challenged to deny yourself, to forget your selfish plans, to die to self-centeredness, and to refuse self-pride. As a disciple of Jesus Christ, you are commissioned to deny your soul and to feed your spirit.

> *For whoever wishes to save his life will lose it; but whoever loses his life*
> *for My sake will find it. For what will it profit a man if he gains the*
> *whole world and forfeits his soul? Or what will a man give in exchange*
> *for his soul?* (Matthew 16:25–26)

In this passage, Jesus strategically chose a word for *"life"* that can also be translated as "soul." In the Western world, it is uncomfortable to address the topic of dying to self; we live in a culture of "self-help," "self-talk," "self-esteem," and "self-regard." However, God's way has never meshed well with the way of the culture. The call to Christ is the call to die to self and to crucify the flesh. If you long to follow Him with every ounce of courage and fortitude you can muster, then you must die to self-centered dreams, self-serving emotions, and foolish imaginations. If you long to live the life that Christ has fashioned for you, then you must also die to emotional excesses.

> *For the Son of Man is going to come in the glory of His Father with*
> *His angels, and will then repay every man according to His deeds.*
> (Matthew 16:27)

The deeds you perform after acknowledging Christ as your Lord and Savior are a reflection of how effectively you have died to self and to your soul. I believe that you can correctly diagnose the health of people's souls by observing their deeds. If your life and actions revolve around a focus of self-pleasure and self-fulfillment, then it might be necessary for you to take your soul back to the cross of Jesus Christ. Conversely, if your life now maintains its health and joy by serving others and pleasing God, then your spirit is vibrantly in charge of your life!

If you will die to your soul today and delight yourself in the Lord, you will experience a rare contentment that comes only from Him. Or, you can have it your way by feeding your soul those empty calories that you mistakenly believe you are unable to live without. If that is your choice, you might gain the whole world but, in the end, you will lose your very soul. The choice is yours and yours alone.

Remember, your spirit stays in sweet communion with the Father, but God longs to maintain authority in your soul, as well. Christ is asking for the loyalty of your soul, no matter what circumstances you face and no matter what dark disappointments you may encounter in life.

PETER AND PENTECOST

After Jesus's ascension to heaven, when the Holy Spirit fell upon the one hundred and twenty disciples in the upper room, Peter was there. And he was miraculously changed from being an impulsive, reactionary, emotional man to being an influential leader in the early church.

> These all with one mind were continually devoting themselves to prayer, along with the women, and Mary the mother of Jesus, and with His brothers. At this time Peter stood up in the midst of the brethren (a gathering of about one hundred and twenty persons was there together).
> (Acts 1:14–15)

Peter was the first one to speak publicly on the day of Pentecost, and he was used by the Holy Spirit to be a mouthpiece for the cause of Jesus Christ. He had been filled with a power beyond himself, and he became a man whose soul was under the control of the Holy Spirit.

THE CALL TO BE LIKE JESUS

Peter's life became a model of what can happen to a person who has learned to guard his heart with the character of God. When you learn to guard your heart and to rein in your speeding emotions, you will have the capacity to reveal the personality of God in every situation in life.

> *Grace and peace be multiplied to you in the knowledge of God and of Jesus our Lord; seeing that His divine power has granted to us everything pertaining to life and godliness, through the true knowledge of Him who called us by His own glory and excellence. For by these He has granted to us His precious and magnificent promises, so that by them you may become partakers of the divine nature, having escaped the corruption that is in the world by lust.* (2 Peter 1:2–4)

Peter's words demonstrate the potential that we all have to live a Christlike life. As ordinary people, we have the capacity to partake of the divine nature! We don't have to be in bondage to disappointment, to the compromise of soul-based living, or to the voice of the enemy himself. We are called to extravagantly demonstrate the very nature of God in the midst of even suffering and pain. It's what Pentecost did for Peter, and it is what Pentecost can do for you!

> *To sum up, all of you be harmonious, sympathetic, brotherly, kindhearted, and humble in spirit; not returning evil for evil or insult for insult, but giving a blessing instead; for you were called for the very purpose that you might inherit a blessing.* (1 Peter 3:8–9)

GUARD YOUR HEART: PERSONAL APPLICATION

1. In Matthew 16:18, why did Jesus call Peter a *"rock"*? What is it in your life that Jesus would affirm by recognizing you as a "rock" in His kingdom? What are some of the ways you have responded to Christ that give your life usefulness in the kingdom?

2. Shortly thereafter, why did Jesus call Peter a *"stumbling block"*? Are there things in your life that might not serve a positive purpose in the kingdom? What are those things?

3. Describe a time when has God pointed out to you that you were pursuing selfish interests rather than His interests. How did you respond to this correction? If you ignored it or rejected it, how will you respond to it now?

4. Consider how your self-centered interests might be a stumbling block to God's purposes for yourself or others. Take all your self-serving inclinations to the cross of Jesus Christ and offer them there, renewing your commitment to Him.

5. (a) In Matthew 16:24, what did Jesus say we must do in order to follow Him?

   (b) In Matthew 16:25, what are the consequences of not following this command?

6. Have you thought about the fact that dying to your emotional excesses is part of dying to self and following Christ wholeheartedly? Surrender all your emotions to Him and allow Him to teach you how to give your spirit full control over your soul.

11

THE DELIGHT OF DESIRE

My husband, Craig, and I were drowning in the joy of raising a large, rambunctious family while trying to build a church, homeschool our clan, and financially keep our heads above water. The small home in which we lived had been built to house a family of four, or at the very most five, but we had seven people crowded into its very limited square footage. Laundry, toys, pets, and children were everywhere!

My mother was a very successful realtor in the area, and she had just been given the opportunity to list a premiere piece of real estate. As she walked onto the four-acre lot, which boasted a three-story brick home, the Holy Spirit whispered to her, *This house is for Craig and Carol.* Even though we knew that we couldn't afford this home, we decided to look at it anyway. (I actually went kicking and screaming but had to submit to my husband and honor my mother!)

The owners of the home were wealthy and well-educated; they were prominent people in the community and leaders in their church. They met us in the driveway of their home, and the wife said to me, "I want to warn you that we are messy, messy people."

I quickly discovered that she was telling the truth! The mess showed in every room of their beautiful and expensive home. Everywhere I looked, there was clutter and disorganization. I saw more dust bunnies than I had ever seen in my life. Additionally, mountains of clothes were piled high on furniture, and stacks of papers rose everywhere, including in the bathrooms. This pricey and lavish home had not been well taken care of.

A similar negligent situation can happen in our hearts. In fact, I often wish that people would warn me of how well they have taken care of their hearts before I agree to enter into a relationship with them. It would save a lot of wasted time and unnecessary trouble if a new friend would just simply confess, "My heart is a messy, messy place. I have not cared for it well."

TAKING CARE OF YOUR HEART

Guarding your heart and keeping it free from emotional clutter, baggage, and grime is the most important assignment of your life. This God-ordained task is more vital than which job you acquire, what level of education you earn, how well you develop your talents, and how much money you make. Your heart affects every other area of your life, so make sure that it is not a messy, messy place.

I AM DELIGHTED!

What delights you? What is the one thing that brings exquisite joy and satisfaction to your heart? Some people gain the greatest satisfaction from having new cars, rich friendships, or excellent entertainment. Others are delighted by state-of-the-art technology, the achievements of their children, or travel to far-flung destinations. But what do the Scriptures tell us about delight?

> Delight yourself in the LORD; and He will give you the desires of your heart. (Psalm 37:4)

The beautiful phrase "delight yourself in the LORD" in this challenge from the Psalms means "to be glad in the Lord, make merry in the Lord, take exquisite pleasure in the Lord." As human beings who are tied to earthbound living, we have taken delight in all of the wrong things; instead, we should be exquisitely pleased in the Lord! We mistakenly suppose that pursuing the desires of our soul will make us happy, when true delight is found in splashing exuberantly in the love of the Savior.

When I first began digging into Scripture and discovered this exciting verse, I falsely assumed that if I showered my love upon Jesus, He would give to me whatever I wanted! I supposed that if I read my Bible in extravagant amounts, I would be able to move into my dream house; or if I sang louder and more robustly at church, I would get to drive a pink Cadillac! Yet this verse holds richer and deeper meaning than my false assumptions could ever realize.

The lovely and sacred truth that Psalm 37:4 teaches is that when I find singular pleasure in the Lord, He will place His own desires in my heart. It is those true desires, given by Him, that He is then able to fulfill and bestow. We erringly assume that pursuing our heart's desires will make us happy. In reality, it is being fully glad in the Lord and allowing Him to establish a desire in our hearts that He Himself will fulfill that will deliver a satisfaction infinitely better than simply being happy! When I delight myself in Him, and He fulfills the desires that He has placed in my heart, it brings me unmatched joy, deep contentment, and the peace that passes understanding.

THE SURPRISE OF GOD!

Craig's mother, Becky, is one of my heroines of the faith. She is a woman of prayer and a student of the Bible. She has loved her family well, and we all grieved with her when her beloved husband, Wesley, went home to be with the Lord. Shortly after Wesley's death, Craig and I and our five children ended up moving nearly a thousand miles away from her. She has one other son, David, who lives three hours away from her.

Becky, whom we all call "Nanny," has spent her entire life "delighting herself in the Lord." When we left North Carolina to serve the Lord in the northeast, she found herself alone and living on a very limited income. It would have been very understandable if she had thrown a pity party or two and stocked up on tissues to wipe her tears. However, she determined not to waste those years of her life and became a pillar of faith in her small community.

On Monday mornings, a group of women gathered in her home to pray for their children and grandchildren. On Wednesday evenings, Becky attended prayer meetings at her church, and on Thursday evenings, she invited a group of neighborhood women into her home for a Bible study. On Friday nights, she played games and had a potluck dinner with other widows. On Sunday mornings, she taught Sunday school and then would often go to a neighbor's house for lunch. Becky was happy and fulfilled during those challenging years because she delighted herself in the Lord in a very lonely season of her life and did not give in to the malaise of her soul. She has found deep delight in loving and serving Jesus!

You, too, will be surprised at how God is able to change the desires of your heart when you choose to delight yourself in Him. Your heart will miraculously mimic the desires of God, and the greatest Gift Giver of all will fulfill your deepest desires. The joy that you will experience will be enormous and purposeful when you delight yourself in Him and all that He is.

OUR UNTRUSTWORTHY HEART

Do you understand yet that you can't always trust your heart? As passionate and enthusiastic as it may be, your heart does not always tell the truth! It is often as conniving as a two-year-old, as persuasive as a smooth politician, and as unstable as a teenage girl in love.

> *The heart is more deceitful than all else and is desperately sick; who can understand it?*   (Jeremiah 17:9)

There are many smart and savvy people in the world today who falsely insist that simply feeling or experiencing a certain emotion validates it, but I don't see that in the Word of God. We have been hoodwinked into believing that every feeling that enters our heart is our reality and that we should embrace it, talk about it, and exhibit it without reserve. Talk-show hosts, humanistic gurus, and New Age enthusiasts all agree—if you feel it...say it.

We must realize that the emotions that endeavor to force their entrance into our souls are not always God-approved. Your heart instantly desires to express what it thinks it wants, and the way it feels in a given moment, but it is necessary to remind yourself often that your heart is not the source of all truth. Your emotions and passions are sly and slippery and usually do not bring genuine stability to your life.

> *I, the LORD, search the heart, I test the mind, even to give to each man according to his ways, according to the results of his deeds.*
>   (Jeremiah 17:10)

I am so grateful that the Lord loves me enough to search my heart! Often, when I have been drowning in the sewage of emotion-driven living, I have been known to cry out, "Lord! Test my heart!" I know that He is able to determine whether my heart is finding its delight in Him or is intent only on pleasing self. In those moments of sheer desperation, I often add these audacious words: "And while You are at it, Lord, test my mind, too!"

My heart and mind are not the litmus test of all truth; God's Word is the compass that will lead me toward truthful and brilliant living. Just like Peter learned from Jesus, I also must learn that my ways, my deeds, and my choices are a reflection of what is allowed to remain in my brain and what my heart is delighting itself in.

God gave you a heart to revolutionize your earthly existence, so that you would know the joy of experiencing heaven even while living on earth. You are invited to desire the very purposes and plans that God desires. You are summoned to align your passions to be in sync with the heartbeat of God Himself! Your loving Father proposes that you choose to discipline your singular personality to mirror the character of God, who is always kind, always true, and always merciful.

> *When my anxious thoughts multiply within me, Your consolations delight my soul.* (Psalm 94:19)

GUARD YOUR HEART: PERSONAL APPLICATION

1. What delights you most in life? Why does it have that effect on you?

2. Psalm 37:4 instructs us to *"delight…in the* LORD." In this context, what does the word *delight* refer to?

3. In what ways has God changed the desires of your heart as you have put Him first in your life and desired to serve Him?

4. If we believe that simply feeling or experiencing a certain emotion validates it and gives us permission to express it, where will that belief lead us?

5. What is the source of truth in your life?

6. Whenever you are caught up in unruly emotions or confused feelings, pray this prayer: "Lord, test my heart and my mind. *'Search me, O God, and know my heart; try me and know my anxious thoughts; and see if there be any hurtful way in me, and lead me in the everlasting way.'*" (See Psalm 139:23–24.)

    After you pray this prayer, be quiet and listen. Expect God to show you what in your life needs to be removed.

12

ALTERED ON THE ALTAR

What we have studied thus far in the section entitled "Guard Your Heart!" are foundational lessons in the dynamics of the human soul. We have learned that the soul is comprised of the mind, the will, and the emotions. When Satan targets a disciple of Jesus Christ, he is only able to come against those three areas or the physical body. The enemy is not allowed to touch a person's spirit.

Your soul, with its strengths and its weaknesses, has been shaped by how well or how poorly you have responded to your life experiences, events, and circumstances. These would include a wide range of situations, such as family life, relationships, socioeconomic advantages or disadvantages, education, travel opportunities, exposure to music, successes, failures, disappointments, and achievements.

Thus, who we are today is the sum of what we have encountered in life and our reactions to those situations. We are hammered and warped by abuse and rejection; we are inflated and propelled by flattery and praise. Human reactions to all life events, whether positive or negative, are poured into the vessel known as "soul" and are blended together to form personality and character.

One's "memory" is actually the spirit reviewing the history and the makeup of the soul. The events that you consider most significant, or the ones that have shaped you to the greatest degree, are never forgotten, no matter how much time has passed. Your natural mind, which exists as a major component of your soul, cannot forget certain incidents due to the fact that those incidents have become part of who you are in your soul.

REDEEMED AND HEALED

Brethren, I do not regard myself as having laid hold of it yet; but one thing I do: forgetting what lies behind and reaching forward to what lies ahead, I press on toward the goal for the prize of the upward call of God in Christ Jesus. (Philippians 4:13–14)

It is impossible to alter the past, but it is possible to lay the past on the altar of Christ as an act of worship. The choice to embrace a heart of worship, in spite of past abuse, disappointment, pain, or regret, will allow God to do a great work in your life. He will finish His beautiful restoration of your soul and revive that which had perished due to neglect or shame.

Every person has experienced some truly good things in life, as well as some terrible events; each individual has walked through successes as well as devastating disappointments. However, for life to be the amazing and abundant journey that it was meant to be, we must allow God to reach into all of our experiences and redeem us from our negative reactions. God's "operating room" is always known for complete and reverent worship. Worship is the channel through which we allow Him to heal the broken and wounded places in our souls.

And we know that God causes all things to work together for good to those who love God, to those who are called according to His purpose. (Romans 8:28)

When the deepest desire of one's heart is simply to love God, bad events can miraculously be transformed by His goodness and glory. An event that had the potential of harming or of paralyzing a person becomes the very incident that propels that individual into God's destiny, when it is covered with heartfelt praise and pure worship. Worship is the miracle cure for which your diseased soul has been longing. And worship is the mighty umbrella that will protect your soul from all of the violent storms that might intersect with your life in the days ahead.

KNOWN FOR STRENGTH!

We are all known for something; there is always a singular characteristic that defines the person that we have become. Some folks are known for their athletic prowess, while others are known for their musical ability. Some people are known for their dishonest dealings, while others are known for their integrity. Some people are known for exhibiting the gift of encouragement, while others are known for their critical comments. Will you be known for emotional stability—or for outbursts of anger or panic? The matter of utmost importance is that our circumstances do not have the power to determine the person that we will become. Again, the determinate is our willingness to worship!

> *How blessed is the man whose strength is in You, in whose heart are the highways to Zion!* (Psalm 84:5)

There is a heavenly highway in your heart, or soul, that will always take you toward worship. When the word *"Zion"* is used in the Bible, it refers to a place of pure worship. "Zion" is that high and holy place where an ordinary man or woman chooses to lay down his or her desires, opinions, and human will in exchange for all that God has and all that He is. "Zion" is where the King is enthroned on our praises; it is where the God of all creation meets with the created. When you clear away the overgrown emotional weeds in your heart and make way for the highway of worship, your life will hold a blessing beyond compare!

> *Passing through the valley of Baca they make it a spring; the early rain also covers it with blessings.* (Psalm 84:6)

With these words, the psalmist is unveiling extraordinary and life-transforming information! The *"valley of Baca"* is a place of weeping, sorrow, and deep disappointment. However, something unbelievable has happened in this place of dark grief, for it has miraculously become a place of blessing. How did this valley of despair become transformed into a place of gentle rain and vibrant growth? It happened because a choice to worship was made, in spite of human pain and anguish.

Worship revolutionizes the worst moment of life so that it becomes a place of fresh growth and blessing. When a person resolves to worship the Father, no matter what has happened this side of heaven, his or her life is transformed; what was once a wicked battlefield becomes a glorious garden of strength and beauty, splendor and delight. While others are dealing with devastation and the remnants of destruction, a worshipper sees only majesty and grandeur as far as the eye can see!

They go from strength to strength, every one of them appears before God in Zion. (Psalm 84:7)

You don't have to give deep disappointment, human pain, and emotional carnage the power to maim or dismantle your life. When you command your soul to worship the Lord, rather than wail in despair, you will be known for extraordinary strength! This strength is not extracted from circumstances but is a gift that God gives to the person who decides to defy his or her current reality with the knockout blow of worship. No longer will you be defined by the weakness into which events and people have pounded you, but you will be known as a person of stellar strength due to your consuming desire to worship!

Teach me Your way, O LORD; I will walk in Your truth; unite my heart to fear Your name. I will give thanks to You, O Lord my God, with all my heart, and will glorify Your name forever. (Psalm 86:11–12)

GUARD YOUR HEART: PERSONAL APPLICATION

1. Have you laid all your past disappointments, pain, and regret upon the altar of Christ as an act of worship? Is there anything particular from your past that holds you back from wholeheartedly following God? If so, what is it? Offer all of your past to Him and choose to embrace a heart of worship, thankfulness, and forgiveness.

2. God wants your life this side of heaven to be an amazing and abundant journey. Ask Him to reach into all your past experiences and to redeem you from your negative reactions to life—transforming you and your circumstances by His goodness and glory.

3. (a) Worship is the channel through which we allow God to heal the broken and wounded places in our souls. Whenever you feel the pain of brokenness rising in your soul, make an active choice to worship and praise God through Scripture and song.

(b) Write down some Scriptures, as well as some lyrics to songs, that are particularly healing for you, and read or sing them each morning and evening.

4. (a) What are you particularly known for in life? What particular abilities or talents stand out?

(b) In terms of your emotions, what are you known for? Restraint or outbursts? Godly confidence or fear? Healthy humility or pride? As you continually make worship a priority in your life, specifically record how your emotions are being transformed to become more like the nature of Christ.

13

THE FEAR FACTOR

Have you ever wondered if there are certain emotions we can verify as having been designed by God to be a healthy part of the human experience? Or are all emotions unhealthy and overly dramatic in nature? And if God created us, His beloved children, as emotional beings, why does the Bible say that the heart is deceitful above all else? (See Jeremiah 17:9.) Why are we unable to trust our emotions to lead us into truth? These are valid questions, aren't they?

As we discussed earlier, some people believe that we should fully embrace and express every emotion—but others believe that emotions should always be stifled and left unexpressed. I believe that the correct response to our emotions probably lies somewhere in the middle of those two extremes. As human beings, there is a full range of emotions that our heavenly Father intended for us to embrace in order to enhance our life journey, not to detract from it. But just as our flesh needs to come under the lordship of Jesus Christ, so do our emotions. When our emotions are either stifled and ignored or wantonly expressed, they can become unhealthy.

THE BIG EIGHT EMOTIONS

Dr. Robert Plutchik, an expert on human emotion, revolutionized the manner in which psychology treated emotions during the 1980s. Dr. Plutchik identified these eight basic human emotions: fear, anger, disgust, surprise, joy, sadness, anticipation, and acceptance. Arguably, there are many more individual emotions than these eight; however, most of the remaining dominant human emotions would fit under the umbrella of the ones noted by Dr. Plutchik.

No one can claim to be a perfect specimen of humanity or of Christianity, and the arena of the emotions is often the place that causes us to slip and slide and eventually sin. Experiencing an emotion is not a sin, in itself; it is how we express and act upon that emotion that may lead us to sin. Since you and I still live this side of eternity, we undoubtedly will be daily bombarded with emotions that we need to manage.

Is it possible to follow after Christ wholeheartedly and not limp along behind one of those eight emotional dominators? Is there a holy and complete way to die to self and to emotionalism? Is it possible to turn one's heart toward Christ and away from sin, even while embroiled in dealing with one of those basic emotional responses to life and to circumstances?

Some of these questions may seem unanswerable to you today, but allow me to assure you that as we study the eight primary emotions and then study God's truth from the sacred pages of His Word, we will discover solid and life-defining answers. Again, we must go to the Word of God with all of our questions, because the Bible is the dynamic Guidebook for life that God has given to all people of every age.

Remember that in this section of the book, you are in the middle of open-heart surgery, and it is essential that you do not spike a fever while undergoing a major operation. Therefore, as we study the eight human emotions, we will also take your temperature from time to time and examine whether or not you may be harboring an infection in one of these areas of emotional response. If you are sick emotionally, it is time for you to get on the path to wholeness and healing!

POWERFUL WEAPONS FOR REFUSING FEAR

The word *"fear"* appears no less than four hundred times in the King James Version of the Bible; I believe it is safe to assume that the Scriptures have something vital to say concerning this basic human emotion. I also believe that we can easily discern what God's will is concerning fear if we extract our information from His Word. Fear is not a hidden subject in the

Scriptures; God addresses it often, and the Holy Spirit gives us a healthy prescription for dealing with it.

One definition of fear is "a distressing emotion aroused by impending danger, evil, or pain, whether the threat is real or imagined." When the soul is dealing with fear, it is in an intense state of stress, whether that fear is merely imagined or springs from a valid source. Fear rears its ugly head when a person believes that something bad is about to happen, either to himself or herself, or to someone he or she loves. When the snowflakes of fear begin to fall in a person's soul, they obstruct an accurate view of what is ahead. Fear causes a blizzard-like whiteout in people's grasp of reality, and those who are dealing with an agonizing stress of fear may lose their way on the road toward the truth.

Most things we fear are only the fictional perceptions of an overactive mind. We "think" something bad is going to happen, so we embrace a spirit of fear. The battle begins in the mind, because an emotion is a thought before it becomes a feeling. Whenever you deal with the emotion of fear— whenever you are afraid of having cancer, of your children leaving home, of the stability of the economy, of the political climate, of some type of disaster occurring, or of a thousand other alarming possibilities in life—you must instantly go to the Word of God. Immediately default to the truth and the promises found in the Scriptures. Do not allow fear to have the last word in your life; let the Word have the last word! You need to remind yourself of who God is and what He has promised to those who love Him. The Bible is filled with the promises of God's divine intervention. You must discover what the Bible has to say about fear and what the Holy Spirit's opinion is concerning this ferocious emotion.

God has not given us a spirit of fear, but of power and of love and of a sound mind. (2 Timothy 1:7 NKJV)

As you are dealing with the stress of human fear, remind yourself that fear is a soul-induced reaction and not a spirit-led response. Fear does not come from the Father, and therefore it cannot reside in our spirits. The fear that haunts you day and night, robs you of your joy, and leaves you sick to your stomach is not from God. And, if it is not from Him, guess who planted it in your mind? There is only one option regarding its source—it comes from old Mr. Deceiver himself. The return address on the envelope of fear is labeled "The Pits of Hell."

Fear has an uncanny ability to turn a thriving believer into a weakling who is unable to accomplish great things for the kingdom of God. The things of which you are afraid become monstrous giants in your life. Satan desperately desires to scare the future right out of you and endeavors to convince you to see all of your tomorrows from his dastardly perspective. However, remind yourself that Satan is the Father of Lies! He is public deceiver number one, and he wants to convince you not to guard your heart. He tries to trick you into giving your heart to a spirit of fear. God, the greatest Comforter in all of eternity, desires for you to guard your heart against any spirit of fear and to trust Him completely. The fabulous result of choosing to guard your heart is that fear will never again be allowed into your well-protected fortress. You will be a fear-free believer!

Christians already possess the powerful weapons that will refuse to allow fear to enter into the boundaries of their hearts. The weapons that God has given us to fight off the enemy's advances in the realm of fear are power, love, and a sound mind. Fear may be a basic human emotion, but you are no longer a basic human! You are a child of God and are filled with the Holy Spirit. The Holy Spirit is never afraid of anything, so refuse fear and get on with your abundant life.

THE CASE FOR CONFIDENCE

If fear has gripped your soul, becoming a loud and loquacious member of your psyche, perhaps it would be beneficial to remind yourself that you are loved completely, fully, and eternally by the One who knows you the very best!

> *Who will separate us from the love of Christ? Will tribulation, or distress, or persecution, or famine, or nakedness, or peril, or sword?*
> (Romans 8:35)

Run into the arms of Christ's love whenever fear threatens to mar the landscape of your glorious future. Remind yourself over and over and over again that there is nothing that has been created or imagined that is able to diminish His love for you or that has the influence to disconnect you from

His love. (See Romans 8:38–30.) His love surrounds you like a shield, and His care is well able to dismantle any of the enemy's schemes concerning your life. You are not the only believer in all of recorded history who has had to look fear in the eye and say, "Get out of my way in the name of the Lord!"

The prophet Daniel was certainly a victim of persecution, but God never left him; He took care of him even in a den of roaring and ravenous lions. (See Daniel 6.)

The distress that Queen Esther encountered when she was made privy to a plot in which her entire people group was about to be assassinated is unlike anything you or I have ever faced. Yet God was with her, and when she prayed and fasted, He gave her a divine strategy to wreck the murderous plot. (See Esther 3–9.)

The patriarch Joseph lived during one of the worst famines in all of human history, yet the Bible tells us that God was with him. The Lord gave Joseph the wisdom and the ability to provide for God's people when the world seemed to be falling apart. (See Genesis 40–47, 50:15–21.)

King Jehoshaphat faced the swords of enemy forces that had the ability to wipe out his entire nation, but God protected him and his people when they chose to worship rather than give in to a spirit of fear. (See 2 Chronicles 20:1–30.)

If God protected and provided for Daniel, Esther, Joseph, and Jehoshaphat, He will certainly do the same for you! Your God is the God of Noah and Moses and Samson; of Shadrach, Meshach, and Abednego. What God has done before, He will do again—of this, you can be very sure!

Just as it is written, "For Your sake we are being put to death all day long; we were considered as sheep to be slaughtered." But in all these things we overwhelmingly conquer through Him who loved us.
(Romans 8:36–37)

The Bible does not promise us that, as Christians, we will never suffer, but it does promise us that the love of God will always be our companion. Think about that for a minute! The love of God is yours in extravagant and immeasurable amounts, and nothing is able to take it from you. You are surrounded by God's love, so rest in that place of unconditional love and dismiss fear with a wave of your authoritative hand. Even when we are facing a difficult or unwelcome situation, we are given the ability to *"overwhelmingly conquer"*! We can overcome in every situation, in every disappointment, and in every hardship because of His great love for us. We don't overcome due to our stunning good looks or our extraordinary IQs. It is not perfect marriages or flawless children that lead us into triumph. Neither is it stable finances, stellar educations, or well-developed talents that give us the power to overcome. It is the love of God, which is lavishly given to us every day and for every situation.

> *For I am convinced that neither death, nor life, nor angels, nor principalities, nor things present, nor things to come, nor powers, nor height, nor depth, nor any other created thing, will be able to separate us from the love of God, which is in Christ Jesus our Lord.*   (Romans 8:38–39)

Paul and the Holy Spirit chose to use an extremely powerful word in their closing ovation to the love of God. They used the word *"convinced."* Paul didn't say, "I *think* I will never be separated from the love of God." The Holy Spirit did not nudge that great and learned apostle to declare, "I *hope* that I will never be separated from the love of God." Paul and his divine writing companion did not even choose to close with, "I *believe* that I will never be separated from the love of God." Paul was *convinced* beyond a shadow of eternal doubt that the all-consuming love of the Father was an unshakable power and a perpetual presence in his life.

The Holy Spirit moved upon the spirit of Paul to firmly claim, in effect, "I know that I know that I know that I know that absolutely nothing will ever have the power to separate me from the love of God, which is in Christ Jesus my Lord!" So take that, fear!

In a courtroom, merely one argument is never satisfactory to absolutely convince a judge of a statement's validity. Paul uses the language of the lawyer in this phrase and presents his case beyond a shadow of a doubt. The word *convinced* is credibly arrived at only when *everything* proves it! That is why heaven is incredulous that a man or a woman who professes faith in Jesus Christ would ever be consumed with fear.

This is a spiritual concept that must resonate in your spirit, because it will never make sense to your soul. Your soul will say, *Of course, there are things to be afraid of!* However, your spirit jumps at the chance to walk in trust. Your spirit knows that your soul tends to embrace the emotional vigor of a scaredy-cat, so understandably the spirit tries to coax the soul into a place of trust and complete faith. Your soul wants to deal only in common sense and current reality, while your spirit always walks in a sense of revelation. Your spirit embraces the love of God and accepts this divine concept as revelation to live by.

DO NOT FEAR!

Every person in the Bible who was called to do something great for the kingdom of God heard the oft-uttered and divinely powerful words, "Do not fear!"

Abraham was told *"Do not fear"* when the Lord called him to move away from his home (see Genesis 15:1), and again when God told him that he was going to miraculously have a son (see Genesis 26:24).

Moses heard those emboldening words from the Lord, *"Do not fear,"* when he was facing an enemy that had the power to destroy the people of God. (See Numbers 21:34.)

Joshua heard God tell him *"Do not fear"* when he led the entire nation of Israel into the Promised Land. (See Joshua 8:1; 10:8.)

David probably heard from the Lord some version of that trio of power-packed words too many times to count. (See Psalm 56:4, 11.)

Likewise, during the events before Christ's birth, Zechariah, Joseph, and Mary were all encouraged by God not to be afraid. (See Matthew 1:20; Luke 1:13, 30.)

As human beings, we all deal with fear at challenging junctures in life, but God doesn't want us to remain in those places of paralyzing anxiety, dread, or terror. He has called us out of fear and into His great love for us.

Even though I walk through the valley of the shadow of death, I fear no evil, for You are with me; Your rod and Your staff, they comfort me.
(Psalm 23:4)

As believers in Jesus Christ and those who find comfort in His trustworthy ways, even impending death should not be able to deliver a spirit of fear to our hearts. Death will simply transport us to Him. Now, remind me, what is there to be afraid of?

ON THE OTHER HAND...

Now that we have established divine boundaries for the unhealthy fear that so often tries to invade our lives, is there a type of fear that is reasonable for us to have? Is there a strain of fear that is acceptable in the life of a Christian? Yes, there is one biblical definition of the word *fear* that will revolutionize your acceptance of this four-letter word. There are places in the Bible where the original words translated into English as "*fear*" mean "to stand in awe of; to reverence, honor, and respect; to tremble for joy at the presence of God." Thus, the Scriptures present the case for exchanging the raw emotion of fear for a type of fear that is a source of outrageous power.

Satan has a counterfeit for every emotional response that God has blessed and ordained. As Christians, our response to all of life's situations should be one of awe toward God in which we are in a state of continual wonder over who He is and what He is able to do. We are called to revere Him every day, regardless of our outward circumstances; we are commanded to recognize Him as the Source of all power, of all purpose, and of each individual destiny. It's our choice: we can either focus on Satan's lies, and therefore embrace the twisted version of fear, or we can focus on God's promises and be in absolute and undeniable astonishment over who He is! Stop being afraid—you have God!

Satan's counterfeit use of fear is for the purpose of causing us to cower before our circumstances and to shake uncontrollably at the possibilities of the unknown. The Bible, however, says that children of God are called to tremble for joy at the very presence of God. (See Jeremiah 33:9.) When your circumstances and the unknown blizzard of the future threaten to stir up fear in your life, your spirit should have the power to immediately draw you into the presence of God and remind you of the promises found in the Bible. Your very gullible soul will endeavor to keep you filled with worry and anxiety, but your spirit should grab your soul by the seat of its slippery pants and drag it into the presence of God, where there is always joy and peace.

The LORD is my light and my salvation; whom shall I fear? The LORD
is the defense of my life; whom shall I dread? (Psalm 27:1)

GUARD YOUR HEART: PERSONAL APPLICATION

1. (a) What is your greatest fear, whether or not it is based in reality?

   (b) How do you usually respond to your fear?

2. Where does the battle with fear begin? Why is this the case?

3. Second Timothy 1:7 (NKJV) assures us that God has *not* given us a spirit of fear. What type of spirit has He given us?

4. While we will all deal with fear at times, God doesn't want us to stay in those places of anxiety or dread. We can counteract fear by living in God's love—by recognizing that His love for us is so high and so deep that nothing can separate us from it. When fear begins to creep into your heart, meditate on Scriptures such as this one:

   For I am convinced that neither death, nor life, nor angels,
   nor principalities, nor things present, nor things to come, nor
   powers, nor height, nor depth, nor any other created thing, will
   be able to separate us from the love of God, which is in Christ
   Jesus our Lord. (Romans 8:38–39)

5. What is one type of fear that is acceptable in the lives of believers? What does this "fear" signify?

6. You have a choice which to focus on: Satan's lies, which instill in you the twisted version of fear; or God's truth and promises, through which a reverence for the Lord—accompanied by power, love, and a sound mind—may be established in you, based on His unshakeable character, love, and protection. Today, make this declaration:

   The battle over fear begins in my mind, so I choose to believe God's truth and promises, and to reject the lies of the enemy. I stand in faith, not in fear. I honor and revere almighty God, who has given me a spirit of power, love, and a sound mind. I rely fully on His unshakeable character, love, and protection to keep me all the days of my life. In Jesus's name, amen.

14

ANGER IS NOT AN ANGRY WORD

Anger may perhaps be the most telling and demonstrative of the dominant eight emotions. As we begin this chapter together, I am going to ask you to answer three questions that just might make you angry!

First of all, "What makes you angry?" Perhaps it is your spouse, who simply makes you so mad you could scream in frustration. Or maybe it is politics or the media. You might be stirred to anger by a noble reaction to an evil such as sex-trafficking or the hunger that little children around the world are suffering.

The second question that I would like to pose to you is this: "How do you express your anger?" Do you scream and throw things? Could you win a gold medal in giving the silent treatment to someone who has offended you? Do you resort to profanity or name-calling? Or do you simply sit and steam at the injustice that is being hurled in your innocent direction? Perhaps you let off your angry steam by making sure that everyone on social media knows exactly how you feel about a certain matter.

And finally, "How quickly do you become angry?" Do you possess an extremely short fuse, so that you are known for flying off at people at the least provocation? Or is your personal wick a lengthy one that burns slowly, but once it reaches the end, you become a human stick of dynamite, causing people to scatter in all directions?

THE "ANGER" OF GOD

Anger is an emotion that we are allowed to engage in because, in itself, it is not sin. God is completely without sin, and yet the Bible tells us that

God responds in anger to certain situations or to certain choices people make. However, He exhibits His anger much differently than we do as human beings, even though we were made in His very image. God's anger is always productive, while our anger, influenced by the fallen human nature, is often destructive.

The "anger of God" has become a religious concept that has thoroughly distorted many people's view of God, preventing them from knowing Him as loving and merciful. Thus, many of us falsely believe that God is angry with us all of the time, and we live in the fear that God is going to cause something bad to happen to us. We think that God is displeased with our behavior and mistakenly assume that He is about to blow venom or burning lava all over our innocent lives. We erroneously suppose that there is absolutely nothing that we can ever do to make God happy, so we cower in fear, just waiting for our just punishment. My friend, nothing could be further from the truth! Listen in.

In the Hebrew, when it says God is angry, it means, "to be displeased; to breathe hard; the blowing hard of the breath through nostrils; to prostrate oneself." Essentially, when God is angry or becomes displeased, He breathes hard and prostrates Himself. Picture it for a minute! What might this imply? When God becomes angry at sin or at human cruelty, He breathes on, and leans as close to, the sinner as He possibly can. He knows that what is needed in our human weakness is more of Him and more of His power in our lives. So He gives more of Himself.

Are you undone yet? Are you just weeping over what God gives to us when we deserve punishment? He gives us His breath and Himself.

His anger is but for a moment, His favor is for a lifetime; weeping may last for the night, but a shout of joy comes in the morning.
(Psalm 30:5)

It is true that God does, indeed, have moments of anger, but He doesn't stay angry for a lifetime; the Bible describes His anger as brief and momentary. He does have the right to be displeased with our rebellious behavior and with our disobedient choices, but His displeasure is limited in length, while His favor lasts for an entire lifetime! His displeasure is only for a moment of history, but His pleasure over our lives extends into all of eternity!

Repeatedly, the Bible declares that God is *"slow to anger"*:

...a God ready to pardon, gracious and merciful, slow to anger, and of great kindness. (Nehemiah 9:17 KJV)

The LORD is merciful and gracious, slow to anger, and plenteous in mercy. (Psalm 103:8 KJV)

Now return to the LORD your God, for He is gracious and compassionate, slow to anger, abounding in lovingkindness and relenting of evil. (Joel 2:13)

How comforting to know that God's anger doesn't come quickly, and when it does come, we can be assured that it will be short-lived. God is not an angry God; He is kind, gracious, and merciful.

However, even Christians have unfortunately allowed *anger* to become an "angry" word. We mistakenly believe that when God becomes angry, He roars and throws things and screams in frustration against the people whom He has created. This is not an accurate picture of how God deals with His displeasure toward us. Remember that when God is angry, He "blows through His nostrils and prostrates Himself." Interestingly, God began His very relationship with mankind by doing something very similar. When He created man, He blew into Adam's nostrils with His very own divine and empowering breath of blessing.

Then the LORD God formed man of dust from the ground, and breathed into his nostrils the breath of life; and man became a living being.
(Genesis 2:7)

When God's breath is blown into us, it calls us to life! Thus, when God is angry with us, He doesn't stomp around heaven and throw His hands up in grief. He doesn't rant and rave, nor does He rub His holy hands together and wonder how He can ruin our day. When God is angry, He never gives one of His beloved children the silent treatment or the cold shoulder. He is not sitting on heaven's throne wondering how He can make us suffer. He never ponders what catastrophe He can send our way. That is complete and utter absurdity!

Rather, God prostrates Himself over the threshold of heaven and blows His wind in our direction. He blows life onto us! God knows that what we need in that moment of displeasure is more of Him! When we make a human error and are not walking in His ways, what we are desperately in need of is more of His life and more of His breath; in that moment of displeasure, the always-giving God blows life on us and leans toward us to help us.

IT IS ABOUT YOU

Now, let's stop talking in theological generalities and make this about you. Let's spend a few minutes examining your own capacity for, and expression of, anger. I am bravely going to interview you again about your potential for anger. How do you deal with your anger? Do you rant and rave, gossip and complain? Do you throw things, criticize, name-call, or raise your voice?

When you are displeased with someone or have been betrayed by someone, perhaps what you should consider doing is what God does. You might just need to breathe Jesus onto their lives! You might also consider "prostrating" yourself in the presence of the one who has caused your anger, because that is what God the Father has done on your behalf. When you are angry, humble yourself and give the anger-inducer more of Jesus. You need to give the person who has angered you exorbitant amounts of mercy, love, forgiveness, and grace, because that is what Jesus has given to you.

A REVOLUTIONARY STRATEGY

It will require a Christlike renewal in each of our lives in order for us to be angry only in the right way and never in the wrong way. We are only human, after all, but we have been exposed to the life-changing call of Jesus Christ. We have been invited to partake of His very nature while living this side of eternity's shore.

> But you did not learn Christ in this way, if indeed you have heard Him and have been taught in Him, just as truth is in Jesus, that, in reference to your former manner of life, you lay aside the old self, which is being corrupted in accordance with the lusts of deceit, and that you be renewed in the spirit of your mind.... (Ephesians 4:20–23)

As a disciple of Jesus Christ, you have learned dynamic life principles from the Word of God and from the sinless life of Jesus. You did have a former life, before Christ, and it still noisily calls your name; one of the greatest problems with the old self is that it is loud and obnoxious. Every day of your life, the old self tries to convince you to be who you used to be. But Jesus is inviting you to be like Him! What a grand invitation, indeed!

For this transformation to be complete, you must *"be renewed in the spirit of your mind."* The renewal takes place in your spirit and in your mind. You must embrace the mind of Christ and take every thought captive to the obedience of Christ. You must set aside time for communion with God so that He is given the opportunity to fully strengthen you and to fill your spirit with all that He has and all that He is.

> *...and put on the new self, which in the likeness of God has been created in righteousness and holiness of the truth.* (Ephesians 4:24)

After you have allowed the Holy Spirit to effect a renewal in your mind and a strengthening in your spirit, then it is time for you to change your wardrobe! You must willfully choose every day not to be who you were before Christ but to be the person whom He has created you to be. What a divine possibility! You weren't created to be like "you"—you were created to be like Him! There is no grander event than that!

You have been called to an entirely new and exuberant way of living; you have been summoned to look, act, and talk like God the Father. This calling includes the submission of all of your emotions to His will and His ways, including your propensity for, and your expression of, anger. You are called to be like Him; you are invited to be holy, even in your emotions.

> *Therefore, laying aside falsehood, speak truth each one of you with his neighbor, for we are members of one another. Be angry, and yet do not sin; do not let the sun go down on your anger....*
> (Ephesians 4:25–26)

This Scripture presents a revolutionary strategy to enable a person to be angry and yet not sin! Lean in...you will want to listen to, and learn from, this incredible philosophy!

First of all, remember to deal with your anger the way that God deals with His anger; prostrate yourself in humility—and in prayer. Breathe in the character of God, and then breathe out Jesus on the one who has angered you.

Then, remind yourself that God's anger is short in duration, and so should yours be. Give your anger distinct boundaries; anger requires a timeline that has a definite ending point. At the very most, you are allowed to be angry for only twenty-three hours and fifty-nine minutes; then, your anger should be over with completely. The problem is that many of us are still angry over things that happened last year, or ten years ago, or forty years ago. I find it necessary to remind myself daily that the anger of God is momentary, and so should mine be. Forgive the person who caused your anger to explode; do not allow another minute to pass in which you hold on to that anger. Long-term anger never hurts the one at whom it is aimed, but only wounds the one who is hanging on to it.

> *...and do not give the devil an opportunity.*   (Ephesians 4:27)

When we process anger in a human way by embracing it and express-ing it through our souls and not our spirits, we make room for the devil in our lives. We give him an opportunity to express himself through our emotional weaknesses. Thus, when you choose to respond to your anger only emotionally and through your soul, the devil is loudly cheering you on. However, when you respond to your anger the way God responds, with humility and with life-giving breath, it is then that the Father will use you to further His kingdom. So, go to the person who has made you angry, and just give them Jesus!

THE EXIT INTERVIEW

Okay, can I ask you a few questions one final time? Now, don't get angry at me, but just allow the Holy Spirit to examine the vein of anger that is within you.

+ "What makes you angry?"
+ "How quickly do you become angry?"
+ "How do you express your anger (how do you act when you are angry)?"
+ "How long does your anger last?"

These questions will help you take your emotional temperature; your answers to these important inquiries will enable you to accurately diagnose the state of your heart.

A fool always loses his temper, but a wise man holds it back.

(Proverbs 29:11)

GUARD YOUR HEART: PERSONAL APPLICATION

1. Answer each question in the last section of the chapter, above, entitled "The Exit Interview."

2. What is your concept of God's anger? How has it defined your relationship with Him?

3. What is your reaction to the description in this chapter of God's response to His anger—that He humbly prostrates Himself and blows the breath of His Spirit on those who have offended Him, giving them more of Himself and His power?

4. Think of someone who has made you very angry in the past. How have you processed and dealt with that anger? Are you still holding on to it? If so, how can you imitate your heavenly Father by "breathing Jesus" on that person according to His mercy, love, forgiveness, and grace?

5. Make a decision to give your anger scriptural boundaries, ensuring that it is short-lived. Renew this decision every time you feel the emotion of anger.

6. Commit these verses to memory to renew your mind regarding God's character and attitude toward you. Repeat them whenever you feel that God is angry with you.

> *The LORD is merciful and gracious, slow to anger, and plenteous in mercy.* (Psalm 103:8 KJV)

> *Now return to the LORD your God, for He is gracious and compassionate, slow to anger, abounding in lovingkindness and relenting of evil.* (Joel 2:13)

15

BE DISGUSTED—BE VERY, VERY DISGUSTED

I deal with fear sporadically, and I often fight off anger, but disgust is an emotion that, honestly, is not a substantive part of my emotional makeup. When I came to the realization of how rarely disgust creeps into the corners of my heart, I wondered if I would be qualified to write on a subject that I am unable to relate to fully. As I prayed about it, I felt God revealed to me that I should actually be disgusted much more often than I am!

The word *disgust* means "to cause loathing to or nausea in"; "to offend the good taste or moral sense of"; "to cause extreme dislike or revulsion in"; "strong aversion." The Holy Spirit has painfully informed me that there are things in this world that I should simply loathe; there are actions that are commonplace in my culture that should tremendously revolt me. Every day, there are events and circumstances that should stir up a harsh aversion in my heart.

Yet, while the actions of a particular person may create feelings of disgust in us, the personhood of that individual should only produce compassion in us. Unequivocally, we should never have an emotional response of disgust in our soul toward someone who has been made in the very image of God Himself. Often, even as believers in Christ, when we are disgusted by the actions of a person, we treat the person himself or herself with disgust, when in actuality what that person needs is love and truth. Let's dig into the Word of God together and discover a healthy prescription for being disgusted solely at the right things and never at the wrong things.

A LIFESTYLE OF TRUTH AND LOVE

I don't often read the "burdensome" book of Leviticus, do you? However, the Holy Spirit has challenged me to dig for truth even in this seemingly legalistic and archaic book of the Bible. The Holy Spirit has assured me that I will find Jesus even in the twenty-seven chapters of Leviticus, such as in this passage:

> *You shall do no injustice in judgment; you shall not be partial to the poor nor defer to the great, but you are to judge your neighbor fairly. You shall not go about as a slanderer among your people, and you are not to act against the life of your neighbor; I am the* LORD. *You shall not hate your fellow countryman in your heart; you may surely reprove your neighbor, but shall not incur sin because of him. You shall not take vengeance, nor bear any grudge against the sons of your people, but you shall love your neighbor as yourself; I am the* LORD.
>
> (Leviticus 19:15–18)

The Bible is clear about how we should deal with the emotion of disgust: we are never to express injustice, partiality, or judgment toward people, who are made in the image of God. The Bible condemns slander, hate, and vengeance, calling us to a lifestyle of truth and love. "Hate the sin, but love the sinner" is an old adage that is a helpful guideline when dealing with the actions of other people. While God doesn't always approve of or even love a person's chosen actions, He always loves the person. God's standard of acceptance and love is our goal. It is reasonable and even expected of us not to approve of the wrong choices of a person; but again, as children of God, our love must extend past the sin to the person himself or herself.

SEVEN GODLY WOMEN

If we are not to be disgusted by people, and yet "disgust" is indeed a basic human emotion, what is it permissible to be disgusted over? I interviewed seven godly and world-changing women, asking each one the simple question, "What disgusts you?" Here are the answers I received from these women, whose hearts desperately desire to please the Lord:

+ Evil—specifically, crimes against children, as well as kidnapping and pornography
+ Gossip [the response of two of the women]
+ Hidden motives and impure intentions
+ Self-pity

+ Walking around with an offended attitude

+ Abuse

These are certainly interesting responses from the hearts of women who desire to exhibit a Christlike character. I believe that some of you, like me, need to be more disgusted by sin, crime, and other evil acts than we have been in the past. This prayer from a man by the name of Bob Pierce should certainly be the prayer of all of our hearts: "May my heart be broken with the things that break the heart of God."[3] How did he come to the place of praying that very vulnerable prayer? Let's look at Bob's story, which is sure to change your view of the emotion of digust.

ONLY FIVE DOLLARS A YEAR

Bob Pierce was a fiery youth evangelist in the days following World War II. He traveled around the world and spoke to thousands and even tens of thousands of people at prestigious conferences and events that were held at large and impressive churches. He was well known for his passionate approach concerning the love of Jesus Christ. The youth of his generation were greatly influenced by this man, who left a mark too great to measure.

When Bob was in a certain city, a missionary woman begged him to speak about the love of Jesus at her day school and orphanage. This woman deeply desired that the abused, abandoned, and lonely children under her care would know about the unconditional love of the Father. Bob readily agreed, and this young, outspoken, vibrant evangelist challenged the young children at the school to accept Jesus as their Lord and Savior, no matter the cost. When the missionary heard Bob's bold words, she was outraged with him. She reminded Bob that she had only requested that he tell the children about the love of the Father, and that she hadn't asked for an altar call.

"These children," she cried, "live in a Muslim culture. If they accept Jesus, they will be shunned for life! Then what will we do? How will we take care of them?"

An eight-year-old girl by the name of White Jade had been in the audience that morning because she attended the day school under the supervision of the missionary woman. White Jade ran home to excitedly tell her father the great news that she had accepted Jesus as her Lord and Savior,

3. See https://www.samaritanspurse.org/our-ministry/history/.

but he was so angry and so disgusted with her choice that he beat her until she nearly died. She was disowned by her parents and was thrown out of the house and onto the streets in an extremely dangerous culture. White Jade was found on the doorstep of the orphanage in a puddle of blood, with her spine exposed.

The missionary, whose name was Tina Hoelkeboer, called for the impetuous and cocky evangelist to come down and see what he had caused to happen. Her words were filled with tears and fraught with frustration as she said, "I already have six children in this orphanage, with no money and no supplies for one more! Look what you have done to this beautiful little girl!"

After calming herself down and cradling White Jade in her arms, Tina brokenly said, "If you will send me five dollars a year, I will be able to take care of this one." Bob Pierce sheepishly agreed, and was moved with great compassion and humility. He went back to America and encouraged Christian families and churches to sponsor children around the world. God gave Bob the idea of providing the sponsoring families and organizations with pictures of the children whom they were supporting. Today, World Vision International, the organization that Bob founded, supports millions of children across the globe because one young man was moved by disgust toward the mistreatment of a child.

As you prayerfully ponder what issues in your life usher the emotion of disgust into your heart, perhaps you, along with me, will pray the prayer of Bob Pierce: "May my heart be broken with the things that break the heart of God."

YOU CAN DO IT!

The Word of God is the most powerful factor we can apply to the condition of our minds, our hearts, and our tongues. I have chosen to close every chapter of this book with a verse or two of life-changing Scripture. For the close of this chapter, I felt there was only one passage that could possibly convey God's heart toward the aspects of human life that should revolt us, change us, and involve us. Disgust should always result in both personal change and personal involvement in answer to the need. This is a long passage, but I humbly ask you to read every single potent word of it.

Don't ignore or rush over any line of this Scripture, but savor it and allow it to guide you as you become more like Christ.

> *Is this not the fast which I choose, to loosen the bonds of wickedness, to undo the bands of the yoke, and to let the oppressed go free and break every yoke? Is it not to divide your bread with the hungry and bring the homeless poor into the house; when you see the naked, to cover him; and not to hide yourself from your own flesh? Then your light will break out like the dawn, and your recovery will speedily spring forth; and your righteousness will go before you; the glory of the LORD will be your rear guard. Then you will call, and the LORD will answer; you will cry, and He will say, "Here I am." If you remove the yoke from your midst, the pointing of the finger and speaking wickedness, and if you give yourself to the hungry and satisfy the desire of the afflicted, then your light will rise in darkness and your gloom will become like midday. And the LORD will continually guide you, and satisfy your desire in scorched places, and give strength to your bones; and you will be like a watered garden, and like a spring of water whose waters do not fail.*
>
> (Isaiah 58:6–11)

GUARD YOUR HEART: PERSONAL APPLICATION

1. Is "disgust" an emotion that you feel only occasionally, or do you feel it frequently?

2. Review the section in this chapter entitled "Seven Godly Women." Then, write down what disgusts you the most. Why do you think it causes this reaction in you?

3. Have you allowed your disgust to make you bitter—or better? In what ways?

4. How might your disgust be leading you to help answer a crucial need in the world? What can you do to transform your disgust into focused intercession for others and constructive action?

5. If disgust is not much a part of your life, begin to pray, as Bob Pierce did, "May my heart be broken with the things that break the heart of God." Be open to what God's Spirit shows you, and record what He tells you.

16

DON'T BE SURPRISED

Most people either absolutely love surprises or dread them! Which group of people do you find yourself in?

When my husband, Craig, and I were about to be married, only six months after we met, my parents decided that the groom needed to know more about his intended bride than he was able to discern in only half of a calendar year of observation. So, his future-in-laws gave this besotted groom a few bullet points concerning his bride's emotional constitution. One of the things they informed him of was that I hated surprises! My dear husband quickly learned not to surprise his wife—anytime, anyplace, or anywhere! Likewise, my children have all discovered that the quickest way to make mom indignant is to surprise her. I like to know what is going to happen next; I like to be privy to all of the possibilities yet to come.

Surprise is one of the eight basic human emotions, so isn't it interesting that some people live for a good surprise, while others recoil from the idea? The definition of the word *surprise* is "to strike or occur to with a sudden feeling of wonder or astonishment as through unexpectedness." Surprise can be filled with fun, elation, and a grand rush of adrenalin. It can stir up a song in the deepest place of your being and even cause your tongue to trip over your heart.

Do you remember those seven godly women whom I questioned about disgust in the last chapter? I also asked them this wonderful question: "What has surprised you the most in life?" Here are their not-so-surprising answers:

+ "That my husband would want to marry me and stay married to me!"

+ "How wonderful the Ritz-Carlton Cancun is!"

+ "How much I love being a mom!"

+ "Surprise! You get to marry Mike! After all we went through for so many years, he was still the one God had for me."

+ "How much my heart hurt when my husband went to heaven."

+ "I am always surprised by kindness in the face of rudeness or injustice because it is against the natural tendency."

+ "I am surprised by what people are able to overcome."

MY OWN SURPRISE

In the early years of our marriage, Craig and I were the parents of two wonderful boys who were two years apart almost to the day. How I loved being a mom to those future world-changing little men! Even so, the deepest desire of my heart was to have another baby...and then another one... and another one.

Then, after years of infertility and painfully sending five babies to heaven before they were old enough to survive outside of the womb, I finally carried another baby to full-term, and we were overjoyed with the gift of our third son, Jordan. After giving birth to this sweet, blond-haired, blue-eyed boy, I deeply desired yet another child, and I talked our infertility specialist into the possibility of another pregnancy. This time, I gave birth to our first daughter, whom we appropriately named "Joy." Craig and I both thought that our family was complete. What could be better than three sons and a daughter? Our days were filled with homeschooling, baseball games, piano lessons, ballet lessons, and friendly basketball competitions at the goal in our driveway.

When Joy was almost four years old, I got the flu—and it lasted for months. I was nauseous all day long and achingly tired. To my absolute delight and surprise, what I thought was a horrible case of the flu turned out to be a pregnancy when I was nearly forty years old! Joni Rebecca, named after both my mother and Craig's mother, is a visual manifestation that God loves to surprise His children. Joni is the best surprise I have ever received, and her sweetness has completed our family in a way I never imagined possible. And guess what? I am not as adverse to surprises any longer because of a surprise that came wrapped in freckles, giggles, and creativity!

NOT A SURPRISE

How should we respond to the emotion of surprise? Mostly, we need to know what *shouldn't* take us unawares. At least two times in the Bible, the Holy Spirit warns us not to be surprised. There are some things in life that shouldn't cause our adrenalin to rush, or cause a rise in our blood pressure, or have the power to overwhelm us with their sudden presence. Let's look at these two places in Scripture where we are instructed not to be surprised.

> *Beloved, do not be surprised at the fiery ordeal among you, which comes upon you for your testing, as though some strange thing were happening to you; but to the degree that you share the sufferings of Christ, keep on rejoicing, so that also at the revelation of His glory you may rejoice with exultation.* (1 Peter 4:12–13)

Trials should never surprise a disciple of Jesus Christ but should always cause us to *"keep on rejoicing"*! What a challenge this is by the great apostle Peter, who spent time in prison, was persecuted for his faith, and died a martyr's death. Peter was crucified in Rome under the empire of Nero Augustus Caesar; according to tradition, he requested to be crucified upside down because he didn't believe that he was worthy to be put to death in the same manner as Christ.

Peter, the incorrigible and the courageous, said not to be surprised when your world falls apart! Don't be surprised when trials come your way. Don't be surprised, but *start to sing praises more loudly.*

Can you do it? When a disappointment or a difficulty enters your personal world, will you choose to reject surprise and to embrace worship? Don't open your mouth in unbelievable incredulity, but open your mouth in song, instead. It's what Peter would do. It's what I am trying to do. And it is what you should do, as well!

The second interesting concept that the Bible tells us not to be surprised at comes from John, who was also known as the Beloved Apostle.

John's heart was expansive, and he was very easy to love. He didn't have the rough edges of Peter, the doubting nature of Thomas, or the sharp tongue of Paul. John was the disciple who never offended anyone and was often in a position to bring peace to relationships. However, these were his words in a letter that bears his own name:

> *Do not be surprised, brethren, if the world hates you.*   (1 John 3:13)

Apparently, the Holy Spirit moved on the heart and pen of John to share this brief bit of coaching advice to the early church. I wonder if John, as well-loved as he was, also wrote this from personal experience. Perhaps he had felt the sting of rejection and had been unprepared to deal with it, and so felt the need to share this parcel of wisdom with others. We will never know what motivated John to write these words, but we do know that it is valuable and inspired advice. When people don't like you, don't be surprised. When others mock your faith, don't be surprised. When the world doesn't understand your Christian principles, don't be surprised. When family members belittle your commitment to the Lord, don't be surprised. Knowing that the world doesn't understand those who have faith in Christ is an unchanging aspect of being a Christian—so don't be surprised.

EXPECT A SURPRISE!

On the other hand, we should always be prepared to see gracious acts from our heavenly Father that may be a surprise to the recipient(s). Let's observe a surprising event found in the book of Acts that involved the enthusiastic Peter and the loving John. (See Acts 3.) These two men were merely doing what they usually did in the afternoon of any given day: they were on their way to temple to pray at the three o'clock hour. Yet this ordinary and daily discipline prepared them for a divine intervention that would surprise everyone around them.

That particular day at the temple, Peter and John came across a lame man who had been unable to walk his entire life. Every day, this man was set down at the temple gate by his friends in order to beg for alms from those who were entering through the Gate Beautiful.

Dr. Luke, a physician, wrote the book of Acts, and he describes this man's infirmity with detailed medical terms in the Greek, with descriptive medical phraseology. The crippled man had a congenital condition that affected his feet. He had paralysis in the base or heels of his feet, and it was especially apparent in the socket of his ankles. His bones had been out of place since birth, and he had never taken a step in his life. When he was a child, his parents had never been able to cheer on his first, wobbling steps. He had never been able to play with the neighborhood boys in the village streets. Luke explains that this man's feet were actually not even fully attached to his legs but dangled uselessly. The condition also affected his muscles all the way to his knees.

During that time in history, there were no surgical options for that condition, nor was there Medicaid or Medicare to take care of the helpless man. His only option for financial provision was to be carried day after day after day to the gate of the temple so that he could beg for his very existence. That particular day, when the crippled beggar noticed Peter and John entering the temple, he asked them for a handout. He was anticipating financial assistance from these two men who were on their way to pray.[4]

When Peter saw this damaged man, he commanded him to look at him straight in the eyes. I believe that Peter and John immediately discerned that this was a divine appointment, and they weren't surprised by the timing of it or by the need of the man. The Bible recounts the fact that this man, who had never walked a day in his entire life, looked at Peter because he was expecting to receive something from him.

Can we press "pause" for just a minute on this story about Peter, John, and the damaged beggar? The Holy Spirit is speaking to me right now, and I have a feeling that He is speaking to you, as well. How many times have I missed a surprise from heaven because I was too busy to be bothered? How many times has God placed a needy person in my pathway when I have walked the other way? How many surprises have I evaded because I wasn't expecting the intervention of God in my life? I must make intercession a daily priority, and I must be aware of, and even welcome, the divine interruptions in my life.

Are you ordering your life in such a way that anticipates a daily surprise or two? What is your schedule on a typical day? What are your

4. Lloyd J. Ogilvie, *Acts*, The Communicator's Commentary, vol. 5 (Waco, TX: Word, Inc., 1983), 79–83.

regular customs that might distract you from receiving a surprise gift from God? So often, the mundane dulls us to the possibility of seeing heaven's entrance into our lives. However, if your daily discipline includes the practice of being faithful in prayer, then you will never be surprised by the things that God does! Put first things first in your life, so that God is able to surprise you with His power. If you long for a surprise of divine proportions, stir up anticipation in your heart and stay on your knees in prayer. More surprises are birthed in prayer than anywhere else. Prayer, when coupled with a divine interruption, always spells the word *miracle*.

Returning to our story, Peter and John met this needy human being at a very particular and well-known place in the city of Jerusalem. As they were passing through the gate named "Beautiful," they had their surprising divine appointment with the disabled man who thought that he needed merely cash. The Gate Beautiful was made of bronze plates and was sixty to seventy-five feet tall; it was also adorned with thick plates of gold and silver. Additionally, the Gate Beautiful was engraved with a spectacular and one-of-a kind vine that ran along the entire top of the gate. This gate was known as "Beautiful" for a reason—it was breathtakingly beautiful. When the sun was high in the sky, the gate sparkled and shone in the afternoon sunshine to such a degree that it was absolutely blinding.[5]

I wonder if Peter had a twinkle in his eyes when he said to the poor, crippled beggar, "You know what? I can't even give you a penny, but I can give you something much better than money—I am going to give you Jesus!" The penniless, paralyzed pauper thought that the only thing that could solve his problems was money, when what he really needed was a surprise! He needed a healing from a Man by the name of Jesus.

Peter told the man to get up and walk in the name of Jesus Christ of Nazareth. He then grabbed him by the hand and jerked him off his feet. The man's ankles instantly became firm and strong! A miracle had occurred! God had done it again!

Dr. Luke uses his medical terminology again in this miraculous description of what was happening in the lame man's lower appendages.

5. Bruce B. Barton, Linda Taylor, J. Richard Love, Len Woods, Dave Veerman, *Acts*, The Life Application Bible Commentary (Carol Stream, IL: Tyndale House, 1999), 43–47; Clinton E. Arnold, gen. ed., *Zondervan Illustrated Bible Backgrounds Commentary: Acts* (Grand Rapids, MI: Zondervan, 2002), 25–26.

This man's sockets were instantaneously and miraculously reset! They popped back into place, and the strengthening was immediate.[6]

The surprise that occurred that afternoon was not that the formerly crippled man had received something from Peter and John; the surprise was *what* he received. Oftentimes, we come to God expecting something of our own design, but the surprise is that He gives us what we actually *need*.

Before we continue with this surprising story, perhaps it would be wise to do a bit of self-examination again. I am humbled and even embarrassed when I review the times when someone has asked me for help and I have offered something only temporary, when what God wanted me to offer was something eternal. I freely gave something tangible, when God was hoping that I would offer the power of His matchless name!

The man at the Gate Beautiful began to walk sturdily and then leap enthusiastically as he praised God with every fiber of his being. Now remember, this had been a congenital birth defect, according to Dr. Luke, and the man had never before had to balance himself on his two legs. In one miraculous moment, the atrophied muscles became strong and flexible; they were not the legs of a wobbling young calf, but the strong, solid legs of a well-conditioned athlete. This was a God-sized surprise!

The temple was very busy at this particular time because it was the hour of prayer. Everyone who had observed the disabled man sitting at the temple gate, day after day and year after year, now saw the same man dancing and glorifying the name of the Lord. What a sight that must have been! What a surprise to everyone there! The purpose of the surprise was to demonstrate the power of God to all of those religious folks who had become accustomed to seeing a decrepit man's begging year after year. The heavenly motive behind this miracle was to turn the hearts of the people toward the wonderful power and grace of God!

> *And all the people saw him walking and praising God; and they were taking note of him as being the one who used to sit at the Beautiful Gate of the temple to beg alms, and they were filled with wonder and amazement at what had happened to him.* (Acts 3:9–10)

---

6. Ogilvie, *Acts*, 79–83.

Let me repeat: the formerly impaired and deformed man had been expecting money, but he received a miracle, instead! Peter had a very interesting reaction to the uproar that the miracle had caused.

> While [the man] *was clinging to Peter and John, all the people ran together to them at the so-called portico of Solomon, full of amazement. But when Peter saw this, he replied to the people, "Men of Israel, why are you amazed at this, or why do you gaze at us, as if by our own power or piety we had made him walk?"* (Acts 3:11–12)

Peter is talking to you and to me in this verse; he is reminding us that we should never be surprised when a miracle occurs. We should never be surprised at how much God loves us, at His goodness toward us, or at His power to perform the miraculous. We should be so aware of His power that we are actually surprised when a miracle does not occur on our behalf. We should know God so well that we *expect* Him to be good! We should bask in His great love and be filled with thanksgiving that we are unable to contain.

We serve a God of miracles—and there is no surprise about that!

> *The men were amazed, and said, "What kind of a man is this, that even the winds and the sea obey Him?"* (Matthew 8:27)

GUARD YOUR HEART: PERSONAL APPLICATION

1. Write down the greatest surprise you have ever experienced.

2. When various trials come into your life, or you are persecuted for your faith, do you expect these difficulties, or do they always take you by surprise? What instructions did the apostles Peter and John give us in relation to trials and mistreatment? (See 1 Peter 4:12–13; 1 John 3:13.)

3. Name several ways you have been surprised by something God has done for you or said to you.

4. Could you be missing out on some of God's surprises—either for yourself or for others through you—by being "too busy" to be a part of them or by not expecting them in the first place? If so, what

can you do to change your priorities, availability, and expectations to align yourself with God's purposes?

5. Your ability to participate in God's surprises—and to gain a greater awareness of His desire to surprise someone with His power and grace—will increase when you raise your expectations for the ways in which He wants to work and when you commit to intercessory prayer.

   (a) Raise your expectations to experience and participate in God's surprises by meditating on this verse:

   > Now to Him who is able to do far more abundantly beyond all that we ask or think, according to the power that works within us, to Him be the glory in the church and in Christ Jesus to all generations forever and ever. Amen.
   >
   > (Ephesians 3:20–21)

   (b) Who will you commit to praying for today who needs a miraculous surprise from God?

17

I CHOOSE JOY!

Joy is a divinely powerful weapon given to us by our Father. He, in His eternal wisdom, knew we would need joy as a supernatural strengthening tool in the very darkest days of our lives. Joy is what turns a mere human being into a fierce fighting hero or heroine. Joy is the best gift you have ever received, because it is the ultimate gift of God's presence!

Do you remember my earlier mention of Dr. Robert Plutchik, the world-famous psychologist who identified these eight basic human emotions: fear, anger, disgust, surprise, joy, sadness, anticipation, and acceptance? Although I do not claim to be an expert on psychology or on human emotions, I must inform you that I disagree with him that "joy" is an emotion.

"Happy" is an emotion that is derived from positive human experiences and earthly events, while joy comes from one place, and one place alone—the presence of the Lord. "Happy" is a response of our soul to outward, temporal circumstances, whereas "joy" lives in our spirit, and it is expressed outwardly as we reflect God's Spirit dwelling within us. Joy begins in the spirit and splashes over into the soul, even when the soul is experiencing an all-time low. Joy is available to us, and is experienced by us, even when circumstances are horrific and devastating. It is not birthed as an overflow of delightful and painless circumstances but is conceived in spite of circumstances. Your soul is able to embrace the joy of your spirit even when there is no reason to be happy. Joy is a miracle, indeed!

One time, a much more naïve and innocent version of me expressed to a dear friend this ridiculous desire: "I am praying that God will make me an expert on joy!" My friend was beyond incredulous at my audacity and instantly replied, "Carol, are you sure that is what you want? Because if you want to be an expert on joy, I can assure you that it is not going to be easy!" I can certify that my dear friend, Linda, was absolutely right. It has not been effortless to become an expert on joy, but without a doubt, it has been worth it.

JOY DEFINED

My beloved fifth-grade teacher, Miss Sullivan, taught her curious class of eleven-year-olds that in order to define a certain word, one should never use the word itself in the definition. The rule that Miss Sullivan taught all of her eager students is an accepted practice that most savvy writers and wordsmiths follow implicitly. I have gone on an all-out search for a definition of the word *joy* that does not use the same word in its explanation, but it has not been an easy or a quick search. I have read definition after definition, and each one has contained the word *joy*. This just seems absurd to the word-lover that I am!

One of the main Hebrew words for "joy" is *simchah*, which is defined as: "joy, mirth, gladness; the joy of God." One of the primary Greek words for "joy" is *chara*, which is defined as "joy, gladness; the cause or occasion of one's joy." Again, these definitions would never do in an English dictionary because the word *joy* is used in the explanation.

After reading these two definitions of the word *joy*, I decided to dig a little deeper. I put on my Sherlock Holmes hat to continue my quest for fuller clarity on the word among the books that had been given to my father by my scholarly grandfather. My grandfather was a Cornell-educated lawyer who left the judiciary and city living in exchange for a rich life of Bible study, vibrant theology, and the call of the farmland. His now dusty and dog-eared books are in my wonderful library of commentaries, Bible encyclopedias, and dictionaries.

I know that I am a grammar elitist, and that most authors and teachers would not expend the mental sweat that I did in trying to determine a complete definition of the word *joy*. But stay with me—it will be more than worth the effort!

Among the stacks of crumbling and tattered books, I found a Bible commentary that was nearly a century old, and in it I discovered this definition of the word in question: "Joy wrought by the Holy Spirit." This meaning resonated more strongly in my frustrated soul because at least it gave credit to the Spirit as being the source of joy. Then, at last, after months of intense research, I came upon the following definition in a Hebrew dictionary I found among my grandfather's archaic but reliable library: "the blessedness that the Lord enjoys around the throne of God Himself." I found myself agreeing completely, enthusiastically, and even tearfully with this connotation of the word *joy*.

What this means is that joy is the atmosphere of heaven! Doesn't that just make you weep?! It is the air that God the Father Himself breathes in every day of eternity. And because joy is heaven's continual gift to me while I walk on planet earth, it is my delight and strength to experience the blessedness that God enjoys on His throne.

Let that reality sink in for a minute! Even though you live in time and not in eternity, you are allowed, even encouraged, to breathe in the very oxygen of heaven. It is not really oxygen that enables you to live another day—it is heavenly joy, which gives you the strength for your ongoing personal journey!

A BABY NAMED JOY

There were a group of ragtag shepherds who lived an inky-black existence. These uneducated men, the lowest dregs of society, spent night after hopeless night taking care of someone else's dumb sheep. They had no chance of promotion or of receiving pay raises; their lives were never going to change from their dark environment and monotonous cycle.

These insignificant shepherds were defined by the most base and disgusting of components that were connected to the herd of beasts under their watch. The sticky drool and disgusting dung excreted by the sheep, and the perpetual baaing of the flock, were all that these hopeless men knew. Day after day after unending day, sheep slobber adorned their robes, sheep dung clung to their toes, and the cacophony of the livestock filled their weary ears.

However, on one unforgettable night, which had begun as a repeat of thousands of other dark, cold nights, the world of these shepherds was suddenly invaded by an announcement of tremendous joy! The heavens exploded in rare and glorious colors as the angels of eternity made a grand pronouncement into the shepherds' hopeless existence:

> *Behold, I bring you good news of great joy which will for all the people; for today in the city of David there has been born for you a Savior, who is Christ the Lord.* (Luke 2:10–11)

The eternal reason that the angels could ecstatically announce that joy had invaded the atmosphere and culture of earth was that joy had come in the *person* of a baby named Jesus. Heaven opened its portals that night, and joy splashed into our lives forever. Jesus came into our inky darkness, and the joy of heaven poured into our discouraged world.

If your world seems hopeless and dark, remind yourself that a Baby was born whom heaven had named "joy." The life of this Baby changed everything for every person in all of recorded history. His presence came to earth, and with Him, He brought the joy of the atmosphere of heaven!

On my kitchen wall hangs a plaque that was given to me many years ago by a friend when I was suffering from debilitating depression. The message on this sign greets me every morning as I walk into the kitchen to brew a cup of coffee; it is a constant companion while I am doing dishes, cooking dinner, and finally turning off the lights after a long day. Written decades ago by a devout Frenchman, these words are morsels of nutrition to my desperate soul:

> Joy is the infallible sign of the presence of God.   —de Chardin

WHEREVER GOD IS

So often, we spend our lives looking for joy in all the wrong places. We mistakenly believe that joy is found in locations like Hawaii, Harvard, or Hollywood. It's not found there. Or we foolishly assume that joy can be found in a person, in a job promotion, or in a prominent position. It's not

I Choose Joy! 169

found there. Neither is joy found in food, in fame, or in fortune. It is simply not there. Joy is fully found in one place, and one place alone. Joy is found wherever God is.

> You will make known to me the path of life; in Your presence is fullness of joy; in Your right hand there are pleasures forever. (Psalm 16:11)

Because we know that nothing is able to separate us from the love of God, which is in Christ Jesus our Lord (see Romans 8:38–39), we also know that nothing is able to separate us from His joy. God is with you perpetually, and you are with Him eternally! He has endearingly bequeathed you with the greatest benefit that comes from His presence: He has brought you the joy of heaven.

When I am being overtaken by the deceit of my emotions, what I really need is more of Him. Thus, when my joy begins to fade and is replaced by, for example, loneliness or depression, I am gently reminded by the Holy Spirit, "Carol, if you lack joy, guess who moved?" In order to cultivate the joy of heaven's grandeur in my puny, ordinary life, I need more of Jesus's presence and more time spent at His beautiful and nail-scarred feet.

I have always loved this quote by the great evangelist Billy Sunday: "If you have no joy…, there's a leak in your Christianity somewhere." All the joy I will ever need this side of heaven is found in hanging out with Jesus! It is found when I relentlessly choose more of Him and less of me; it is found when I understand the value of intimacy with the Lover of my soul. Joy is a heartfelt and strenuous discipline that only the desperate are brave enough to choose. I must choose His presence no matter what.

JOY IS THE OPPOSITE OF WEAK

By now, you understand that the enemy wants to influence the activities of your soul, but remember that he is unable to touch that which flourishes in your spirit. Joy was always meant to be the muscle that flexes itself in your spirit when life is roaring around you.

> Do not be grieved [or depressed], for the joy of the LORD is your strength.   (Nehemiah 8:10)

The enemy desires that you live in a constant state of debilitating, relentless depression and discouragement. He knows he is unable to change the fact that you are heaven-bound and have been guaranteed eternal life. He can do absolutely nothing about your entrance into heaven's gates. Since he can't touch your eternal life, what he attempts to do is to tarnish your abundant life here on earth.

The devil does not want you to be strong. This diabolical laughingstock of a shadow of absolute nothingness wants you to be the weakest version of yourself, and he goes about trying to accomplish this in a singular way: he attempts to steal your joy. The devil is not after your marriage, your health, your finances, your children, or your relationships. What he is really after is your joy, and the way he seeks to access your joy is *through* your marriage, your health, your finances, your children, and your relationships. Don't let him do it!

You have a loving and glorious God who wants to inject you with His joy. It is God's miraculous, perpetual joy that will deliver strength to your life this side of heaven's glory. Do not let the devil have the joy that Jesus died to give you. Stand toe-to-toe and nose-to-nose with the accuser of the brethren and engage in a defiant staredown. Whatever else you let go of, don't let go of your joy!

If you release any of your joy to the enemy, it will turn you into a weak, whining, and ineffective Christian, because *"the joy of the LORD is your strength."* Other than your salvation, I believe that your joy is the most valuable commodity you have been given for this life. The powerful gift of joy is able to give you indomitable strength during your days of pain and trauma. If there is anything the devil hates more than a Christian, it is a *joyful* Christian. Your joy is what will give you the strength to fight and to carry on with fortitude and tenacity every day of your life.

It is not strength that gives you joy, but it is joy that gives you strength! If you wait until you are strong to experience joy, you will never know joy as a reality. You must choose joy even in your weakness because it is then that strength will come rushing in!

A GARDEN OF JOY

Everything I know about farming, I learned from my dad, who was a farmer during the Depression and into the years of World War II. As a little girl growing up, I was my dad's sidekick in the acre family garden that grew behind my childhood home. Although my agricultural education is not extensive, I do know one of the most basic principles of farming, illustrated by this example: when a farmer plants cucumber seeds, cucumbers will grow. Aren't you impressed with my vast knowledge? I also can assure you that when a gardener plants sunflower seeds, smiling sunflowers will grow in that very piece of soil. The old adage "You reap what you sow" is verifiably true in every branch of agriculture, horticulture, and botany. If you plant radish seeds, you will not harvest carrots. If you plant a rosebush in a certain place, there is no need to worry that turnips will grow there. Relatedly, when two giraffes come together to mate, they will not produce a baby porcupine.

However, there is a verse whose imagery leads me to contemplate a seeming exception to this valid and scientific rule:

Those who sow in tears shall reap with joyful shouting. (Psalm 126:5)

If your life has held nothing but pain and sorrow and tears, let me assure you that it holds more potential for true joy than does the life of someone who has always had that proverbial white picket fence guarding the tulips of his or her life. The Bible says that God is able to take all of your tears and miraculously enable you to reap a harvest of joy and rejoicing. How is this even possible? Lean in and listen to the heart of God concerning the tears and pain of your life.

God takes our tears of disappointment and sadness, fertilizes them with His presence, and, out of that place of deep pain, causes an abundant harvest of joy to spring forth. You are never immune to such a miracle or left out of this promise. Only God is able to take your worst defeat, your greatest pain, and your moment of raw sorrow and turn it into His miraculous and irreplaceable joy. Only God.

AT THE CROSS

And finally, there is one more Scripture that must be included as part of our exhaustive research into the meaning of joy and how to apply it to our lives.

Surely our griefs He Himself bore, and our sorrows He carried.

(Isaiah 53:4)

Jesus took all of our sins and shame to the cross of Calvary so that we would no longer be in bondage to those damaging and toxic chains. He forgave us completely by His powerful blood and wiped away every spiritual consequence of sin. If that were all that Jesus had done, it would have been enough. It would have been *more* than enough. But this truth ricochets through the ages: not only did Jesus take our sins to the cross, but He also took every grief that we will ever experience and every sorrow that has ever tormented our lives. Jesus has gently removed our grief and our sorrow from us and has laid them at the foot of Calvary.

George Whitefield, the eighteenth-century theologian and one of the founders of Methodism, knew personally the truth of this great exchange that happened at Calvary. He expressed it in his words, "I was delivered from the burden that had so heavily oppressed me; the spirit of mourning was taken from me, and I knew what it was to truly rejoice in God my Saviour."[7]

Yes, Jesus took your grief and sorrow so that you would no longer have to carry them on your own. He has relieved you of the bondage that sorrow and grief bring to a person's life. Just as your sins are gone, so are your sorrows. Jesus has replaced your sins with His eternal forgiveness, and He has replaced your grief with the joy of His everlasting presence!

Create in me a clean heart, O God, and renew a steadfast spirit within me. Do not cast me away from Your presence and do not take Your Holy Spirit from me. Restore to me the joy of Your salvation and sustain me with a willing spirit. Then I will teach transgressors Your ways, and sinners will be converted to You. (Psalm 51:10–13)

GUARD YOUR HEART: PERSONAL APPLICATION

1. Write down your own definition of "joy." How does this definition compare with the idea of joy being the atmosphere of heaven, created by God's own presence?

2. When has God's joy suddenly and unexpectedly broken through your negative feelings or distressing circumstances and filled your heart? Describe how it happened.

7. George Whitefield, quoted in *Awakened by the Spirit* by Ron M. Phillips (Nashville: Thomas Nelson, 1999), 120.

3. Have you ever mistaken happiness for joy? What types of happiness have you pursued, thinking that they would bring you joy?

4. In what way is experiencing God's joy a choice on your part? How can you choose joy in your present circumstances?

5. On the cross, Jesus took your grief and sorrow so that you would no longer have to carry them on your own. He desires to give you the joy of His everlasting presence. If you are currently struggling with depression or discouragement, pray this prayer:

> Dear Heavenly Father,
>
> Your Word says that Jesus bore all my griefs and carried all my sorrows when He died on the cross for me. He has removed them from me, just as He has taken my sins away. I ask you to replace my feelings of deep sorrow and grief with your joy as You fill me with Your Spirit and presence. I love you, Lord, and I thank You for exchanging my sadness and misery for your abundant joy! In Jesus's name, amen.

6. Commit this Scripture to memory:

> *Do not be grieved* [or depressed], *for the joy of the* Lord *is your strength.* (Nehemiah 8:10)

18

NEVER SAD AGAIN

It's time for another interview with that heart, or soul, of yours. Let's take the temperature of your heart by asking a few questions that will help you to pinpoint areas where the emotion of sadness has infiltrated your heart.

First of all, what makes you sad? Think of the saddest moment in your life and analyze the cause of that sadness.

Second, how do you react when you are sad? Do you weep and wail and whine? Or do you retreat inside yourself and become despondent and unreachable?

My third question is this: have you ever made someone else sad? Think soberly about that possibility for a minute; perhaps you can think of a time when your actions or your words have brought sadness to someone's life. Have you taken the time to rectify the situation?

THE SOURCE OF SADNESS

One succinct dictionary definition of sadness is "something that brings emotional pain, unhappiness, or misery." Often, sadness occurs when we simply don't like our circumstances and are powerless to change them. Here are some other, more specific, sources of sadness:

+ being ignored or mistreated

+ wanting more than one is able to accomplish or access

+ comparing oneself with others

+ being disappointed about something

The truth is that there are hundreds of reasons why the emotion of sadness may invade a person's life. The good thing about sadness is that, generally, it is a passing reaction to a specific event. Sadness is not the same as depression; depression is long-lasting and pervasive, while sadness is temporary and limited. However, depression often springs out of sadness if the sadness is left untended and is allowed to multiply.

SAD FACES

Joseph, of the Old Testament, was spending time in prison through no fault of his own. The wife of his master, Potiphar, had accused the young, handsome Joseph of sexual harassment, which was verifiably untrue. Potiphar's wife was actually the one who had sexually and aggressively pursued Joseph, and he had repeatedly turned her down, so she spitefully defamed his character. After Potiphar heard his wife's accusations against their slave, the innocent Joseph landed in a sordid Egyptian prison.

Yet the Lord was with Joseph even in that prison, and Joseph quickly found favor with the chief jailer. The jailer put him in charge of all of the prisoners, and Joseph became a trusted member of the supervisory staff, even though he, himself, was a prisoner.

While Joseph was in prison, the pharaoh's cupbearer and baker both offended the ruler, and they landed in the same prison. Joseph was put in charge of these men and apparently got to know them quite well. One night, the cupbearer and the baker both had dreams that upset them greatly. When Joseph came in the next morning to attend to the two men, he quickly discerned that something was not right with them.

> [Joseph] *asked Pharaoh's officials who were with him in confinement in his master's house, "Why are your faces so sad today?"*
> (Genesis 40:7)

These two men were sad, and it showed on their countenances. Oftentimes, sadness that is birthed in your circumstances will not remain just in your heart but will be plainly seen on your face. In all probability, the cupbearer and the baker were sad for these accumulated reasons: they did not like prison, they didn't understand what was going on in their lives, and they had each had a perplexing, disturbing dream. Sadness often enters a person's heart when he or she is disappointed in the circumstances of life and sees no hope for the future.

What is amazing to me about this story is that Joseph was not sad. Although he had been mistreated by his brothers, sold into slavery in Egypt, and then unfairly placed in prison, there is nothing in the Bible that indicates Joseph may have been dealing with sadness. Instead, he obviously had it in his heart to take care of others and to stay true to his character.

When we are more aware of the Lord's presence than we are of our disappointing circumstances, we are able to overcome sadness, miraculously step away from our own pain, and encourage others. In Genesis 39, Joseph was dealing with separation from family, with enslavement, false accusations, and imprisonment. Yet four times in that chapter, the Bible states that the Lord was with Joseph. (See verses 2–3, 21, 23.) And remarkably, five times in the same chapter, it says that the Lord either blessed Joseph, showed him favor, or caused him to prosper. (See verses 2–3, 5, 21, 23.)

In the midst of Joseph's discouraging and frustrating circumstances, the Lord was with him and had His wonderful hand on his life. When I feel life crowding in on me, and I sense sadness creeping its way into the corners of my heart, I often remember the story of Joseph, and I remind myself that the Lord is with me and that He is intent on blessing me right where I am. Like Joseph, if I can be more aware of the Lord's presence than I am of my own human pain, then any sadness will quickly pass, and I will be able to minister to others.

WHERE IS JESUS?

One of the saddest stories in the entire Bible is certainly the account of the crucifixion of our Savior, Jesus. Let's review what happened in the lives of His followers after that heartbreaking event.

It had been three long days since Jesus had been crucified; He had been laid in a borrowed tomb, and a heavy stone had been rolled into place, closing up the grave. The tomb had been sealed so securely that no one was able to disturb it. Pilate had ordered his soldiers,

Make it as secure as you know how.   (Matthew 27:65)

On the first day of the week following the crucifixion, Mary Magdalene and the *"other Mary"* (*"Mary the mother of James,"* according to Mark 16:1) went to Jesus's grave, and when they arrived, they were instantly and completely shocked at what they found in that ancient cemetery. The stone had been rolled away by an earthquake, and a shining angel from heaven greeted these unsuspecting and grieving women. (See Matthew 28:1–4.) The angel told them,

> *Do not be afraid.... [Jesus] is not here, for He has risen, just as He said.*   (Matthew 28:5–6)

The angel instructed the incredulous women to go and tell the disciples that Jesus had risen from the dead. He also informed them that they would see Jesus with their very own eyes in Galilee. (See verses 7–10.) However, most of the disciples dismissed the women's remarkable message.

> *But these words appeared to them as nonsense, and they would not believe them.*   (Luke 24:11)

However, when Peter and John heard this unbelievable news from the women, they ran to the tomb to see for themselves what had happened. (See Luke 24:12; John 20:2–8.) Peter and John, who had been in the inner circle of friendship with Jesus, were compelled to discover the truth. Peter—the impetuous one, the one who had walked on water, who had rebuked Jesus, and who had cut off a man's ear while trying to defend his Lord from arrest by the Roman soldiers and officers of the chief priest and Pharisees—barged into the empty tomb. This was an act of sheer bravado, because a tomb was a sacred, holy place. Peter ripped into the tomb, gasping for air, with sweat pouring down his face, but all he found was an empty grave. No one was there. The body of Jesus was gone!

> *But Peter got up and ran to the tomb; stooping and looking in, he saw the linen wrappings only; and he went away to his home, marveling at what had happened.*   (Luke 24:12)

Two other followers of Jesus were walking along the road to Emmaus that very day; as they were walking, they couldn't help but talk about what had happened to Jesus. It was the question that consumed them, haunted them, and confused them. *What had happened to Jesus, and why?*

> *And behold, two of them were going that very day to a village named Emmaus, which was about seven miles from Jerusalem. And they were talking with each other about all these things which had taken place.*
>   (Luke 24:13–14)

A Man joined the two grieving disciples and engaged them in conversation. Although He walked with them for a distance, they didn't know who He was, and they told Him about their sad circumstances.

> *While they were talking and discussing, Jesus Himself approached and began traveling with them. But their eyes were prevented from recognizing Him. And He said to them, "What are these words that you are exchanging with one another as you are walking?" And they stood still, looking sad.*   (Luke 24:15–17)

Why were these formerly vibrant, empowered disciples sad? What had caused the malaise that was growing in their hearts? The answer, of course, is obvious to those of us who know the history of Jesus and His resurrection. For these disciples, however, all they were aware of was that Jesus's body was gone—He was nowhere to be found. He had been killed like a criminal and buried in a tomb that didn't even belong to Him, and now the tomb was found to be empty. Where was Jesus?

The two disciples had placed themselves in a state of sadness because they were disappointed and heartbroken over their circumstances. Jesus wasn't where they thought they would find Him, and their sadness prevented them from seeing Him when He showed up to walk with them. He was right there with them, but their sadness robbed them of the joy of that moment.

There is much we can extract from this story, but one of the primary points is that often our sadness will skew our perception of who God is and where He is. Our sadness just might keep us from recognizing Him, and we will mistakenly presume that He is removed from us when He is not far away at all. Perhaps the greatest lesson from this tender story is that sadness will blind us to the joy of His presence.

EASTER PEOPLE

My life was greatly impacted by the chaplain at the Christian university I attended in the 1970s. Brother Bob Stamps was similar to what Peter must have been like—enthusiastic, dynamic, and charismatic. A graduate of Wheaton College and Asbury Theological Seminary, he had also earned a doctorate in systematic theology from St. John's College, Oxford. Bob was one of the greatest theologians of our day. He unfolded the Scriptures with warmth and depth, and he taught generations of students how to celebrate the Eucharist with the proper combination of celebration and reverence. And how Bob loved to teach about the resurrection of Christ! It was the theme of his life and the grand connecting point in every spiritual truth that he taught. I will always remember what Brother Bob said about sadness: "We are an Easter people, and nothing can ever really be sad again!"

It has been well stated that the resurrection of Jesus Christ is either absolute truth, or it is the greatest lie in all of history. If you believe that Jesus is the Son of God, that He was God in the flesh, born of a virgin, was crucified and buried, and was raised from the dead, then you are part of what is known as the great eternal company of "Easter People"! We are the people who glean our entire identity from the life of Jesus Christ.

Whenever I am tempted to allow sadness to take up residence in my heart, I remind myself that I belong to Easter and that Easter belongs to me! Because of Jesus and the empty tomb, nothing can ever really be sad again. His resurrection trumps the power of sadness in my life, and His presence delivers joy!

A joyful heart makes a cheerful face, but when the heart is sad, the spirit is broken.   (Proverbs 15:13)

GUARD YOUR HEART: PERSONAL APPLICATION

1. (a) What types of things cause you to be sad?

    (b) What was the saddest moment of your life? Why?

    (c) What are you sad about right now?

2. (a) How do you ordinarily react to your sadness? What do you usually turn to when you feel sad?

(b) How did Joseph react to his own distressing circumstances? What was the reason he responded in those ways? How can you respond in the same ways, despite your situation?

3.   Have you ever caused someone else to be sad? Describe the circumstances. What can you do to bring about reconciliation with, or to encourage, that person?

4.   We have learned from the story of Jesus's disciples after the crucifixion that our sadness can blind us to the reality—and the joy—of His continual presence in our lives. Fill your mind with Scriptures like the following, spoken by Jesus, to remind yourself that He is always with you, no matter what the circumstances.

> *I will never desert you, nor will I ever forsake you.*
>
> (Hebrews 13:5)

> *I am with you always, even to the end of the age.*
>
> (Matthew 28:20)

5.   Reread the last section in this chapter, entitled "Easter People." Write down what it means for you personally to be part of the "great eternal company of 'Easter People.'"

19

THE ANTICIPATION OF THOSE WHO WAIT WELL

Do you recall the singular excitement that anticipating Christmas brought into your heart when you were a child? Do you remember that the days never seemed to end during the apparently longest but very best month of the year? Even now, decades later, I look back and am reminded of the trouble that I had falling asleep as I contemplated the delicious delight that belonged only to Christmas morning. In the days leading up to it, night after night, my heart pounded, my toes wiggled, and I dreamed of the sweet moments that December 25 would give me to savor.

Or do you remember how, as a young student, you couldn't wait for summer vacation to begin? As you tried to concentrate in class, it seemed that all of those imaginary yet energetic butterflies in your stomach threw a lively party day after day. Although the waiting time for enjoying those weeks without school seemed never-ending and arduous, somehow you felt a magnetic pleasure in just contemplating the freedom that summertime would deliver.

DON'T KEEP ME WAITING!

For many of us as adults, the years have quickly flown by, and it can often seem as if there is less and less to truly anticipate in life. No longer do we look ahead; instead we look back with longing for what used to be. Rather than anticipating the glorious delight that tomorrow may bring, we walk backwards through life paralyzed by the memories, both good and bad, of yesterday. The child still inside each one of us wishes there was something to truly look forward to, but the adult version of us has grown to dread having to wait for a long-anticipated and much-prayed-for event. As we wait, we do not anticipate anymore—we worry. We no longer have the need to contain our excitement; instead we must discipline ourselves to stir it up!

Where has our anticipation fled to? Is there any way to connect our human hearts to the reassurance that there is, indeed, a solid reason to live in a place of divine expectancy?

For a Christian, anticipation is so much more than an emotion; anticipation is the unwavering expectation that God's goodness will write the end of all our stories. As we anticipate His intervention, we participate in the growth spurt that the act of waiting brings to the spirit of a disciple of Jesus Christ. While we wait, while we hope, and while we expect God's goodness to manifest in our lives, our faith will grow to gigantic proportions! Waiting—and stubbornly expecting God's faithfulness to have the last word in our life—is the most vibrant spiritual vitamin known to mankind. Believing in the eternal goodness of God and His unfailing love for His children as we wait for His hand to move in our lives will add priceless value to our common existence. As the psalmist wrote,

> *Rescue me, O my God, out of the hand of the wicked, out of the grasp of the wrongdoer and ruthless man, for You are my hope; O LORD God, You are my confidence from my youth. By You I have been sustained from my birth; You are He who took me from my mother's womb; my praise is continually of You.* (Psalm 71:5–6)

Unfortunately, I believe that the march of time and the devastation of disappointments many of us have experienced have stolen our ability to anticipate the goodness of God in all of our life circumstances and events. Several years ago, a grieving widow tearfully confessed to me, "There is nothing to look forward to anymore. There is nothing about life that gives me any hope." As she said those words, I understood her pain. I recognized that death had stolen something precious from her; the passing of her beloved husband had robbed her of the ability to anticipate the joy that was yet to come. Thus, whatever our circumstances, let's resolve to renew the optimism of anticipation and to allow our childlike expectation to become a strengthening part of our walk with Christ.

I have heard it said, "Young girls with dreams grow up to be women with vision." Have you noticed that if you ask a child what they would like to be when they grow up, they quickly recite an entire list of possibilities? "A nurse, a teacher, a fireman, a librarian, a veterinarian, and a circus performer," one of my grandchildren has gleefully declared when asked that question.

However, if you ask an adult what his or her dreams might be, the answer is most often expressed in silence or in stuttering. Why is it that as we grow older, we lose our ability to anticipate what God might have for us in the days to come? Perhaps it is time for each one of us to raise our hopes, to dream again, and to anticipate God's goodness in the future days of our lives.

"IN THE WAIT"

While we are longing for a prayer to be answered or for a hope to become tangible, we often find ourselves wrestling with God "in the wait." However, that is the place where our anticipation can be most beautifully refined and most powerfully transformed.

> *Do you not know? Have you not heard? The Everlasting God, the* LORD, *the Creator of the ends of the earth does not become weary or tired. His understanding is inscrutable. He gives strength to the weary, and to him who lacks might He increases power. Though youths grow weary and tired, and vigorous young men stumble badly, yet those who wait for the* LORD *will gain new strength; they will mount up with wings like eagles, they will run and not get tired, they will walk and not become weary.* (Isaiah 40:28–31)

These extraordinary verses, spoken by the prophet Isaiah nearly three thousand years ago, deliver strength to the weary and bestow power to those who lack might in the twenty-first century. The strength God gives to those who find themselves "in the wait" is unlimited and comes in as many ways as there are facets to the eternal character of God. The Lord is lavish in giving emotional strength, physical strength, and spiritual strength to all of us who spend time waiting and hoping. There is no end to His creativity as He gives His eternal fortitude and matchless energy to His children. If you have found yourself lacking in anticipation, perhaps your focus has been solely on some future event rather than on the Creator, the Giver of strength and endurance.

For just a moment, I want to say a word especially to older adults. You are completely mistaken if you believe that strength, vigor, and power are attributes of only the young. If you believe the Bible, then you must also believe that when a person chooses to wait upon the Lord and anticipate His miraculous intervention, God will assuredly deliver new, resilient strength to his or her personal life. When you pause to access the strength of God and anticipate His perpetual goodness, you will gain the capacity to run beyond your human endurance and will not even be out of emotional breath. Your vitality will not lag, nor will your heart race with the challenge of it all. You will have the vigor to go the distance—and then to go some more! However, this incredible surge of heaven's power and strength into your human frailty will be possible only when you choose to wait upon the Lord and anticipate, with gratitude, all that He has for you.

Therefore, if you are in your golden years, do not use this season in life as an excuse to lie down, give up, or retire from productive activity, because your age has absolutely nothing to do with the energy and vitality that is headed your way from heaven's resources. God is not done with you yet! Get in the starting gate and in the take-off stance, regardless of the date on your birth certificate. Do not sit around waiting to die, but peacefully and hopefully wait for God's strength to revitalize your weary bones. Wait on God to give you the ability to literally change the world—that goes for anyone, whether you are fifteen years old…fifty years old…or eighty years old.

Regardless of your age, background, or situation, you must eagerly expect and joyously anticipate the promise that God will indeed reward you with His vitality as you read your Bible and enter into worship every day, and as you engage in vibrant, daily prayer. Those are the disciplines of fortitude that will enable you not only to receive strength from the Lord, but also to apply to your daily walk the strength that you receive.

In addition to participating in those helpful and hopeful daily disciplines, which result in God's power flowing into your life, there might also be times and seasons when you will feel a need to specifically and directly entreat God for His power. I have discovered that the best part of anticipation is sharing it with the Father, such as in the following prayer:

> God, I need You! This situation is too difficult for me to handle in my own strength. Would you give me Your power? Would you give me a word from the Bible that I can apply to this situation? I am waiting, Lord, for all that You have for me. I am anticipating Your goodness in my life. In Jesus's name I pray, amen.

A POWERFUL GIFT FOR RESTORING ANTICIPATION

There are various Hebrew and Greek words that are translated as *"wait"* (or some form of the word) in our English Bibles, among whose meanings are "to expect," "to look eagerly for," "to hope for," and "to lie in wait for." As you "wait well" in God's presence—with expectation, eagerness, and hope—and devote yourself to prayer, you can assuredly anticipate some opportunities that will require the strength of God. In the book of Acts, it was when the disciples prayed and *waited* that they were given the power of heaven's entry into all of their life's circumstances.

> *Gathering them together, [Jesus] commanded them not to leave Jerusalem, but to wait for what the Father had promised, "Which," He said, "you heard of from Me; for John baptized with water, but you will be baptized with the Holy Spirit not many days from now." ...These all with one mind were continually devoting themselves to prayer, along with the women, and Mary the mother of Jesus, and with His brothers.* (Acts 1:4–5, 14)

I believe that pure anticipation will be restored to our hearts as we receive the power of the Holy Spirit and begin to share His divine perspective on life.

THE JOY OF THE WAIT

Besides the meanings noted above, there is a Hebrew word translated as *"wait"* in the Bible that signifies "to bind together, to hold fast to something." Thus, as you truly and absolutely anticipate the goodness of God to intervene in your life circumstances, you also need to participate in another activity. You must bind your life so intimately to the life of the Father that His strength literally and thoroughly becomes your very own portion of power.

This term for "wait" was actually used in the ancient Hebrew culture for "a gathering of waters." When the water from two separate streams becomes combined, it is impossible to distinguish which parts of the water came from which stream. Likewise, when water is poured from two different pitchers into a third pitcher, it is impossible to discern which molecules of water came from a certain pitcher. So it is with the strength of the Lord; when you "gather yourself" to the Lord and intimately bind yourself to Him, it is as if His strength becomes your own strength. You won't be able to discern where your strength ends and where His begins!

Receiving the strength of the Lord is the joy of the wait! Strength overpowers worry, and joy diminishes dread, while you bind yourself to the nature and the character of God Himself.

Yes, one of the most miraculous and amazing aspects of the strength God provides is that He does not give mere human strength to His waiting children. Rather, He gives of His own divine source of strength. During the difficult days of life, if what you needed was mere human strength, then a self-help guru, a psychology course, or a trip to Hawaii might deliver what you required. However, what you need is strength beyond human strength; you need more of God! You desperately need His strength to be gathered inside of you—and you will receive it while you wait and while you pray. You will be strengthened as you anticipate seeing the goodness of God.

> *I would have despaired unless I had believed that I would see the goodness of the* Lord *in the land of the living. Wait for the* Lord; *be strong and let your heart take courage; yes, wait for the* Lord.　　(Psalm 27:13–14)

HOPE TRIUMPHS

Perhaps the best way to understand the joy of anticipation is simply to define it as "hope." Genuine hope has the powerful capacity to banish worry from one's mind and to neutralize fear in the depth of one's soul. Hope triumphs over despair and gives a dazzling brilliance to even the dreariest of times spent "in the wait."

> *Be strong and let your heart take courage, all you who hope in the* Lord.　　(Psalm 31:24)

Here is my own simple yet life-changing definition of *hope*: "believing that the goodness of God will intervene in my circumstances." A Christian must believe, with his or her whole heart, that experiencing God's goodness is not a remote possibility but a solid reality. As those who serve the God of all hope (see Romans 15:13), you and I can be unwaveringly confident that His goodness has not eluded our temporary circumstances; we can be assured beyond a shadow of a doubt that His eternal goodness is inevitable in all that concerns us.

The truth of Romans 8:28 is not a religious platitude—it will deliver a reason for you to hope again!

And we know that God causes all things to work together for good to those who love God, to those who are called according to His purpose.

God has been to your future, and it is good because He is good! It's time for you to lay aside the weight of your past, to bury the devastation of your disappointments, and to gain fresh strength for the days that are ahead.

That's *anticipation*.

GUARD YOUR HEART: PERSONAL APPLICATION

1. What events did you especially anticipate with excitement when you were a child (for example, Christmas, vacations, or birthdays)?

2. (a) Has your sense of anticipation diminished or even disappeared as you have grown older? If so, why do you think this has happened?

   (b) Do you usually worry about the future rather than look forward to it?

3. In this chapter, the biblical sense of *anticipation* is defined as "unwavering expectation that God's goodness will write the end of all our stories," and "believing that the goodness of God will intervene in my circumstances."

   (a) What happens to our faith when we live according to this type of anticipation? How does godly anticipation cause us to grow and mature spiritually?

   (b) What kind of strength does God provide for us as we wait for Him to intervene in our circumstances?

4. How will you kindle anticipation of God's goodness and grace in your life?

5. If you are facing a particularly difficult situation, instead of worrying, draw close to God, "binding" yourself to Him, and receive His own divine strength in your life. As you do, remind yourself of the following Scriptures:

   > *Be strong and let your heart take courage, all you who hope in the LORD.* (Psalm 31:24)

   > *And we know that God causes all things to work together for good to those who love God, to those who are called according to His purpose.* (Romans 8:28)

20

I ACCEPT!

Acceptance" is an interesting emotion, isn't it? I am not sure that I would have listed it in the top eight identifiable human emotions, as Dr. Plutchik did. However, since he is the expert and I am the novice, we will consider what his intentions might have been in naming acceptance as one of the primary emotions.

As human beings, we all have the ability to either accept or reject another person; we show our acceptance by the words that we speak, as well as by our actions. Additionally, our body language and attitudes strongly communicate whether we accept someone or have placed that person on our "reject list." Likewise, we each have the option of receiving someone else's apology or refusing it. Moreover, we have the choice whether to accept our own life with grace and gratitude, or to always be striving for something new or different. And there are many other examples we might give for our capacity to accept or reject.

Actually, the longing to simply be accepted is one of the deepest human desires. We yearn for God to accept us just the way we are, and we desperately hope that the Lord is filled with mercy and compassion toward our weaknesses and failures. Oh, how I love for God to listen to me when I speak, and not to reject the words that I say in His presence!

O accept the freewill offerings of my mouth, O LORD, and teach me Your ordinances. (Psalm 119:108)

Just as I long for God to accept me and to extend lovingkindness and mercy to me at my very worst moments, I need to frequently remind myself that unconditional acceptance is what others long to receive from me, as well. The people in my family, at my workplace, and in my group of friends simply desire to be accepted, to be shown forgiveness even when they don't deserve it, and to be extended compassion and grace. Most people simply want me to listen to them, just as I want God to listen to me.

What a glorious and beautiful gift acceptance can be! It is more valuable than a gift box from Tiffany's or even a large inheritance. If we are able to love someone freely and without reproach, it bestows more honor on that person than a degree from an Ivy League university would dispense. If we are inclined to lavishly and generously splash words of encouragement and kindness on others, it will bring more delight to them than a trip to an exotic location would provide. Thus, when you or I freely and graciously accept the personhood of someone else and acknowledge his or her importance as an individual, we give that person the most costly and treasured resource known to mankind—the resource of acceptance.

ACCEPTANCE AT ITS FINEST

The Holy Trinity is perhaps the most consequential demonstration of the model of acceptance that is available to us. The Trinity, as you know, is the Three in One—the Father, the Son, and the Holy Spirit. Essentially, the Father is the Creator, the Son is the Savior, and the Holy Spirit is the power. God is the King of Heaven who sits on the throne, Jesus is the Prince of Peace who even now makes intercession for us, and the Holy Spirit lives in us as Comforter and Wisdom. While there are three persons of the Trinity, they are all in one accord. For example, the Trinity is total goodness. The Bible talks about God's *"abundant goodness,"* how Jesus *"went about doing good,"* and how the Holy Spirit works all things together for our good. (See, for example, Psalm 145:7; Acts 10:38; Romans 8:28; Philippians 2:13.)

The picture that the Trinity demonstrates is acceptance at its finest. As members of the body of Christ, we are to live according to the acceptance of the Father, Son, and Spirit by receiving each another as one, even though our roles differ and our callings vary.

> *Therefore, accept one another, just as Christ also accepted us to the glory of God.* (Romans 15:7)

What great news, and what a difficult challenge, is packed into this one short verse! Christ accepted each one of us when we were hard to love, when we were lost in sin, and when we lived in darkness. He accepted us as one of His own before we ever accomplished any great task, led anyone to Christ, or sang a solo in church. He accepted you, and He accepted me, which brought glory to God! In this verse, Paul and the Holy Spirit are in agreement about this vital truth: when we accept one another, we will bring glory to the Trinity. As a matter of reminder, one of the reasons we are still breathing in oxygen and living this side of eternity is to bring glory to God! Thus, this verse indicates that part of the reason we are still alive is to accept one another the way that Jesus Christ has accepted each one of us.

The word *"accept"* in this introductory letter that the apostle Paul wrote to the church in Rome has a beautiful yet challenging meaning. Among the shades of its definition are the following: "to take as one's companion; to take or receive into one's home with the idea of kindness; to grant access to one's heart."

EGR

Our family has often utilized a secret code language. Raising five rambunctious, creative, and individual kids while serving in full-time ministry has required this covert dialect. Often, when we needed to communicate something to our children that we didn't want anyone else to understand or to overhear, we would break into our cryptic communication.

It would often happen after church service on Sunday mornings. As the pastor of a growing church, Craig would frequently, of necessity, be dealing with a long-winded person or perhaps listening to an especially needy person's most recent disappointment. During these seemingly interminable moments, the children would understandably become impatient or hungry. Then, the five tiny saints that God had given to us would impatiently ask me when we could leave, when we could eat, or when their dad was finally going to be free to leave the sanctuary. With a smile, and with a sparkle in my eyes, I would bend down to look right into their McLeod blue eyes, gently take their little faces in my hands, and say, "EGR." That was our code for "extra grace required." And with that simple phrase, my children could accept the situation and the person. They knew in that moment that their daddy was giving Jesus to someone in pain. We longed for our children to see the big picture of ministry and not just their own momentary needs. We longed for our children to love the people to whom their dad and I were called; we also made it a priority that, as McLeods, we treated everyone with rare kindness and acceptance.

Acceptance is often a difficult choice to make and usually requires dying to self, to personal preference, and to personal comfort. However, just as Jesus accepted you to the glory of God the Father, so must you accept others—and that will also bring glory to God! So, perhaps the most important bridge you can build in accepting others is "EGR." There will be people whom God strategically places in your life who need your EGR. When you give grace to challenging and fractious people, you are accepting them just as Jesus accepted you!

WHO NEEDS YOUR ACCEPTANCE?

Is there someone who needs access to your heart? Perhaps even now you are being reminded of an individual whom you have been keeping at arm's length. The world is filled with people who have been rejected, scorned, and thrown aside, and Jesus has given you the extraordinary job of rescuing them from the clutches of sin and darkness. Perhaps it is your acceptance of a person that will lead them into the arms of Christ. Oftentimes, our soul wants to reject people who are difficult to love, who are dysfunctional, or who come with troublesome habits. But it is your spirit that must make the final call about these challenging folks. If your spirit has been in active fellowship with the One who accepted you, then you will have the grace and the strength to accept other people, no matter how jagged they might seem on the surface.

Do not just gloss over this chapter and stubbornly believe that the Holy Spirit does not want to challenge you with regard to those whom you have rejected in your life. Perhaps it is your husband who is aching for a greater degree of acceptance from you; maybe it is your mom or your dad from whom you have been keeping your distance. If you are a parent, have you been quietly ignoring the difficult child who requires extra love and atten-tion from you? There are all types of people whom we might have refused to allow entrance into our hearts—from the loquacious to the prickly to the cruel. Today is your day to open up your heart and accept the people whom God has strategically placed in your pathway.

Remember, when we accept each other, we bring glory to God the Father! When you welcome a person into your life, it's almost as good as a full-blown worship service. I believe that God strategically places troublesome and problematic people in our lives to strengthen our love muscle. He knows that there are certain people who need more of Jesus, and so He trusts you to minister to their unstable lives. If you respond to other people with your soul rather than with your spirit, your soul will probably become impatient and frustrated with them, and you will walk away from irritating people. Your soul easily rejects demanding people, but your spirit accepts them with the grace and love of the Father.

DON'T ACCEPT IT

Nevertheless, as a Christ-follower, you are allowed to set some healthy boundaries concerning the degree of acceptance to which you are called to adhere. What is *unacceptable* is behavior that is dishonoring to God. Again, the old adage rings true that it is possible to love the sinner but hate the sin. It is possible to love a person while not condoning that person's behavior. Parents are able to make this distinction daily while raising their children. I adored my two-year-olds, but their temper tantrums were unacceptable behavior; I delighted in my teenagers, but sassy talking was unsatisfactory in our home.

> *Listen to counsel and accept discipline, that you may be wise the rest of your days.* (Proverbs 19:20)

Thus, it is feasible to accept a person but not their behavior, yet we can also believe the best about a person even while knowing the worst. The church is not to be known as "The Fellowship of the Religious" or "The Body of the Holier-than-Thou." We must remind ourselves that we are "The Fellowship of Sinners Who Have Been Redeemed by Grace"!

> *By this all men will know that you are My disciples, if you have love for one another.* (John 13:35)

These words of Jesus, spoken two thousand years ago, penetrate our hearts today as we consider how we are to treat the people in our lives. Acceptance is a gift of the heart that we freely extend to others, whether or not they deserve it. The world will know that we are Christians by our love for one another.

Acceptance is a choice that we must make in many life situations. Most important, we must choose whether to accept or reject the words of Christ. We must choose whether or not to accept the person of Christ as our Lord and Savior. Acceptance is the foundational emotion of our relationship with Jesus, and it governs all of our relationships with other people.

Acceptance is invariably accompanied by kind thoughts, kind words, and kind actions. The powerful benefit of kindness is that it usually causes a softening of heart in the person to whom it is aimed. Always remember, with joyful anticipation, that your kind acceptance of a challenging person in your life may be all it takes to lead him or her to Jesus.

> *Or do you think lightly of the riches of His kindness and tolerance and patience, not knowing that the kindness of God leads you to repentance?* (Romans 2:4)

GUARD YOUR HEART: PERSONAL APPLICATION

1. Do you generally feel accepted by others? Why or why not?

2. When you are accepted by others, how does that make you feel?

3. What do we know about God's acceptance of us, based on the following Scriptures?

   > *Therefore, accept one another, just as Christ also accepted us to the glory of God.* (Romans 15:7)

   > *[God] chose us in [Christ] before the foundation of the world, that we should be holy and without blame before Him in love, having predestined us to adoption as sons by Jesus Christ to Himself, according to the good pleasure of His will, to the praise of the glory of His grace, by which He made us accepted in the Beloved.* (Ephesians 1:4–6 NKJV)

4. When we accept other people in the name of Christ, what spiritual result does this bring about?

5. How does your soul respond to troublesome or difficult people, as opposed to your spirit? In what way will you direct your spirit to control your soul under such conditions?

6. Who in your life especially needs some "EGR" (extra grace required) from you? Write down the names of two people toward whom you will actively seek to demonstrate the love and acceptance of Christ—knowing that He has accepted you despite your own mistakes, failings, selfishness, and moodiness. Commit to pray for these two people frequently, and ask God to fill you with His love for them, so it can flow through you to them.

PART THREE
GRACE YOUR TONGUE!

21

STICK OUT YOUR TONGUE AND SAY, "AHH!"

It is time for you to stick out your tongue and say, "Ahh!" Have you done that dreaded but extremely vital self-examination lately? Now—look in the mirror as you do it.

Do you have it? Do you have "mouth disease"? Are you infected with an "oral bacteria" of the very worst kind? Have the germs of the culture attached themselves to your vocal chords? Is your tongue rife with verbal viruses?

What is it with women and their words? What is it with *anyone* and their words? We are definitely defined by the stuff that proceeds out of our voice boxes. The organ that lies between our pearly whites has the capacity to control our very lives. The vile eruptions that come tumbling unbridled out of that lovely orifice called the mouth are often what color our relationships and the atmosphere of our homes.

Our words have the propensity to direct us, to define us—and to drive us. It is as if we are compelled by a force of nature to continually talk, and we often refuse to stop talking until we have the very last word in every conversation and in every argument.

The anchor verse that will change the way we talk is found in Proverbs, the book of wisdom that is changing our thought processes, giving boundaries to our emotions, and now will impact the way we speak. Perhaps you have previously read it and wondered what application it had for your life:

> *Death and life are in the power of the tongue, and those who love it will eat its fruit.*   (Proverbs 18:21)

The stark reality is that, someday—in the not-too-distant future—you are going to be forced to eat the fruit of what you have chosen to say. When dealing with the tongue, your options are twofold: you can speak life or you can speak death. There is no middle ground between those two choices. There is no gray area when it comes to the words that you speak. That's it. Just life or death. Which will you choose?

When you understand that you have the power to speak life or death every moment of your existence, it will underscore the fact that controlling your own tongue will be one of the most vital endeavors of your life. First, you must take every thought captive to the obedience of Christ; next, you must guard your heart faithfully; finally, you must put a bridle on your tongue. If you don't first think something or feel something, then, in all probability, you will never say it. Any idea or opinion begins in the mind, travels to the heart, and finally comes out of the mouth.

Perhaps there is no other life matter that we should take more seriously than the matter of the tongue. The ability to discipline your tongue is more important than the number on your bathroom scale, more essential than your education, and more profitable to you than climbing the corporate ladder. Consistent discipline in the attempt to manage your mouth will create more beauty than will a home that is attractively decorated, and provide more true wealth than will a full retirement fund.

According to the always-applicable truth of the Bible, your tongue has the power to control the type of life that you will enjoy in all of your tomorrows. Will your life be a fruitful one? If you can maintain godly government over your tongue, your life will be one of joy and peace; you will cultivate a home atmosphere that is warm and inviting, and you will maintain friendships that flourish.

Conversely, if you refuse to regulate the discharge that comes out of the cavity that lies beneath your nose, your life will be dry and brittle. Nothing beautiful will grow in your life, and you will be known for "halitosis" of the very worst kind!

IT'S CONTAGIOUS!

The Hebrew word that is translated *"death"* in Proverbs 18:21 means "fatal disease or pestilence." When you choose to spew angry words on a person, when you select to be negative and critical, or when you determine to gossip, you might as well be exposing yourself and those who are within hearing distance of your words to a highly contagious and fatal disease.

Speaking about what is contagious, I love watching young moms and the different stances they take on exposing their precious children to common, childhood illnesses such as chicken pox. Some moms are laid back and just say, "Well, they are going to get sick with it someday anyway, so we might as well get it over with now." More cautious mothers use appropriate wisdom in what their children are exposed to, but they do continue on with daily activities and adventures. Then there are those moms who have a true phobia when it comes to germs, and they "Clorox" everything in sight! They might as well build a bubble around their home, so terrified are they that one of their dear little earthlings might become ill with a runny nose.

When Craig and I had our first child, Matthew, every time the pacifier came out of his mouth, we threw it away and plucked a new one out of the sterilized packaging. No dirt was going to touch the lips of our precious, darling boy!

When we had Christopher, just two years later, we could no longer afford the volume of new pacifiers that our previous behavior required, so we placed his discarded pacifiers into boiling water on the stove. Every evening, whether a pacifier had been thrown to the ground or not, it received the boiling treatment under my watchful eyes.

Then, when we had our third son, Jordan, I would merely run his dirty pacifiers under running water at the kitchen sink. I wasn't picky about the temperature of the water; hot or cold water would do. I justified that it was clean enough after a dousing of fresh water from my kitchen spigot.

When our fourth child, Joy, would throw a beloved pacifier out of her mouth, I would simply put it in my own mouth to clean it off. Just a quick lick, and it was as good as new to go back into her little rosebud mouth.

And finally, with baby number five, Joni Rebecca, I didn't bother to replace, to boil, to rinse, or to lick. I would just pick the pacifier up off the ground and put it efficiently back into her mouth.

We can laugh at the way we have parented over the years and how diligently or how casually we have protected our children from germs, but the truth is that none of us would knowingly expose our children to a fatal disease. There is not a compassionate or concerned person who would willingly bring bacteria or viruses into breathing distance of their loved ones.

Yet, if it is true that our tongues hold the capacity to pour serious and life-altering matter on those whom we love, it is vital that we examine the words that we speak and the tone of voice they are spoken in. The Holy Spirit is speaking to you, and He is reminding you that words have power for good *and* power for evil. Words can bring life, and words can destroy. Words can revive, and words can kill.

The word *"death"* in Proverbs 18:21 can also mean "violence or destruction." The words that we choose to speak to another person who is made in the image of God can actually cause damage to their soul and may destroy their very future. Sometimes, we destroy other people by our careless words; other times, we destroy ourselves by them.

What are your words doing to the people whom you love the most and know the best? Are your words infested with negative ideas and attitudes that are destined to infect those you love with mental and emotional diseases like insecurity, rejection, and a failure to thrive?

LIFE IS WHAT YOU GET!

When you speak God's Word over people, when you convey words of kindness, when you choose to be positive rather than negative, and when you bless others even in the face of cruel treatment, the Bible says that you will receive life! The Hebrew word translated *"life"* in the above verse is *chay*, which means "prosperity or welfare." *Chay* was also used as a salutation or a blessing, and as a form of greeting.

In the Western world, when we greet someone, we often use phrases such as, "Hello!" or "Nice to see you," or "How are you doing today?" However in the ancient Hebrew world, when a man or a woman walked down the street, they would declare *"Chay,"* or a form of that word, as they greeted friends, acquaintances, business associates, and family members. This Hebrew greeting communicated the very principle that the verse from Proverbs is trying to convey. When the Hebrews declared *"Chay"* upon one another, they were wishing all who were listening the gift of life, prosperity, and welfare.

People in the ancient Hebrew culture knew that their tongues held the very power of determining a person's future days. As they welcomed one another with the word *"Chay,"* they were saying it with the absolute assurance that by using this simple yet enthusiastic greeting, they were changing someone's life for the better.

THE POWER OF THE MUSCLE

Another foundational belief of the Hebrew culture was that the tongue had as much influence on their prosperity, their health, and their future as did their hands. Unlike our society today, people in that culture depended chiefly upon their ability to use their hands to accomplish the tasks that needed to be done each day.

People used their hands to caress their children and to till the land on which they planted their crops. Their hands were their primary instruments when milking the family goats to obtain daily sustenance, and for pounding in the pegs for the tents in which they lived. Their hands held the power of guiding camels across the desert in blinding and ferocious sandstorms. As they considered everything that their hands accomplished each day, the people of the Hebrew nation knew that their tongues held at least as much power in their lives.

With their tongues, they expressed their love for their children, and they spoke daily blessings over their land. With their tongues, they provided a caring atmosphere that brought emotional sustenance to their families and created a warm and loving environment in which to live. They also believed that their tongues had the God-given power to direct them through any storm in life.

In the modern, Western world, the belief that our tongues hold inherent and God-given power has been lost in the maze of emotion-driven living. This belief in the power of the tongue was indeed born in the heart of God and expressed through the Holy Spirit. Perhaps it would be beneficial for you if you rediscovered this rich way of living and renewed your family through the power of your tongue.

202 Guide Your Mind, Guard Your Heart, Grace Your Tongue

The same holds true for you as it did for the ancient Hebrews: your tongue holds at least as much power in determining your future as do your hands—and your education, your marital status, your socioeconomic level, the type of the neighborhood in which you live, and your health insurance plan. Your tongue is a greater determinate of your family's future than who lives in the White House, what size dress you wear, or what the media has to say on any given day. Your words have the power to influence, to determine, and to frame your very future. You must use your tongue as an instrument of blessing, a provider of health, and a tool that only builds and never destroys. Additionally, since *"death and life are in the power of the tongue,"* it is up to you to declare a rich and vibrant life over everyone else who comes in contact with your speech.

RECIPE ROULETTE

Thus, not only do your words have the power to declare life or death as they cascade out of your mouth, but they are also cooking up a recipe for your life. You are going to eat your words someday, whether you like them or not! The words that you choose to speak in moments of searing emotion and of tremendous disappointment are planting the crops for your future; the words that come out of your oral cavity will determine the harvest in your life that you will eventually either enjoy or detest.

Knowing that the Bible expresses the immutable fact that you will one day eat your words, consider this: are the words you are currently speaking sweet or sour? Are they health-producing or are they carcinogenic? This is not recipe roulette! Remember, you can accurately determine the future health of your life by what you are saying today. The words that you speak truly matter as you build a family legacy and as you partner with God in His plans for your life.

The one who guards his mouth preserves his life, but he who opens wide his lips comes to ruin. (Proverbs 13:3)

As you learn to grace your tongue, just as you have learned to guide your mind and guard your heart, you will ensure that your life remains safe, uncluttered, and undefiled. If you can regulate the words you allow to proceed from your mouth, your life will be vibrantly healthy, regardless of the circumstances that come your way.

However, if you open your lips wide and say whatever you feel like in the moment, you are setting yourself up for destruction. You have the power to destroy your life with words of venom, impatience, and anger. Remind yourself daily and in every stressful situation that your words have the capacity to determine your very destiny.

BACK TO THE FUTURE

The idea of influencing the future with one's chosen words is not just a primitive point of view extracted from a bygone culture, but it is thematic in the Word of God. Joseph of the Old Testament prophesied his future to his brothers decades before it came to pass. (See, for example, Genesis 37:5–10; 42:1–6.) We will never know how Joseph's life would have turned out if he had not spoken words of hope and authority over his young life; however, what we do know is that those prophetic words, combined with Joseph's unfailing faith in the Lord, led him to a strategic place of leadership from which he could preserve the emerging Israelite nation from extinction. (See, for example, Genesis 50:20.)

The grieving widow, Ruth, declared that nothing but death would part her and the mother of her deceased young husband. Ruth made a verbal commitment to remain true to her now childless and widowed mother-in-law, Naomi, and her words determined her very future. (See Ruth 1:16–17.) Rather than speaking of her grief and of the unfairness of her life, and rather than refusing to go on, Ruth's strong words crafted a future for herself and Naomi that was filled with hope and promise. We will never know how Ruth's life would have turned out if she had not spoken those words of deep respect and lifelong devotion to her destitute mother-in-law; however, what we do know is that her chosen words framed her life with security and with stability, and she became the ancestor of a royal line. (See Ruth 4:13–22.)

The Jewish people, in exile and subject to the Persian Empire, were about to be annihilated by the devious plot of Haman, but Queen Esther's uncle, Mordecai, did not join in the verbal panic attack that everyone else was participating in. Instead, he spoke purpose and divine destiny over the life of the beautiful queen: *"And who knows whether you have not attained royalty for such a time as this?"* (Esther 4:14). We will never know how Esther's story would have turned out if Mordecai had spoken words of anger and worry concerning this disastrous situation, but what we do know is that Mordecai's powerful words propelled Esther into her very destiny, and once more God's people were preserved. (See Esther 4–7.)

Therefore, if you are sick, don't talk about everyone in your family who has died too young; instead, these are the words that should come out of your mouth:

> *I will not die, but live, and tell of the works of the* Lord.
> (Psalm 118:17)

If an unexpected bill arrives and you don't know how you will pay this debt, rather than worry and whine, get your tongue into agreement with God's Word:

> *And my God will supply all your needs according to His riches in glory in Christ Jesus.* (Philippians 4:19)

If you have been unable to conceive a child and desperately want to hold a baby in your arms, rather than doubt God and spend time in emotional pain, perhaps you should consider declaring these powerful words:

> *For this [child] I prayed, and the* Lord *has given me my petition which I asked of Him.* (1 Samuel 1:27)

When you are concerned about the lifestyle of one of your children and the choices he or she is making, use your tongue to declare these promises of God:

> *Even so it is not the will of your Father which is in heaven, that one of these little ones should perish.* (Matthew 18:14 kjv)

> *All of your sons will be taught of the* Lord*; and the well-being of your sons will be great.* (Isaiah 54:13)

> *Let our sons in their youth be as grown-up plants, and our daughters as corner pillars fashioned as for a palace.* (Psalm 144:12)

Don't allow your tongue to have a free-for-all lifestyle but give it strict boundaries that are set by your mind, which now thinks the thoughts of

Christ, and by your heart, which is extremely well-guarded by the Word of God. Your mind gives your mouth fodder from which to speak, and your heart is the motor that kick-starts your mouth. Again, if you don't think something, you will never say it, and if you don't feel something, you will never speak it! The only dictionary from which you extract the words that you are allowed to speak should be the Bible!

Set a guard, O LORD, over my mouth; keep watch over the door of my lips. (Psalm 141:3)

GRACE YOUR TONGUE: PERSONAL APPLICATION

Reread our anchor verse for gracing the tongue:

Death and life are in the power of the tongue, and those who love it will eat its fruit. (Proverbs 18:21)

1. Here are some questions to ask yourself as you apply the principles in this chapter to your life:

   (a) Think about the words you typically say every day. Are your words and your tone of voice infected with negative ideas and attitudes that result in tearing people down, or are your words graced with positive, kind, and encouraging expressions that build people up?

   (b) What effect do you think your words are having on the people you love the most and know the best?

   (c) What effect are they having on you?

   (d) What influence are your words having on the acquaintances and even strangers you interact with?

2. (a) Think of some of the people and events in your life that have impacted the words you use the most often and the tone in which you speak them. Do you need to forgive anyone who has impacted you negatively?

   (b) Now, think of someone who has impacted your life in a positive way by the words they have chosen to speak. How can you emulate this person?

(c) What is a "trigger" in your life that compels you to speak in a negative manner? Is it your finances? A difficult person? Your children? How can you ensure that this "trigger" never does any long-term damage again?

3. One way or another, we will all have to eat the fruit of what we have chosen to say. What kind of seeds are you planting for your future and your destiny? If you could use one word to describe the banquet feast that your words have prepared, what would that word be?

4. We have learned that the Hebrew word translated *"life"* in Proverbs 18:21 is *chay*, which means "prosperity or welfare," and that *chay* was used as a form of greeting in which the Hebrews spoke words of life and prosperity over their families, friends, acquaintances, and business associates. What "chay" words can you speak to your family, friends, neighbors, coworkers, business associates, and acquaintances today?

5. Review this significant verse about the use of the tongue:

    > *The one who guards his mouth preserves his life, but he who opens wide his lips comes to ruin.* (Proverbs 13:3)

    (a) In what ways can you make a point to guard and grace your tongue today?

    (b) What specific biblically-based declarations will you make with your mouth concerning your current difficult circumstances?

6. If your tongue has been out of control—either as a habit or in a recent stressful situation—ask your heavenly Father to forgive you according to the sacrifice of Jesus on your behalf and to help you learn to speak words of grace and life, no matter what the circumstances.

22

LEAST FAVORITE OF ALL

I have so many favorite Bible verses and passages that they could fill an entire book of their own! When I teach the Word to a group of spiritually hungry and thirsty women, I am known for saying, "And *this* is my favorite Scripture!" The problem is, I say that same six-word statement multiple times, even within one teaching session!

However, there is only one verse in the Bible that I can clearly say causes my heart rate to accelerate, my blood pressure to increase, and my mouth to immediately go dry. This singular verse, found in the otherwise wonderful book of Matthew, shakes me to the very core every time that I read it:

> *But I tell you that every careless word that people speak, they shall give an accounting for it in the day of judgment.* (Matthew 12:36)

Do you understand why these words of Jesus bring sheer terror to my soul? For every careless word that I have ever spoken, or will ever speak, someday I will have to tell Jesus exactly why those particular words came out of my guilty mouth. Every unkind word that I have ever spoken to my husband, every sassy word that I ever communicated as a teenager to my mom, every word of gossip that I have ever repeated, will require an accounting with the Father. Every critical word that I have expressed concerning men and women made in the image of God, every word of anxiety or worry, every impatient word that I ever articulated to one of my precious toddlers, will necessitate an explanation to the King of all Kings. In that moment, I know what will be going through my mind; I will be thinking, *What **was** I thinking!*

> He who guards his mouth and his tongue, guards his soul from troubles. (Proverbs 21:23)

If you thought it was hard to guard your heart, or soul, just wait until you try to grace your tongue! If you have not already been successful at guarding your heart, your tongue will prattle on well beyond any hope you might have of grasping it or taming it. It is true that our heart does not want to be guarded, and so, in reality, our unguarded heart has no business at all trying to guard our tongue. The heart should never be allowed to determine the words that we speak, because, as we have noted, the Bible says that our hearts are deceitful above all else. If it weren't for the help of the Holy Spirit, what an emotional-verbal mess we would be in!

It is your spirit that needs to take control and have the final say, not only about what is in your heart, but also about what you are allowed to speak. Your spirit, which is filled with faith, power, and the Word of God, should be given the authority to determine what words come out of your human mouthpiece.

SLOW DOWN, RIGHT NOW

So often, in conversations with women, I hear phrases that are akin to fingernails on the chalkboard of life. These women who love the Lord and would call themselves Christ-followers often say needless words such as these:

- "Well, I just don't understand what God is doing! If I were God, I would certainly do it this way…."
- "I am just angry at God, and I might as well tell Him. He already knows how I feel, so I am going to let Him know how upset I am!"
- "God never answers my prayers. I pray and pray and pray, and He never responds. What's up with that? I feel like my prayers are just hitting the ceiling."
- "God is just so slow! I wish that He would move more quickly on my behalf."

Those statements—and others like them—always bother me, based on my theology. I have never felt comfortable correcting God or complaining about Him, have you? Our words matter, and what we say about God matters; just because we think something, doesn't mean we need to say it. Just because we feel something, doesn't give us the clearance to speak it.

> *Do not be quick with your mouth, do not be hasty in your heart to utter anything before God. God is in heaven and you are on earth, so let your words be few.* (Ecclesiastes 5:2 NIV)

Thus, before you regurgitate your verbal vomit on your Father, and before you throw a bucketload of stinking thinking His way, perhaps you should pause and take the time to acquire heaven's perspective on your personal situation. It is empowering to know that, as believers, we are able to access God's opinion on all of our situations because we now have the mind of Christ.

> My [daughter], *give attention to my wisdom, incline your ear to my understanding; that you may observe discretion and your lips may reserve knowledge.* (Proverbs 5:1–2)

If you desire to speak with the wisdom and knowledge of God, then you must listen to Him in His Word. You must daily ask for the mind of Christ to trump your personal thought processes. If you ask for His wisdom to supersede all of your heart plans, you will enjoy the possibility of using your lips in a wise and discreet manner. When your words echo the words of Christ, you will actually seem smarter than you are, rather than more foolish than you are! Your words will become a fragrant bouquet of blessing and a life-giving source of nutrients to everyone who comes in contact with them. You will also ensure that you are able to relish a future that is healthy and prosperous.

THE WOMAN WE LOVE TO HATE!

Don't you just love to hate that infamous "Proverbs 31 Woman"?! Who is she, anyway? I have always thought of her as Miss America, Mother Teresa, and Mary Poppins all rolled into one perfect persona. However, when I compose myself and cease to judge her unfairly, I understand that there is a bounty I can glean from her life by lingering in the verses of that chapter in Proverbs. If we note carefully how the Holy Spirit describes the tongue of this unforgettable piece of femininity, we can learn what is perhaps one of the loveliest and most powerful lessons of all.

> *She smiles at the future. She opens her mouth in wisdom, and the teaching of kindness is on her tongue.*   (Proverbs 31:25–26)

The reason this woman is able to smile at the future is that *"she opens her mouth in wisdom, and the teaching of kindness is on her tongue."* When you begin to open your mouth in wisdom because you think like God thinks, you will be able to smile at the future, as well.

The Hebrew word translated *"teaching"* in this verse can signify "habit or discipline." This exemplary woman is in the habit of speaking kindly; she has disciplined her tongue to speak only kind perspectives, kind words, and kind phrases. She has forgotten how to gossip, how to be critical, and how to complain, because her basic routine is bathed in kindness. She has a kind heart, and therefore she exhibits kind speech. No wonder she can smile at the future! The smorgasbord from which she will eat all the days of her life will be seasoned with grace and sweetened with forgiveness.

How I long to be like her! The legacy I desire to leave is not one of self-promotion, nor is it one of amassing a fortune or acquiring degrees or jewels. The legacy I long to leave is a legacy of wisdom and kindness. How about you?

> *Do not let kindness and truth leave you; bind them around your neck, write them on the tablet of your heart.*   (Proverbs 3:3)

GRACE YOUR TONGUE: PERSONAL APPLICATION

1. Which careless words you have spoken to other people do you especially regret saying?

2. What types of negative statements have you made *about* God, or *to* Him, that reflected a lack of faith or respect (even if, at the time, you didn't think about it in that way)?

3. After answering question 2, think about how you might have expressed your pain or desires to God in a way that was truthful

but also reverent and based on His Word. As you consider your answer, meditate on the following verses:

> *And when you are praying, do not use meaningless repetition as the Gentiles do, for they suppose that they will be heard for their many words. So do not be like them; for your Father knows what you need before you ask Him.* (Matthew 6:7–8)

> *For we do not have a high priest who cannot sympathize with our weaknesses, but One who has been tempted in all things as we are, yet without sin. Therefore let us draw near with confidence to the throne of grace, so that we may receive mercy and find grace to help in time of need.* (Hebrews 4:15–16)

4. What type of legacy would you like to leave concerning the words you speak? Write down a sentence or two describing that legacy.

23

TWO WOMEN AND THEIR WORDS

One aspect of studying the Word of God that has revolutionized my entire being has been taking a close look at the lives of men and women in the Bible who have endeavored to live for God and for His purposes during their journey on earth. As we read their stories, we sometimes see them "getting it right," while at other times we observe the abysmal failures in their lives. However, we can always learn life principles and astounding lessons from these men and women, who weren't so different from you and from me. They might have dressed differently, cooked in a different manner, and lived in tents or hovels rather than in houses, but their hearts were on an adventure to find God and serve Him, just as our hearts are.

> *For whatever was written in earlier times was written for our instruction, so that through perseverance and the encouragement of the Scriptures we might have hope.* (Romans 15:4)

The Holy Spirit strategically and purposefully chose exactly which life stories—lived out thousands of years ago—to place in the Bible so that God's people, even those of us in the twenty-first century, would receive encouragement and hope from them, and so we would be able to learn how to persevere.

A DIATRIBE OF DISAPPOINTMENT

Women who have "mouth disease" and therefore have trouble controlling their tongues are common in every generation, and can be found at every juncture of human history. Perhaps you know some women like that;

or perhaps you regretfully belong to this far-too-large sorority! The same women who have trouble taming their tongues also have trouble believing the promises of God; if a woman truly locks her life onto the promises of the Father, it is evident in her speech patterns. The women in the Bible are given as examples for those who follow in their footsteps, and, unfortunately, those women who have spoken poorly have had to eat their words for generations! Sarah, also called Sarai, was one such woman.

> *Now Sarai, Abram's wife had borne him no children, and she had an Egyptian maid whose name was Hagar.* (Genesis 16:1)

Abram's beautiful wife, Sarai, was disappointed to the core of her being. She desperately wanted a baby; she ached to hold a little one in her arms. Desiring to be a mother is a God-given desire, but for Sarai, that desire was unfilled decade after decade. While most of her friends were becoming mothers, Sarai had maintained her hope. However, now that her friends were welcoming grandchildren and even great-grandchildren, she had become frenzied beyond comfort, so deep was her longing.

Sarai's desire to be a mother was not sinful or inappropriate; nonetheless, what she said concerning her situation smacked of pain rather than of promise. She did not choose her words according to her faith in God, but she verbalized her deeply wounded perspective and her emotional pain.

> *So Sarai said to Abram, "Now behold, the LORD has prevented me from bearing children. Please go in to my maid; perhaps I will obtain children through her." And Abram listened to the voice of Sarai.* (Genesis 16:2)

Out of her emotional pain, Sarai came up with a human plan for God and for her husband. God had already promised Abram that he would have a child, so perhaps Sarai was just trying to help Him out by controlling her husband's actions with her words. We can learn from the life of Sarai that God doesn't need our help or our opinions in order to follow through on His promises. He is quite capable of fulfilling the promises that He has given without our intervention. God fulfills every promise that He makes, and He doesn't need our human manipulation or control to get the job done!

Another lesson we can learn from the tongue of Sarai is that the words of a wife have power in the life of her husband. Knowing that this is true, if you are married, it is vital for you to search out God's opinion on a matter before you give your husband an earful of your own opinion. It would be a wise decision to take your words to the altar before you ever speak them to your spouse. In this particular situation with Sarai and Abram, it is conceivable to believe that Abram was not forced to take Sarai's advice. Abram, after all, had a mind of his own, and he could have refused to do what Sarai wanted him to do.

I extend grace to Abram for his actions in this story because he had been dealing with a disappointed woman for decades. Month after month, year after year, he had heard Sarai express her longing and pain, and he had grieved with her. At this time in history, it was not uncommon for a man to have more than one wife or to utilize his wife's maid for conjugal purposes. The sad moral of this story is that, in Abram and Sarai's generation, even the people of God had compromised and caved in to the ways of the world. It was never God's will for a man to have more than one wife; but Abram, like so many others before him and after him, responded to the call of the culture.

If you are mentally defending Sarai in this story and conjecturing, *Well, Abram didn't have to go in and sleep with her maid*, that idea may hold a sliver of truth. We must remind ourselves that Sarai will be the one who answers for her own words on the day of judgment. Abram will answer for his actions and his choices, but Sarai will answer for her words.

After Abram had lived ten years in the land of Canaan, Abram's wife Sarai took Hagar the Egyptian, her maid, and gave her to her husband Abram as his wife. He went in to Hagar, and she conceived; and when she saw that she had conceived, her mistress was despised in her sight. And Sarai said to Abram, "May the wrong done me be upon you. I gave my maid into your arms, but when she saw that she had conceived, I was despised in her sight. May the LORD judge between you and me." (Genesis 16:3–5)

The nerve of Sarai! Now she places blame on Abram for her disappointment and her emotional pain. Abram can't win with Sarai! He had only done what she had insisted that he do. And, to add insult to injury,

Abram would now have a child to hold and to play with. Sarai would still have nothing...absolutely nothing. Hagar now despised Sarai for her inability to bear a child, and we can assume that formerly they had been as close as sisters might be.

Sarai's human "fix" hadn't really remedied anything, and she was still barren. She realized in hindsight that giving Abram the ability to have a child with Hagar had created a precious bond between her husband and her maid. And, due to her disappointment, Sarai made Abram feel guilty for the outcome of the words that she herself had spoken. Later, when Sarai observed Abram enjoying the little boy born to Hagar, she felt absolutely ravaged on the inside.

When a person chooses to speak out of a heart filled with disappointment and pain, words of blame will eventually begin to flow, as well. Sarai was filled with resentment, envy, and regret. The cry of her heart was, *Why did I ever suggest that Hagar and Abram make a baby together? What was I thinking?*

The answer to that question is that Sarai had not been thinking; she had been emoting. Her improper and ungodly emotions had gushed out of her mouth in an effort to manipulate and control. Sarai had spoken words that reflected her discouragement and her misery rather than the promises of God. Also, as is clearly seen in this story, Sarai locked into a solution that reflected the flawed culture rather than the character of God.

Although God restored this situation and gave Abram and Sarai— whose names He changed to Abraham and Sarah to reflect His purposes for them—the baby boy that He had promised to them, this elderly couple still had to digest the fruit of Sarah's mouth. And the world is actually still eating the fruit of Sarah's words. Abram and Hagar's son, Ishmael, became the father of the Arab nations, while Isaac, Abraham and Sarah's son, became the father of Israel. Sarah's disappointment and verbal control issues have ricocheted through the centuries so that, thousands of years later, in the twenty-first century, society is still dealing with the conundrum of Ishmael and Isaac.

VERBAL VESUVIUS

Let's look at another biblical family whose example continues to instruct us today. Once more, the husband, Elkanah, had two wives; and once more, one wife was barren, while the other was known for her fertility. But this time, the barren wife spoke words aligned with God's will; this choice transformed her own circumstances and even brought a revolutionary blessing to the people of God.

As we have noted, the practice of having two wives was never God's way, but Elkanah had compromised with what was accepted in the culture of his day.

> *Now there was a certain man from Ramathaim-zophim from the hill country of Ephraim, and his name was Elkanah the son of Jeroham, the son of Elihu, the son of Tohu, the son of Zuph, an Ephraimite. He had two wives: the name of one was Hannah and the name of the other Peninnah; and Peninnah had children, but Hannah had no children. Now this man would go up from his city yearly to worship and to sacrifice to the LORD of hosts in Shiloh. And the two sons of Eli, Hophni and Phinehas, were priests to the LORD there.* (1 Samuel 1:1–3)

Even though Elkanah had made a choice to compromise with the culture with regard to his marital state, he remained a man who deeply desired to honor God with his life. Every year, he went to the temple to worship the Lord and to make a sacrifice on behalf of his family.

> *When the day came that Elkanah sacrificed, he would give portions to Peninnah his wife and to all her sons and her daughters....*
> (1 Samuel 1:4)

The implication of this Scripture is that Elkanah's wife Peninnah had given him many children; she was the ancient model of "Fertile Myrtle" or "The Old Woman Who Lived in a Shoe." Yet Hannah, whom he especially loved, had never been able to give him a child.

> *...but to Hannah he would give a double portion, for he loved Hannah, but the LORD had closed her womb.* (1 Samuel 1:5)

Although Hannah had been denied the love of children, she did possess the love of her husband. Elkanah loved Hannah dearly, and he demonstrated his love to her by his heartfelt actions. It is puzzling to me that a man in that society would visibly show love toward a wife who was unable to give him children. In that day, a man's value was determined by the number of children he produced, specifically by the number of sons he fathered. If a man's wife stopped producing children for him, he generally rejected her and found another wife, usually a younger model. In that patriarchal society, women had no more value to a man than did his favorite cow. Peninnah was Elkanah's producer, yet the Bible states that Elkanah adored his wife Hannah.

Although the Bible doesn't specifically recount exactly why Elkanah was so smitten with the barren Hannah, as we continue to read this portion of Scripture, I believe that we will find the answer in its description of each woman's personality and tongue.

> [Hannah's] *rival, however, would provoke her bitterly to irritate her, because the* LORD *had closed her womb.* (1 Samuel 1:6)

Peninnah fully expressed her resentment against Hannah because Hannah was the one who received the benefit of Elkanah's sweet love. Peninnah apparently had one goal in life—to get under Hannah's skin and to remind her of all that she was lacking. Peninnah took great delight in mocking Hannah and in the obvious fact that her rival was unable to conceive and bear children. Peninnah aimed her barbs at Hannah's deepest pain, and then picked at that emotional scab until it was raw and bleeding.

Have you ever fully expressed your anger toward a person, as Peninnah did to Hannah? Like the volcanic Mount Vesuvius, we mistakenly believe that we must give full vent to an unstoppable eruption of unkind thoughts, outrage, and judgments toward a person who is made in the very image of God the Father. Often, in the awkward silence after a volatile discharge of justifiable or unjustifiable anger, the one who has erupted realizes that it wasn't worth it. It just wasn't worth it at all.

Let's contrast the reactions of the two women to their circumstances. Even in her disappointment, Hannah was lovable; yet even in her abundance, Peninnah was fractious. Our tongues are often not a true reflection of our circumstances in life. Hannah was a woman who had guarded her heart well, even during the difficult days of life. Peninnah, although blessed beyond measure with children, allowed anger and spite to enter her unguarded heart.

WHAT IS AN ANGRY WOMAN TO DO?

We will come back to the Old Testament soap opera of Hannah and Peninnah in just a bit, but for now, let's talk about you, your anger, and your tongue. When anger threatens to raucously roll out of your heart and burst through your mouth, what is the solution? What is the proper way to express anger?

> Now the deeds of the flesh are evident, which are: immorality, impurity, sensuality, idolatry, sorcery, enmities, strife, jealousy, outbursts of anger, disputes, dissentions, factions.   (Galatians 5:19–20)

The Holy Spirit, who is the leading Authority on all things to do with emotions and the spirit, states that *"outbursts of anger"* are one of the *"deeds of the flesh."* He immediately follows this instruction with a reminder to Christians that we are to be controlled by the Spirit of God, not by the pull of the flesh. (See Galatians 5:22–24.)

There will certainly be events and people in our lives that will cause anger to knock on the doors of our souls, and we will struggle with how to express our anger. But a verbal attack is not a healthy way to process the emotion of anger. When it is time to discuss your anger with the person involved, you must only speak the truth in love. Your words, even if you are dealing with a difficult and tense situation, must be birthed in patience and in kindness.

Most people are angered by situations and events in life that are actually mere inconveniences, and they allow that ridiculous anger to flood over their tongues and onto the lives of unsuspecting and innocent people. The greatest mistake that one can make in dealing with anger is to allow that anger to become a verbal weapon.

THE VALUE OF ENCOURAGING WORDS

Perhaps you already know how Hannah's story turned out. Elkanah, her husband, assured her of his love by the very words that he spoke to her. Although Peninnah was as mean as a snake and attacked Hannah with every word she spoke to her, Elkanah, with his words, exhibited the gift of encouragement.

It happened year after year, as often as she went up to the house of the LORD, [Peninnah] would provoke [Hannah]; so [Hannah] wept and would not eat. Then Elkanah her husband said to her, "Hannah, why do you weep and why do you not eat and why is your heart sad? Am I not better to you than ten sons?" (1 Samuel 1:7–8)

Peninnah's words to Hannah were perpetually cruel; Elkanah's words to Hannah were always tender and caring. Elkanah could have chosen to be frustrated by the tension between his two wives, but instead he chose to love and encourage the victim. Elkanah's words changed Hannah's perspective and gave her the strength to make a positive step toward God.

Then Hannah rose after eating and drinking in Shiloh. Now Eli the priest was sitting on the seat by the doorpost of the temple of the LORD. [Hannah], greatly distressed, prayed to the LORD and wept bitterly. She made a vow and said, "O LORD of hosts, if You will indeed look on the affliction of Your maidservant and remember me, and not forget Your maidservant, but will give Your maidservant a son, then I will give him to the LORD all the days of his life, and a razor shall never come on his head." (1 Samuel 1:9–11)

Hannah refused to pour out her pain on other people; she poured out all her pain before the Lord. Even though she was deeply disappointed and hurt, Hannah didn't make Elkanah's life miserable, and she didn't seek revenge on the heartless Peninnah; she took her heart issues to God. Her pain propelled her into His presence, where there is always fullness of joy.

While Hannah was pouring out her heart to the Lord, the priest Eli was watching her. At first, he thought that she was drunk, but later he recognized that he had observed a woman in deep intercession with the Lord. When Eli entered into a conversation with this humble woman, the Holy Spirit spoke through him and promised Hannah that she would indeed have a son. (See 1 Samuel 1:12–17.)

[Hannah] said, "Let your maidservant find favor in your sight." So the woman went her way and ate, and her face was no longer sad. (1 Samuel 1:18)

When we go to God with our pain, rather than vent to other people, we are healed and renewed. Hannah's countenance had changed not because she had spoken her piece to Peninnah or because she had defended herself. She was changed by the word of the Lord and by time spent surrendering her emotions to Him.

Hannah's story had a happy ending because she took her disappointment to the throne room of God Almighty. She chose to pour out her deep longing before the Lord, and He heard her heart cry. Hannah was given a miracle child, Samuel, whom she gave back to the Lord. After she willingly gave this precious little boy to the Lord, the Lord blessed her with five more children! Hannah and Elkanah's first son, Samuel, changed the course of history for the people of God. Samuel was the last judge of Israel, and he anointed the first two kings of Israel.

Peninnah, however, was never heard from again. After the reference to her mean spirit and her vicious tongue in 1 Samuel 1, her name is never mentioned again in the Bible. Perhaps from these two women we can learn that our tongues have the power to craft our very destiny in the purposes of God, not only in our own generation but also in generations to come.

In our culture, we have compromised God's truth by believing that it is a healthy choice to allow one's emotions to rampantly direct one's tongue. We have mistakenly agreed with the philosophy that when we are mistreated, a normal response is to wretch endless anger on the cruel prognosticator. That is not a healthy response, and that is not normal—that is a deception. If you can't say something in God's presence, then it should not be said at all.

> *If you have been foolish in exalting yourself or if you have plotted evil,*
> *put your hand on your mouth.*   (Proverbs 30:32)

GRACE YOUR TONGUE: PERSONAL APPLICATION

1. (a) In the biblical story about Abram and Sarai, what were the results—for Sarai and for future generations—of her ill-spoken words to her husband?

    (b) Sarai's desire to be a mother was not wrong or inappropriate. If she had taken her pain and disappointment to the Lord in prayer, what might she have said differently, based on His promises and faithfulness?

2. What will you do the next time you are tempted to give advice to someone (or to just vent at someone) based on your raw emotions rather than on faith and God's Word?

3. In the second biblical story, did you find yourself identifying more with Peninnah or with Hannah? Why? What emotions may have contributed to your answer?

4. Have you ever talked badly about someone or criticized them out of rivalry or jealousy? If so, what would have been a better response? How will you apply that better response in the future?

5. What does it mean to speak the truth in love, even under difficult and tense situations?

6. (a) In what way did Elkanah's encouraging words help Hannah to make the best response to her distressing situation?

    (b) When Hannah went to God with her pain, instead of venting to her husband or others, what were the results—for her emotions and her circumstances? What results can we expect when we do the same?

24

A MATURE MOUTH

The problem with my tongue is that it is just so slippery; trying to control my tongue is like trying to hold a wiggly, squiggly fish in my hands. I seem to be able to control the other muscles in my body so much more effectively. I can convince my leg muscles to walk and even to run; I can certainly discipline my arm muscles to hold weights and to carry heavy objects. I can even, from time to time, put my stomach muscles to good use and force them to hold in that midsection bulge. But my tongue is an entirely different, and much more defiant, muscle to conquer!

All of the members of our physical bodies represent two distinct functions: a physiological one and a spiritual one. The purpose of my physiological mind is to store knowledge and to learn new information; but my spiritual mind was created to embrace and cultivate the mind of Christ. My hands possess the physical function of performing daily and mundane tasks; for spiritual purposes, however, my hands were made to serve and to bless others. My biological heart holds an extremely important role in my physical makeup because it must pump blood throughout my body in order to keep me alive; however, my spiritual heart is meant to love Christ passionately and to love those things that He loves. With my biological tongue, I am able to taste and to communicate. However, what is the spiritual function of the tongue?

A SCALPEL OR A TONGUE?

What do you do for a living? What is your chosen career? Your answer might be "administrative assistant," "accountant," "nurse," "homemaker," or "engineer." However, in my opinion, no matter what your vocation, you are really a teacher!

> Let not many of you become teachers, my brethren, knowing that as
> such we will incur a stricter judgment. (James 3:1)

Regardless of what university degree you have earned or who writes your paycheck, I believe that you are called to be a teacher. Each one of us has the significant and unmatched calling of teaching others with our very lives. Someone is always observing how you live out, walk out, and talk out your Christianity. Your life, by the example of the choices you make on a daily basis, offers the strongest teaching moment that others may ever have the opportunity to witness. Every word that you speak has the capacity to give out either good information or bad information. Each sentence that you utter has the potential to teach a positive character lesson or a negative one.

People in most professions utilize a chief instrument for carrying out their work. For a mechanic, it might be a wrench. For an accountant, it is certainly a calculator. An architect's most important career tool, these days, is a computer program. A nurse, of course, is unable to get through the day without a thermometer or a stethoscope; for a surgeon, it is a razor-sharp scalpel.

Some professions, by their very nature, utilize more exacting and potentially dangerous instruments than others. For example, a scalpel has the potential to do much more severe damage than a calculator is able to do. Yet the most dangerous instrument for people in any profession is a piece of equipment that is especially utilized by teachers—the tongue. The tongue is the most potent and formidable instrument because it has the capacity to bring enormous healing—or do inestimable damage.

A SLIPUP

> For we all stumble in many ways. If anyone does not stumble in what
> he says, he is a perfect [mature] man, able to bridle the whole body as
> well. (James 3:2)

The Hebrew word translated "stumble" in the above verse is most accurately translated as "slip up." I can certainly relate, can you? As I vulnerably shared with you at the beginning of this chapter, throughout my life, my tongue has been as slippery as a banana peel! I slip up more often than I care to admit on my two-ounce hyperactive piece of muscle. I never "plan" to say something mean or exaggerated; it's not that I premeditate sin in the area of my words. I am just so often caught off guard, and then…I slip!

My friend, the first step to controlling your tongue is to admit that you have a problem.

> *If we say that we have no sin, we are deceiving ourselves and the truth is not in us.* (1 John 1:8)

I admit that I have a problem, and it is my tongue! I keep an unending mental list of words that I wish I had never said, had said differently, or had never even thought about saying. I barely go through a normal day without wishing I could take back a phrase that I uttered, or having to correct something that I have misquoted, or sadly desiring that I had said something in a kinder tone of voice.

No matter what other areas of life you have under operative control, I am sure that, like me, nearly every day, you wish you could press rewind on various words that you have spoken.

GROW UP!

Control over one's tongue is a mark of Christian maturity. How well you are able to control your tongue is truly a litmus test of how well you have guarded your heart. The most mature among us exhibit the most control in the area of the tongue. The words that come out of a person's mouth are the defining gauge as to whether that person is a toddler Christian, a third-grade Christian, an adolescent Christian, or a full-grown and mature disciple of Christ.

When a baby is just learning to speak, everything that precious little one says sounds like gibberish. The words that a toddler expresses are nonsensical sounds and deliver no deep meaning to anyone at all except perhaps the baby's adoring mother. Due to an inability to communicate effectively, a baby would never be asked to make a speech at the UN or to anchor the network news. Neither would a toddler be given the opportunity to preach in front of thousands.

It is easy to discern how mature a person is by the statements that come out of his or her mouth. If you choose to gossip or to say bitter words, that is like speaking baby gibberish. If you worry out loud, you are just a toddler in the faith. However, if words of kindness, wisdom, encouragement, and praise are alone allowed to exit the opening under your nose, then you are mature.

If you desire to be used by God for greatness in His kingdom, then you need to learn to control your tongue. The Lord will give amazing opportunities to serve Him, and He will open magnificent doors, for those whose tongues are fully under the control of the Holy Spirit.

BRIDLE YOURSELF

Now if we put the bits into the horses' mouths so that they will obey us, we direct their entire body as well.   (James 3:3)

In this verse, the apostle James and the Holy Spirit are teaching the benefits of controlling one's tongue. When your tongue is under control, your entire life will be positively affected. Your home will be peaceful, your marriage will be healthier, and your friendships will flourish. You will be a woman of heavenly excellence!

James uses a vivid illustration concerning how profitable a well-placed bit can be in the mouth of a horse. It is the bit, or the full bridle, that enables the rider to control the horse's entire body. Likewise, it is your tongue that controls your entire body.

Horse trainers know the importance of putting the bridle on the horse not while the animal is on the open range, but when it is safely contained in its stall. It is nearly impossible to insert a bit into a horse's mouth out in an expansive field while the horse is grazing. When the horse sees the bridle, it will either run away or become difficult to manage. However, in the confines of the stall, the procedure is accomplished easily and with little opposition.

I, too, must insert a bit into my mouth while I am in a "contained" area, such as during my private times with the Lord; I must give myself verbal boundaries before I find myself in the openness of challenging and stressful situations. I must strictly establish the confines to which my tongue must adhere prior to engaging in difficult conversations or in emotionally charged moments in life.

Before my beloved husband forgets to take out the trash, I must decide that I will speak only loving, encouraging words to him.

Before my precious children talk back to me, I must predetermine how I will respond to their lack of respect.

Before I spend time with women who gossip, I must determine that I will never enter into a conversation that is rife with half-truths and negative comments.

Before potentially divisive topics, such as politics, ever come up at the office, on social media, or in the church, I must decide how I am going to respond to them.

MY TONGUE, MY PEN, MY PHONE, MY KEYBOARD

Because I am so very cognizant of my extreme weakness in the area of my tongue, I have set some very clear boundaries for my life. The following are the perimeters I have established not only for my tongue but also for all the methods of communication that I employ, including my pen, my phone, and my keyboard! Perhaps you should consider embracing these, as well:

1. I am not allowed to lie or exaggerate. Not once. Not one time. Ever.

2. I am not allowed to put someone else down. Not once. Not one time. Ever. (Not even in jest.)

3. I am not allowed to develop close relationships with people who gossip or who are negative. Never. Not one. Ever.

4. I am not allowed to gossip about others made in the image of God. Not once. Not one time. Ever.

5. I am not allowed to tell my side of the story simply to make myself look better. Not once. Not one time. Ever.

6. I am not allowed to murmur or complain or whine. Not once. Not one time. Ever.

7. My tongue will be used only as an instrument of encouragement
    and as a tool of praise. Always. All the time. Forever and ever.

Those seven principles are my self-made bridle, and I remind myself of
these principles often. I must keep my bridle on at all times!

A TWO-OUNCE RUDDER

I love the language that James uses in the third chapter of his book,
that extraordinary chapter that deals with the tongue! His illustrations
are both vivid and practical; I have also felt that I could develop a valuable
friendship with this half-brother of Jesus.

As we have noted, James first discusses the great responsibility and
hazards of being a teacher in the body of Christ, then he challenges all of us
to grow up to maturity. His third point is delivered by painting a picture of
a horse that has been controlled by a bridle. And now, for principle number
four, he uses the illustration of a rudder on a ship. James is a wordsmith of
the very best kind and the Rembrandt of verbal pictures!

Look at the ships also, though they are so great and are driven by strong
winds, are still directed by a very small rudder wherever the inclination
of the pilot desires.   (James 3:4)

The society in which James lived was both agrarian and commercial.
The ships in the days of the New Testament were among the largest and
most powerful structures then known to mankind. Even thousands of
years ago, ships moved tons of cargo across uncertain waters. These ships
were directed chiefly by the trade winds on the seas. However, one facet of
a ship that was more important in determining its direction than even the
trade winds was the rudder. The rudder was a tiny piece of workmanship
on the underside of the massive ship. The operation of this minuscule blade
redirected the flow of water to the opposite side of the hull; rudders are
used, even today, to enable a boat to move in the opposite direction from
which the current is flowing.

It is simple to apply this illustration to our lives and to the power that
our tongue wields. Your life is the great ship that James is referring to, and
your circumstances are the winds that blow your ship across the ocean of
life. Your tongue is the petite rudder that has the power to redirect the

water to set you in an entirely different direction from your circumstances or from the culture in which you live.

When you see a storm approaching on the horizon of your life, and you anticipate a ferocious wind that is certain to blow you off your chosen course, your tongue can redirect the flow of water so that you will still reach your desired destination.

Thus, if you receive a bad report from the doctor, rather than moaning and groaning and calling the funeral home to make advance arrangements, your tongue can boldly declare,

You are the Lord who heals all of my diseases! (See Psalm 103:3.)

When an unexpected bill comes in the mail, and there is no extra cash with which to pay it, the rudder of your life should firmly state,

And my God will supply all [of my] *needs according to His riches in glory in Christ Jesus.* (Philippians 4:19)

If you feel yourself tottering emotionally and wonder if you are headed for a breakdown, remember that your tongue was created to agree with the truth of God's Word, and declare,

The Bible says that God always leads me in triumph in Christ Jesus, my Lord! (See 2 Corinthians 2:14.)

Use your tongue as an authoritative weapon to steer yourself *out of* storms and not *into* storms. Since the Bible explains that your tongue was created to have the same power over your life that a rudder possesses over a ship, make sure that you use your rudder to your advantage. Utilize your tongue to diminish the influence of the winds of circumstances and to ensure that you are going toward God's plans and purposes for your life.

CHANGE YOUR LIFE

What this discussion has been leading to is that if the desire of your heart is to live a powerful, overcoming, and significant life, then you must change your language. Use only positive words, no matter how you feel; say only kind words, regardless of how others talk. All change begins with a choice.

Personal counselors understand this dynamic life philosophy. They believe that if you are able to change the language you speak, then your emotional preferences will actually change, as well. If you can be convinced to speak positively rather than negatively, it is possible for you to slowly but effectively alter the manner in which you process events and circumstances.

This substantive philosophy delivers great hope to people who are in the depths of despair or who tend to worry their way through life. James knew this approach to be effective, as well; thus, he illustrated the fact that changing the direction of the rudder is certain to alter the direction of the ship.

Let me remind you again that your tongue weighs only about two ounces, but it has the power to control your entire life, and its force can be felt for generations. If you struggle in the area of your tongue, put the bridle on. Give yourself verbal boundaries and refuse to say another negative word. As you begin to speak only positive responses and positive opinions, you will become a positive person. If you determine that you will never again worry out loud but will always speak words of trust and faith, you might actually even adjust your personality bent.

> *My* [daughter], *if your heart is wise, my own heart also will be glad; and my inmost being will rejoice when your lips speak what is right.*
>
> (Proverbs 23:15–16)

GRACE YOUR TONGUE: PERSONAL APPLICATION

1. In this chapter, we are reminded that we are all teachers, in the following sense: the examples we set by what we do and say provide others with either a positive character lesson or a negative one. What type of lessons are you communicating to those around you?

2. What do the words you use—and the words you choose not to say—indicate about your level of maturity in Christ?

3. (a) Make a concrete list, such as the one in this chapter, of boundaries you will set for what you will allow yourself to say and what you will not permit yourself to say.

   (b) Determine ahead of time how you will apply this list to specific situations in life, such as difficult conversations or emotionally charged moments. Be prepared for the many situations you will face where the answer of your tongue will set either a good result or a bad result in motion.

4. In what ways do James's analogies about the horse's bit and the ship's rudder help you to understand the power and potential of your own tongue—as either a positive or a negative force—and what you can do to control it?

5. If you recognize that your life is being blown off-course by your negative attitudes and reactions, or your ill-conceived words, begin to use positive words, in agreement with God's Word, to redirect your life toward His plans and purposes. Write down specific verses with which the "rudder" of your mouth can steer you to a safe shore.

25

FIRE, WATER, AND FIGS

Have you ever set fire to someone else's home? I sincerely hope not! Have you ever been accused of arson? Probably not. However, James is not so sure about our innocence in the setting of certain types of fires. He happens to believe that, perhaps unknowingly, we are guilty of the horrific crime of cruel arson.

> *See how great a forest is set aflame by such a small fire! And the tongue is a fire, the very world of iniquity; the tongue is set among our members as that which defiles the entire body, and sets on fire the course of our life, and is set on fire by hell.* (James 3:5–6)

A VERBAL ARSONIST

If our tongues are not bridled but left uncontrolled, they can be guilty of arson! They might be paltry in size and rarely seen, but they are able to inflict a great deal of scorching and destruction.

Only the mentally or emotionally deranged would take a match and set fire to someone's home, car, family pictures, or other valuables; very few people are diagnosed as that twisted or cruel. However, in the unseen world, which is more real than the world we see with our eyes, we participate in a horrific act of arson whenever we are unkind to someone with our tongues. When you or I choose to ridicule someone, a life is unfairly engulfed in vicious and fierce flames. Likewise, when you or I choose to spread an unsubstantiated rumor, we scorch something very precious in a person's life.

232 Guide Your Mind, Guard Your Heart, Grace Your Tongue

My tongue has sent scorching, biting flames into people's lives more times than I want to remember. All that has been left, after my tongue has done its damage, is a charred and ruined mess. It can take only one small spark, or one small rumor, or one minor untruth, to set an entire life on fire. Only one tiny, unkind or cruel word may be required to destroy a person's reputation for years.

James is very clear where this predisposition is born—it is conceived in hell. Fire comes from fire; the fire that your tongue spreads was collected in the fires of hell. The enemy often tries to influence the choices that our tongues make, but there is a way to stop his influence and set him on the run. Remember that James and the Holy Spirit have first told you that you must put that bridle on; then you must be the captain of your ship and use your rudder to steer the ship out of turbulent waters and torrential storms. Finally, you must determine that your tongue will never set another fire.

WHAT ARE YOU BOASTING ABOUT?

> *So also the tongue is a small part of the body, and yet it boasts of great things.* (James 3:5)

Perhaps the malady of the mouth with which you are infected is not worry or negativity but enthusiastic and relentless boasting. The Hebrew word translated "*boasts*" in the above verse is *aucheo*, which means "to make a show or to be foolish." My tiny tongue can boast about some very impressive things in life. Can yours? James is cautioning all those who will listen to his warning not to allow the tongue to get too big for its hinge. This is sage advice that has resonated with people through the ages. An important aspect of tongue control is to be careful who you talk about, what you talk about, and *how much* you talk about certain things and people. (For example, if you are anything at all like me, you and I might need to take a breath from time to time and let somebody else talk about their children or grandchildren!)

In ancient sacred writings, when a person was known for boasting and for pretense, that person was regarded as a fool. Often, when I am tempted to let the world know how magnificent my children are and how brilliant my grandchildren are, I must pray, "Jesus! Save me from myself! Cure me from foaming at the mouth about my family!"

But then, the Holy Spirit gently reminds me that I am, indeed, called to boast about certain things in my life. The Bible actually applauds me for boasting about one thing in particular:

> My soul will make its boast in the LORD; the humble will hear it and rejoice. (Psalm 34:2)

Boasting, in the best sense, is not inherently a sin; however, the challenge is in the object about which, or about whom, the boasting is being done—and the spirit in which it is done. If you are going to boast, make sure that you are boasting about the right things and not about the wrong things. When you choose to boast about the Lord, the Holy Spirit will be cheering you on!

AN ECHO FOR DECADES

While your tongue has the ability to set people's lives on fire through negativity and callous speech, always remember that it also has the power to elevate people's lives with positivity and encouragement, especially those who are closest to you. Will the words you deliver be positive or negative? When you choose to declare the Word of God over your family and upon those whom you love, heaven unleashes blessings—and hell shakes! When your speech is flavored with grace, and when the words from your tongue are lavishly generous with understanding, you are causing someone's life to flourish like a well-watered garden. Your tongue is able to bring new growth into a person's world and to deliver extraordinary health to their relationships. What divine possibilities!

The effects of verbally encouraging someone can last for years. I distinctly remember the life-changing words that my second grade teacher, Mrs. Margaret Dombrowski, spoke over me when I was only seven years old. She told me that I had the talent to be a writer. What? I could barely read *Green Eggs and Ham* when she told me that I could write books such as Laura Ingalls Wilder and Louisa May Alcott had written.

I have never forgotten that September afternoon at the elementary schoolhouse on Main Street in my small, western New York town. Mrs. Dombrowski, a war bride from Australia, handed me her own copy of *Little House in the Big Woods* and said, "Carol, I believe in you. You were made to be an author. Read this book and learn how to write a beautiful story."

234 Guide Your Mind, Guard Your Heart, Grace Your Tongue

I gulped in that book over one short weekend and came back to school on Monday morning asking for the second in the "Little House" series of books. By Friday, I was desperate to read the third installment.

Mrs. Dombrowski began to write quotes by Wordsworth, Tennyson, and Lincoln on my daily assignments. Although I was unable to understand the nuances and meanings of all of the words, what I did understand was that I had a teacher who believed in me, and she demonstrated it by the words she spoke over me.

That year in the second grade flew by; Mrs. Dombrowski handed me volume after volume after volume, and the books I read during that period gave me the ability to travel in my mind through time and across continents. When June arrived, and my second grade year was coming to a dreaded end, Mrs. Dombrowski left me a "message in a bottle." In my second grade yearbook, these were the words that she wrote to a little girl who was then only eight years old:

> To thine own self be true, and it must follow, as the night the day, thou canst not then be false to any man. —*William Shakespeare*[8]

Those words that Margaret Dombrowski wrote in her perfect penmanship in my thin yearbook were probably not meant for the eight-year-old Carol. She must have known they would later resonate in the heart of the twelve-year-old preteen Carol…and the eighteen-year-old college freshman Carol…and the thirty-seven-year-old mother Carol…and the sixty-two-year-old grandmother Carol.

Just as I remember the encouragement of Mrs. Dombrowski from nearly sixty years ago, I know that our own words can have staying power for others. Your words can live beyond the situation in which they were spoken, and your words can live beyond even the years of your life. Use your words to encourage someone else to live a great life! Use your tongue as an instrument of grace and healing.

TAME IT!

> *For every species of beasts and birds, of reptiles and creatures of the sea, is tamed and has been tamed by the human race. But no one can tame*

8. *Hamlet*, Act I, Scene III.

the tongue; it is a restless evil and full of deadly poison.

(James 3:7–8)

Here is another reminder from James about the potency of the tongue. Mankind is so brilliant that he is able to tame every species of animal, but the one creature that remains out of his control is that squirming body part known as "the tongue." You will never control your tongue with your own power or in your own strength; it requires a partnership with God. I am utterly powerless against the wiles of my tongue when I try to tackle them in my own strength. I need God to help me attack every verbal virus that has infected my body.

James and the Holy Spirit chose to utilize profoundly strong and even frightening phrases in the last few verses that we have studied. Again, these phrases serve as a warning as to the true nature of some of the words we choose to speak:

…is set on fire by hell. (James 3:6)

…is a restless evil and full of deadly poison. (James 3:8)

James holds absolutely nothing back as he fully diagnoses the source of the sickness that has invaded our ability to use our tongues for their proper purpose. The battle for control of the tongue is a spiritual battle, and the enemy doesn't intend to leave quietly or without an intense fight.

LOCK IT UP!

Like most mothers, when my children were toddlers, I installed locks on all of the lower kitchen cabinets and bathroom cabinets, because those were the places where the cleaning supplies were stored. I knew that the chemicals with which I cleaned my home could poison my sweet children if they ever got into them and drank from them, so I ensured that no little hands would be able to open those specific cabinets. My precious babies were absolutely not going to ingest any of those poisons as long as I was the mom!

Then something happened that showed me how the very words of my mouth could be dangerously toxic to my children, as well. The ages of our five children are spread out by nearly fourteen years, so I was dealing with the independent attitudes of teenagers at the same time that I was potty training toddlers. One evening, I was frustrated with one of the teenagers and said something in anger that I never should have said. The conversation had been intense, and this particular child had pushed me to my maternal limit. Yet rather than defaulting to my verbal boundaries, I allowed my soul to have the last word, and it wasn't a pretty one.

The next morning, when I was reading my Bible in the early hours of the day, I came upon this particular verse from James, which we looked at above:

> But no one can tame the tongue; it is a restless evil and full of deadly poison. (James 3:8)

I realized that my tongue was doing as much damage to my older children as I feared the cleaning supplies would do to my younger children. The Holy Spirit clearly spoke to me that day with this admonition: *"Carol...you need to lock up your tongue!"*

I got the message loud and clear from the greatest Communicator of all. The only time that I ever took those cleaning supplies out was to clean with them; similarly, the only time that my tongue should be allowed out was when I was encouraging others, speaking the truth in love, and worshipping the Lord. Other than for those foundational reasons, my tongue needed to stay safely locked up where it was unable to do any long-term, poisonous damage.

GUARD YOUR SOUL FROM TROUBLE

It is obvious that the contemporary wisdom of our culture encourages people to assert themselves verbally. We have foolishly bought into the New Age lie that it is healthy to say everything that we think, feel, and believe. Pop psychologists, television personalities, and media gurus imprudently advocate the philosophy of speaking out and refusing to stifle oneself. I have not found that same wisdom in the Word of God. The Bible calls us, as children of God, to apply self-discipline and to think of others as more important than ourselves. Here is some wisdom advice from the book of Proverbs, some of which we have looked at in previous chapters:

If you have been foolish in exalting yourself or if you have plotted evil, put your hand on your mouth. (Proverbs 30:32)

If that advice, which comes from the wisest man who ever lived, doesn't sober you, let these words settle in your soul:

A fool does not delight in understanding, but only in revealing his own mind. (Proverbs 18:2)

And if you are not thoroughly humbled yet, let me share one more breathtaking verse with you:

He who guards his mouth and his tongue, guards his soul from troubles. (Proverbs 21:23)

I am a great observer of people, and I also find pleasure in the lost art of eavesdropping! In public places, I often covertly listen in on conversations of which I am not a part. Although I really have no business overhearing what is being said, I gain terrific insights by paying attention to the verbal exchanges in these random discussions of strangers. I have overheard comments such as these:

"Well...somebody had to tell them off!"

"It sure felt good to get that off my chest."

"I gave her a piece of my mind!"

"Maybe what I said will do him some good."

"I feel better for having said it."

If you can pretend that you were listening along with me, then you, too, will hear that all of those phrases were said with a whole lot of pride and a bit of self-justification thrown in. My diagnosis is that if you have to rationalize what you have said, then maybe you shouldn't have said it at all.

OUCH!

Are you beginning to understand the true reasons why God gave you a tongue? He gave you a tongue to praise Him, to speak His words, and to encourage others. Those are the only three directives for which your tongue was created. There is no other reason. You weren't designed by God to rattle on senselessly. The Lord didn't give you a tongue so you could slice and dice people, or so that you could murmur, complain, and whine.

Yes, you were graced with a tongue in order to bring rich praise and glory to God's name! Your tongue is your primary instrument of worship.

And my tongue shall declare Your righteousness and Your praise all day long. (Psalm 35:28)

You have a tongue for the purpose of declaring God's will and His words over people, situations, and events. You have a tongue that was created to speak His wisdom from His mind.

This book of the law shall not depart from your mouth, but you shall meditate on it day and night, so that you may be careful to do according to all that is written in it; for then you will make your way prosperous, and then you will have success. (Joshua 1:8)

You have been given a tongue to encourage other people every day.

But encourage one another day after day, as long as it is still called "Today." (Hebrews 3:13)

In his heartfelt letter, which is overflowing with wisdom and God's point of view, James continues to teach concerning the importance of the words that we choose to speak:

With [the tongue] *we bless our Lord and Father, and with it we curse men, who have been made in the likeness of God; from the same mouth come both blessing and cursing. My brethren, these things ought not to be this way.* (James 3:9–10)

Can you say, "Ouch!"? James is cutting straight to the heart of the issue in this simple yet complete discussion. Your tongue must submit to the higher authority of the purposes of God. Thus, your tongue must not be "double-minded." Unfortunately, we have habitually used our tongues for polar-opposite purposes.

We are thrilled to lift our voices in worship on Sunday mornings, and to immediately follow that worship with cheerful and encouraging conversations with those with whom we fellowship. Yet the same tongues that gave glory to God and encouraged mere acquaintances at church with heartfelt and gracious words soon rip mercilessly into family members who have disappointed us in some minor way. Our tongues quote the Word of God in prayer meetings, but later they gossip about others while we meet with friends over a cup of coffee. James is heartbreakingly clear as he begs us to rethink how we are utilizing this most precious gift of the tongue, saying, in effect, "My sisters, these things ought not to be this way!"

If your tongue is not worshipping the Lord, then lock it up. If your tongue is not declaring the mind of Christ, then lock it up. If your tongue is not encouraging others, then lock it up.

"WE BUILD! WE DON'T TEAR DOWN!"

Craig and I raised five opinionated, exuberant, vociferous, and loquacious children, all in one very small home on an extremely small salary. But oh, the joy that was in that home is still inexpressible to me! However, it wasn't always olive branches and sweet, idyllic days. As I described earlier, our children were spread out in age over a nearly fourteen-year span, so that, at the same time I was dealing with driver's training for my teenagers, I was dealing with potty training for my toddlers. At the same time I was conjugating Latin verbs with the two older boys, I was reading Dr. Seuss books to the younger ones. When the older ones were clamoring to be more independent, the little ones were still superglued to my legs and sleeping in my bed.

Additionally, exhibiting five distinct personalities, the children were loudly expressive with their opinions, preferences, feelings, and tempers. As a result, I embraced a motto that expressed my core belief as a mother: "In this home, we build! We don't tear down!"

Every time one of my delightful children was having a full-blown meltdown at someone else's expense, I quickly asked, "Were those building words or tearing-down words?" This is a question I must ask daily and consistently, even now that my children are no longer the ones prompting the question. I ask it of myself. God gave each of us a tongue as a source of encouragement. Let's use it as such!

In the classic, allegorical tale *Pilgrim's Progress*, John Bunyan enlists a character by the name of "Talkative" to illustrate something that is a significant downfall for many of us. When he is abroad, Talkative is known as a saint, but in his hometown, he is known to be a devil. Unfortunately, this is the story of many of us, and it is time for us to change. Our tongues must cooperate with the rhythm that God sets for our lives. It's a consistent rhythm of worship, encouragement, and wisdom. The cadence remains the same, whether one is at home, at church, or in the marketplace. The meter never changes or varies from the one that has been set by the Great Conductor Himself: *Worship. Encouragement. Wisdom.*

A PURE HEART

When God wants to do a cleansing and rejuvenating work on your tongue, He first starts in your brain and in your heart. He gives you a brand-new mind, and then a heart transplant, knowing that your tongue is an extension of your mind and your heart. As you endeavor to change the manner in which you speak, you will quickly realize, as has been emphasized, that this is a job you and God must do together. It is not possible for you to control your tongue in your own strength—you need to partner with the power of God to get the job done.

> *Does a fountain send out from the same opening both fresh and bitter water? Can a fig tree, my brethren, produce olives, or a vine produce figs? Nor can salt water produce fresh.* (James 3:11–12)

James finishes his teaching on the tongue with one final, vivid illustration. Thus far, he has wisely compared the tongue to a bit in a horse's mouth, a rudder on a ship, a fire in a vast forest, and deadly poison. Now, James compares the tongue to a fountain that is a continual source of water.

Water brings vibrant life to every living thing; without water, we would quickly die. People, animals, and plants all need water to survive and even to flourish. The water cycle in nature is a constant reminder of God's care for our needs, and His brilliant plan of life.

James clearly points out that it is impossible for both fresh and bitter water to come from the same fountain. It just can't happen. Similarly, we are able to release only what is already inside of us. If you have allowed bitterness to remain in your mind and heart, then your tongue will produce bitter "water." If you have allowed mercy and grace to exist in your mind and heart, then your tongue will gloriously produce fresh, restoring "water."

"Can a fig tree, my brethren, produce olives, or a vine produce figs?" In an earlier chapter, I mentioned how my dad had been a farmer, and how, when I was a girl, I helped him in the family garden, learning a simple but essential lesson: like produces like. It is impossible for a fig tree to produce olives. What an absurd idea! Likewise, rosebushes don't produce turnips, and pine trees don't grow baby carrots. The point that James is emphasizing is that we will merely produce the fruit of what we have allowed to grow inside our mind and heart. If your mind is renewed, your words will be renewed. If your heart is forgiving, your words will be forgiving.

An ancient proverb that is often quoted in relation to this Scripture passage places the final exclamation point on the coaching of James:

If a cup is filled only with good water, it cannot spill even one drop of bitter water, no matter how badly it is jarred.

OUR CHALLENGE

Oh my—how I have been challenged by the words of James and the Holy Spirit! How about you? Why don't we spend some time on our faces in the presence of God as we allow Him to take control of our out-of-control muscle known as the tongue? We can't do it without Him and His power.

I long to have my heart purified so that my words are only pure. I long for every word that comes out of my mouth to demonstrate the Jesus who vibrantly lives inside of me. I long for more of Him and for less of me.

Search me, O God, and know my heart; try me and know my anxious thoughts; and see if there be any hurtful way in me, and lead me in the everlasting way. (Psalm 139:23–24)

GRACE YOUR TONGUE: PERSONAL APPLICATION

1. (a) What source does James say sets the tongue on fire, causing us to speak destructive words? What does the answer tell you about

the nature of the battle you are engaged in for control of your tongue?

(b) Have you ever thought of your careless, unkind, or spiteful words as "setting fires" of devastation in other people's lives, as the apostle James describes? Does that image change your perspective about the negative comments you have made? Why or why not?

2. (a) What negative thoughts would it be best for you to "lock up" permanently because of their deadly potential, especially if verbalized?

    (b) Replace those negative thoughts with specific expressions of praise for the Lord and encouragement for others.

3. Have you allowed your tongue to get too big for its hinge? Do you find yourself continually boasting about your accomplishments, the talents of your family members, or your prosperous life? If so, change your focus—humbly "boast" about the Lord and His qualities and accomplishments in order to give hope and encouragement to others who need to know about God's love, power, and faithfulness.

4. (a) Have you had someone in your life, like Mrs. Margaret Dombrowski, who encouraged you by his or her words and had a long-lasting impact on the course of your life? If so, write down the name of this person. Then, record what he or she said that lifted you up and helped you to fulfill a particular dream or to become more than you ever thought you could be. If the individual is still living, why not reach out to him or her with a letter or card expressing your appreciation?

    (b) Think of someone younger than you in your own sphere of influence whom you could encourage in a similar way, and make a specific plan to do so.

5. Have you ever been guilty of offering beautiful songs of worship to the Lord—only to shortly thereafter gossip about someone or speak sarcastic words to a family member? Make a commitment that your worship of God will not end up being mere lip service but will reflect a purity of heart that flows over into loving and

considerate relationships with other people. Walk in God's rhythm for your life: *Worship. Encouragement. Wisdom.* Write these three words on several three-by-five cards and place them where you will see them regularly.

6. We can't tame the tongue on our own; we must be willing to allow the Spirit of God to transform our speech patterns. Make a point to spend time in prayer asking your heavenly Father to take charge of your out-of-control tongue and to make it a means of blessing for others.

26

POWER WORDS

Now that we all are experts on what not to say with our muscular tongues, it's time to discover additional practical application concerning the God-designed use of the tongue. While it is vital to know what *not* to say, it is perhaps even more important to understand what we *are* allowed to say! As the rudder of your life, your tongue must steer your very existence toward safe and untroubled waters. And the course that leads us to an abundant life is found in using our tongues in the manner that God has ordained.

BORN TO PRAISE GOD

God gave you a tongue so that you could declare His high praises in your everyday life. From Genesis to Revelation, it is clear that we were created for praise. We were created to lift our voices in song to the One who made us, who loves us, and who redeemed us. Praise is what delivers value and purpose to our lives. And praise has the power to miraculously change a common life into a rare and significant one.

I have come to realize that there is something about the character of God that *relishes* the praise and thanksgiving of His children. He takes pleasure in the praises of His people—He literally basks in the songs that we sing. The Bible says that God makes Himself at home when His people are praising Him:

> But thou art holy, O thou that inhabitest the praises of Israel.
> (Psalm 22:3 KJV)

God makes Himself at home when we choose to worship Him no matter what is happening in the circumstances of our lives. Perhaps the reason that you have felt far from God at times is that you have stopped praising Him. When you praise Him, He will show up! When you praise His name, He puts His feet up and relaxes; He sets up camp and stays where your worship is the most exuberant!

> *Let everything that has breath praise the* LORD.   (Psalm 150:6)

Thus, as long as you are still breathing, your job description this side of heaven is to use your tongue as an instrument of praise. And, because we are made in the image of God, it makes sense that we would enjoy the same things that God enjoys. People enjoy your expressions of praise directed toward them, just as the Father who made them enjoys expressions of praise directed toward Him. Your spouse, your children, your parents, your siblings, your coworkers, and your pastor were all made in the image of God, with His heart. God's heart responds to praise, and so will theirs. It is not prideful or vain to enjoy encouragement from others; it is simply the nature of God being reflected in our humanity. The desire to be appreciated is therefore a desire that is placed in people by God. Nobody enjoys being critiqued or criticized, and neither does God. It hurts the very heart of God when one of His beloved children falsely believes that it is his or her job responsibility to complain about Him or to needlessly question Him.

Remember, you were given a tongue to worship God the Father and to encourage His children, who were made in His likeness! The following are some practical ways in which you can do this.

THANKSGIVING IS NOT JUST A HOLIDAY

First of all, be exuberantly and outrageously thankful every single day of the calendar year. Your goal in life should be to become the most vocally grateful and thankful of anyone who is alive at your moment in history. There should be no one who is more enthusiastic and consistent in his or her praises to God the Father than you are!

Each day, keep a running list of every single thing for which you are appreciative. But it is not enough to make a list—making the list is merely where it begins. Choose the highlights of the day and read them out loud to someone—your spouse, your child, or another family member. If you live alone, you can read them over the phone to a friend—or even speak them to your pet if you have one! If no one else will listen to you, say them out loud to the Holy Spirit; I have learned that He is a great listener, indeed!

Next, use social media as a place for giving thanks boldly and often! Don't hold anything back, but make a choice to daily post about something positive or wonderful that has happened to you—whether "small" or great—and how grateful you are for that particular blessing. This is not an occasion for boasting about yourself, but rather for pointing others to the love of God and His desire to guide, help, and protect them in similar ways. So be humble and sensitive to others in your posts as you openly express your gratitude to God.

Additionally, enlist the use of a "Thankfulness Journal" in which you chronicle the thoughts of appreciation in your heart and the words you have spoken out of gratitude. Before you lay your head on the pillow every night, list at least three outstanding treasures that have marked the hours of that day. Likewise, instead of worrying at night when you are in bed, thank God for all that He has done for you in every season of your life.

Often, we are consumed with what we don't have and with what is lacking in our lives, and we are exhausted by disappointments and discouragement. However, the daily habit of focusing on, and speaking about, the gifts that the hand of God has bestowed upon you—whether those gifts are common or uncommon—will put a spring in your step and renewed joy in your heart. Remember that joy and thankfulness are not so very far apart!

If you only recount your disappointments on a given day, your life will soon become a human tragedy. However, even in the very worst of times, we can all make the amazing discovery that we have someone or something for which to be grateful. Rehearse your blessings, out loud, over and over and over again. Hit rewind and mention them again and again and again.

In these ways, you can become a perpetual thanksgiving machine. The month of November will have nothing on you—you will be the most audaciously grateful person in all of recorded history!

God gave you a tongue because He trusted that you would use it to bring Him glory. Giving thanks should be the designated sweet spot in every believer's life; every home run that we hit on the field of life should be conceived in, and resound with, heartfelt gratitude. Each one of us should become a world-renowned expert on the subject of appreciation. When there is a lull in a conversation, begin to talk about the blessings you and others have received. When discussions turn to gossip, default to gratitude. Every conversation should be a healthier one because your voice is a part of it. Raise people to your level of praise; do not lower yourself to their level of complaining.

The atmosphere of every room should miraculously transform when you walk into it; every meeting you attend should be a time of encouragement and positive reinforcement simply because your voice is being heard. Every evening spent at home with the family you love should be a bounty of thankful sentences, phrases of gratitude, and words of affirmation. One of my goals in life is to be the most thankful woman of my entire generation! In this chapter, I have encouraged you to embrace the same goal. I dare you to beat me at it!

DECLARE THE WORD

You were given a tongue not only for praise, worship, and encouragement, but also to declare the Word and the will of God. The Word of God is an all-powerful weapon that is meant to usher His will into your circumstances. God's Word should have the final say, every time—for each situation and throughout the day. There should not be a single situation or event in your life that is not impacted by the jurisdiction of the Word that you have hidden in your heart.

"For My thoughts are not your thoughts, nor are your ways My ways," declares the LORD. "For as the heavens are higher than the earth, so are My ways higher than your ways and My thoughts than your thoughts. For as the rain and the snow come down from heaven, and do not return there without watering the earth and making it bear and sprout, and furnishing seed to the sower and bread to the eater; so will My word be which goes forth from My mouth; it will not return to Me empty, without accomplishing what I desire, and without succeeding in the matter for which I sent it." (Isaiah 55:8–11)

God's Word is guaranteed by the Holy Spirit to do a mountain-moving, Red-Sea-parting, bread-multiplying, water-into-wine, "impossible" miracle in your life! Open your mouth and declare the Word of God, and see what God will do for you. Rather than whine and complain and speak disparagingly, splash the Word of God all over your circumstances, and then just watch what it will accomplish!

I have a list of confessions that I daily declare over every situation that concerns me and those whom I love. These declarations have become increasingly precious to me as I have seen God do a transforming work in me. This transformation has occurred—and is occurring—simply because I am a woman who has determined to see things from God's perspective and not from my own.

When I am dealing with a difficult person who is nearly impossible to love, this is the declaration of my mouth:

I can do all things through Christ who strengthens me.
(Philippians 4:13 NKJV)

When someone has willfully used his or her words to discourage me, I speak forth this:

"It is more blessed to give than to receive," so I am going to be a giver today. I am going to give words of encouragement and not of discouragement. I am going to give blessings to everyone I meet, even those who discourage me. (See Acts 20:35; Matthew 5:43–48; Romans 12:14.)

When I am dealing with judgmental and critical thoughts toward someone who has been made in the image of God, I often repeat this:

I will "[take] *every thought captive to the obedience of Christ."* My mind must line up with the mind of Christ. Lord, I give You my mind today. I refuse to think unkind thoughts and will only meditate on good and pure things. (See 2 Corinthians 10:5; 2 Corinthians 2:16; Philippians 4:8.)

When Craig and I are struggling in the areas of our finances or need a breakthrough in provision, I declare:

You are the God *"who supplies seed to the sower and bread for food."* Thank You that You are able to *"multiply* [my] *seed for sowing and increase the harvest of* [my] *righteousness."* Thank You, Father, that Your Word says I *"will be enriched in everything for all liberality, which through* [my life] *is producing thanksgiving to God."* Your Word says that *"the ministry of this service is not only fully supplying* [our] *needs…, but is also overflowing through many thanksgivings to God."* I thank You, Father, in advance for the provision that is coming our way. (See 2 Corinthians 9:10–12.)

When I am sick, I pray out loud,

You are the Lord who heals all of my diseases! (See Psalm 103:3.)

When I am struggling in the area of destiny or a lack of change in my circumstances, my favorite Scripture to shout is this one:

"The LORD will accomplish what concerns me; Your lovingkindness, O LORD, is everlasting; do not forsake the works of Your hands." I am a work of Your hands! (See Psalm 138:8.)

The Word of God will do an outside work on your circumstances and an inside work on you! When you use your mouth to declare the promises of God, it will change your perspective on your situation. Your mouth was made to declare God's plans over your disappointments and human pain. Your tongue was created to affirm everything that God has ever said. It was not meant to be a puppet on a string, mimicking the faulty thoughts of your mind and the unguarded contents of your heart. Instead, it was designed to be a beautiful echo of the perfect mind and the pure heart of God.

Like apples of gold in settings of silver is a word spoken in right circumstances.   (Proverbs 25:11)

GRACE YOUR TONGUE: PERSONAL APPLICATION

1. What is the primary purpose for which we were created?

2. In this chapter, we have learned that God *relishes* our heartfelt praise and worship. Does this perspective change your attitude

toward and practice of worship? Why or why not? If so, in what ways?

3.   Write down something specific with which you can praise or encourage each of your immediate family members or closest friends. Then, communicate it to them today or at the next opportune time.

4.   (a) Write out a heartfelt statement of thankfulness or gratitude that you can communicate on social media today, and then post it. Make a practice to do so daily.

     (b) Whenever others post positive and thankful statements on social media, encourage them by posting a supportive response.

5.   Keep a list and/or a "Thankfulness Journal" in which you daily record what you are grateful for. Read aloud from it to someone else or to yourself each day.

6.   Before going to sleep at night, think of at least three good things that happened during that day for which you are thankful. Record them on your list or in your journal.

7.   Write down various declarations of faith, praise, and thanksgiving—as illustrated in this chapter under the section "Declare the Word," as well as in previous chapters—that you can proclaim in the daily challenging situations you face. This will instill Scripture and biblical principles in your mind and heart so that your words will always be filled with affirmations of the Word of God for your life.

CONCLUSION: A TRIPLE-THREAT OFFENSIVE— YOUR MIND, YOUR HEART, AND YOUR TONGUE

MIND READING

After reading this book, have you come to the realization that I can read your mind? Yes, that's right; I am a verified expert at reading people's minds. The way I am able to read your mind is quite simple—by listening to the words that come out of your mouth. If the words that proceed from your oral cavity are warm and kind, seasoned with grace, and reflective of forgiveness, then I am fully assured that your mind is taking on the characteristics of Jesus Christ. Conversely, if you speak words of anger, bitterness, and unforgiveness, I know *exactly* what you are thinking. But in that case, my friend, quite frankly, your mind is a foul-smelling cesspool of anger and bitterness, and it harbors the refusal to forgive!

> *Death and life are in the power of the tongue, and those who love it will eat its fruit.* (Proverbs 18:21)

In earlier chapters, we discovered that this verse has a twofold meaning when it is fully applied. First of all, the words that you speak to others are loaded with either life or death. You can kill people's self-respect, destroy their marriages, assassinate their potential, annihilate their dreams, and murder their futures with the negative words you speak to them. Or, you can propel people into destiny, cultivate their health, bless their relationships, and fertilize their dreams and potential when you speak God's words to them.

Second, remember this: your words can also bring either death or life to *you*. Your words help determine your capacity to love your spouse, to nurture your children, and to encourage your parents. What you say determines whether your future will be fruitful and abundant—or shriveled and dry.

"*...and those who love it will eat its fruit.*" Accordingly, someday, you are going to eat the words that you have chosen to speak today. Does the menu of tomorrow look appetizing or disgusting? Only you, my friend, are able to determine the flavor of what is yet to come. Will the banquet of your life be serving that which is sweet and delightful? Will you be munching on the fruits of the Holy Spirit? Or will you be dining on bitter and sour morsels, and reluctantly trying to swallow the unappetizing deeds of the flesh?

GUIDING OUR MINDS

> My [daughter], *give attention to my wisdom, incline your ear to my understanding; that you may observe discretion and your lips may reserve knowledge.* (Proverbs 5:1–2)

The only possible way for your lips to express knowledge and wisdom is for your mind to pay attention to the wisdom of God. Wisdom begins in the brain and then filters through the heart and mouth. If you think wise thoughts, you will become a wise person! Our anchor verse for the study of the mind has given us pervasive and astounding clarity about this reality:

> For as [a person] *thinks within himself, so is he.* (Proverbs 23:7)

You must think wise thoughts before you have a wise heart. If you adopt a wise mind, you will not have a foolish heart, because your heart will take its cues from your brain, the nerve center of your life, in the thoughts that you think. When you have determined to be a wise person, your heart will begin to beat with wisdom and godly judgment. Accordingly, when the wisdom that has been exhibited in your brain influences your heart, which is filled with grace, you will discover that you have the supernatural ability to live a powerful life!

...which things we also speak, not in words taught by human wisdom, but in those taught by the Spirit, combining spiritual thoughts with spiritual words.   (1 Corinthians 2:13)

This is how we become truly wise in all of our ways. Those who are wise in all areas of life have submitted their minds to the control of the Holy Spirit, have allowed the Holy Spirit to transform and renew their thoughts (see Romans 12:2), and have taken every thought captive to the obedience of Christ (see 2 Corinthians 10:5). To have wisdom is to think like God thinks.

GUARDING OUR HEARTS

Watch over your heart with all diligence, for from it flow the springs of life.   (Proverbs 4:23)

All of the issues of your life are determined by the feelings that you willfully allow to simmer in your heart. If you can train yourself to think wise thoughts and to be transformed by the renewal of your mind in Christ Jesus, then your heart will begin to play "Follow the Leader" with your brain. Your emotions will start to mimic the profound wisdom that has been given to you by the One who is known as Wisdom. It may take a while, but be patient! A new way of living is about to revolutionize your emotions, your decisions, and your words.

Do you remember the astounding fact that an emotion travels eighty thousand times faster than a thought? Your thoughts are like the Pony Express, while your emotions are like e-mail. Knowing this helps us to understand why it is so much easier to control a thought than it is an emotion. Your thoughts are more easily maintained and contained than your heart is able to be controlled. But there is no end to the power you will experience in your life when your emotions embrace the wisdom that your mind offers! When your heart decides that it will live in subjection to the wisdom of the mind, your wise emotions will arrive at the decision-making center eighty thousand times faster than your thoughts will. Therefore, when you guard your heart with the wisdom that the mind offers, then the spontaneous, swift decisions you make will honor the Lord and His authority.

Your emotions should be carrying the information that has been given to them by the wisdom of the mind of Christ, which is preeminent in your brain, rather than by the soulish responses of the heart, which are sickeningly deceitful. (See Jeremiah 17:9.) That is why it is essential to guide your mind into thinking only the truth. The atmosphere that is cultivated in your mind determines to a great degree the atmosphere of your life. To put it another way, the quality of your thoughts determines the quality of your life.

GRACING OUR TONGUES

> *The heart of the wise instructs his mouth.* (Proverbs 16:23)

Your tongue is not a solo act or a one-man band. It only has the capability of speaking the words that are conveyed from either your mind or your heart. Remember, your tongue is the shadow-dancer of your heart and your mind. When your heart has become wise and noble due to the influence of the mind of Christ, it has the authority to retrain your tongue. Your mature heart, which is no longer a place of fantasy, worry, or criticism, now has the capacity to coach your tongue to be an instrument of grace and gentleness.

Thus, the potential of tomorrow is conceived in your mind, travels to your heart, and finally reveals itself in your tongue. Your tongue is intrinsically, and by God's design, forever and irretrievably locked to the processes of your mind and heart. Your mind must think it, and your heart must feel it, before your tongue is capable of saying it.

> *But the things that proceed out of the mouth come from the heart, and those defile the man. For out of the heart come evil thoughts, murders, adulteries, fornications, thefts, false witness, slanders.*
> (Matthew 15:18–19)

Let me remind you just one more time that your tongue is not your problem; the actual source of your mouth disease can be found in your heart. Once your heart has been renewed, refreshed, and cleansed, your tongue will have no problem at all giving a timely word, and in season. (See, for example, Proverbs 25:11; 2 Timothy 4:2.) Your speech will be a joy to the people around you, and everyone will be waiting with bated breath to hear what you have to say next. Your tongue will be an agent of grace!

THINK, LOVE, AND SPEAK LIKE GOD DOES

> *The good man out of the good treasure of his heart brings forth what is good; and the evil man out of the evil treasure brings forth what is evil; for his mouth speaks from that which fills his heart.*   (Luke 6:45)

Yes, the clear evidence of what you have allowed to live in your heart is demonstrated by the words that you speak. When you have filled your heart with the treasures of the Word of God and with the wisdom that comes from the mind of Christ, your tongue might just become the very best part of you! There is a generation waiting for the treasure, the comfort, and the hope that only you are able to verbalize. There is a hungry world that longs to feed itself on the feast that your tongue is able to cook up.

God gave you a mind to think like He thinks. He gave you a heart to love like He loves. And He gave you a tongue to speak exactly like He does!

Think like God thinks, fill your heart with the very things that fill His heart, and speak what Christ would speak if He were walking on earth today. Did you know that Christ is actually here right now? He is here because He lives in you! And He is aching to use your mind, your heart, and your tongue to demonstrate His character in the world at this very moment in history.

> *I will give you a new heart and put a new spirit within you; and I will remove the heart of stone from your flesh and give you a heart of flesh. I will put My Spirit within you and cause you to walk in My statutes.*
> (Ezekiel 36:26–27)

> *The Spirit of the Lord God is upon me, because the Lord has anointed me to bring good news to the afflicted; He has sent me to bind up the brokenhearted, to proclaim liberty to captives and freedom to prisoners.*   (Isaiah 61:1)

ABOUT THE AUTHOR

Carol McLeod is a popular speaker at women's conferences and retreats through her ministry, Just Joy!, and is the author of a number of books, including *Defiant Joy*, *Holy Estrogen*, and *Joy for All Seasons*. Carol hosts both a daily radio show, "Defiant Joy! Radio," which is broadcast in major markets across America, including Sirius XM FamilyTalk Radio 131, and a daily podcast, "A Jolt of Joy!" on the Charisma Podcast Network. Her blog, "Joy for the Journey" (formerly "A Cup of Tea with Carol"), has been named in the Top 50 Faith Blogs for Women.

After her 2013 devotional *21 Days to Beat Depression* had nearly 100,000 downloads in the first month, YouVersion picked it up, where it has been read close to 300,000 times in three years. Carol has nine other devotionals with YouVersion and also writes for *Ministry Today* and *Charisma*. She is a frequent guest on and has cohosted *100 Huntley Street*. Her teaching DVD *The Rooms of a Woman's Heart* won a Telly Award in 2005 for excellence in religious programming. The first Women's Chaplain at Oral Roberts University, she currently serves as Chaplain on the university's Alumni Board of Directors. Carol has been married to her college sweetheart, Craig, for nearly forty years and is the mother of five children in heaven and five children on earth. She and her husband have recently moved to Tulsa, Oklahoma, where Craig serves as the North American Director for Global Partners, a missions' organization that plants churches in remote areas of the world.